URBAN LATIN AMERICA

The Texas Pan American Series

Urban Latin America

The Political Condition from

Above and Below

by Alejandro Portes and

John Walton

University of Texas Press

Austin

The Texas Pan American Series is published with the assistance of a revolving publication fund established by the Pan American Sulphur Company.

Library of Congress Cataloging in Publication Data

Portes, Alejandro, 1944–
    Urban Latin America.

    (Texas pan-American series)
    Bibliography: p.
    Includes index.
    1. Cities and towns—Latin America. 2. Poor—Latin America.
3. Power (Social Sciences) I. Walton, John, 1937–   joint author.
II. Title.
HT127.5.P67   301.36'3'098   75-23171
ISBN 978-0-292-72961-2

Contents

Tables

Preface

The idea for this book emerged from a series of conversations
held at the University of Texas at Austin during 1972. Our individual experiences in research and teaching about Latin America had led us to the judgment that the exponential increase of
published materials in this field was not matched by systematic
attempts to organize what was known around a few major
themes. Whether one was seeking a book for classroom use
that incorporated a broad coverage of the recent literature or a
work that assayed the current status and future directions of
research, little appeared available. In our separate work we had
approached the Latin American city from very different perspectives. One of us had concentrated on the structure and
dynamics of urban elites, in particular the developmental consequences of various configurations of power. The other had
focused on the poor sectors (called at the time "marginal"
groups), their political orientations, and their forms of organization. We subsequently came to believe that these different
perspectives offered suitable points of triangulation for bringing
together what was known about power and poverty in urban
Latin America. Such integration, through contrast, could not
provide an exhaustive coverage of all the relevant material.
Rather, a selective effort was made to synthesize those themes
that seemed most crucial for understanding the present situation.

It would be impossible to list here all those who have contributed directly or indirectly to the materials presented in this
book. They range from dedicated field workers and informants
to those colleagues in Latin America and the United States who

have provided us with useful ideas and suggestions. We owe a special debt of gratitude to the Institute of Latin American Studies at the University of Texas at Austin for a stimulating intellectual environment and for generous support with the processing of successive drafts. In particular, members of the Urban Studies Group of the Institute are thanked for their many informed observations and for the vital setting for discussion of comparative urban studies. Our students and research assistants who gave generously of their time and effort in the gathering of data and compiling of sources include Reynaldo Cué, Carlos Dávila, Michael Hennessy, Enrique Ogliastri, Adreain A. Ross, and Lindsay Woodruff. This brief testimony bears little relationship to the value of their contributions or to our gratitude. Finally, our wives, Nancy and Priscilla, deserve very special thanks. As social scientists in their own rights they have been actively involved in our research from the early days of field work through the penning of these lines. In addition to offering support they have made substantial contributions to our work and merit our greatest appreciation.

Alejandro Portes
John Walton

URBAN LATIN AMERICA

1 Introduction

Comparative urban research is a new and growing field aimed at generalizing our knowledge of urbanization and urban social organization cross culturally. Recent years have witnessed the appearance of specialized professional journals devoted to comparative urban studies as well as several collections of articles dealing with the city in Europe, the Middle East, Africa, and Latin America.[1] Because of its recency much of this literature has appeared in an unintegrated form, usually as distinct essays that are not linked together in any conceptual or theoretical schema. The purpose of this volume is to begin to integrate within a single theoretical framework much of the research on Latin American urban social organization. Each of our essays stands alone and can be read without reference to the others. Yet we believe that in combination they complement one another and constitute a holistic perspective.

Whether explicitly or implicitly conceptual in orientation, most urban research can be located within one of three distinctive traditions. With respect to urban studies in the United States, Scott Greer identifies these "images of the city" as based on a governmental, geographic, or economic conception of the unit of analysis.[2] In closely parallel terms, we would suggest that most comparative urban work could be classified within the traditions of *policy and planning, ecology and demography,* or *economics.* Within the policy-and-planning approach are studies focused on comparative public administration or public service delivery in such areas as housing, health, welfare, transportation, land use, and so forth.[3] The ecology-demography tradition, of course, has concentrated on processes of urbanization, migration, population, mobility, and settlement patterns. Finally, economic perspectives have emphasized the role of the city in economic development, regional *growth poles*, the labor force in urbanization, centralization-decentralization, and so forth.

The theoretical perspective and the organizational theme of this volume differ from the foregoing; in some senses they attempt to transcend them. That is, we assume that questions of urban planning, ecological patterning, and economic development are ultimately *political* questions, that a fundamental understanding of these processes or outcomes must rest upon an analysis of *political control and the mechanisms of access to power*. The planning of services, the use of land, and the decisions about development do not occur in a vacuum but may be instructively viewed as variable and problematic outcomes of the struggle for power and access to power among competitive urban groups.

More specifically our title refers to "studies from above and below" because we have attempted to bring together the formidable research literature on Latin America that deals separately with the political behavior of elites and masses. In the many hundreds of titles that touch on these groups, we know of few that endeavor to examine the *interface* between elites and masses, to simultaneously understand the political behavior of relatively powerless groups in terms of the interests and actions of those that hold power. Yet, it should be stressed that in this analysis we have not foreclosed on the issue of how political power is distributed in Latin American elites, or on what the consequences of its distribution may be. We regard the question as problematic and anticipate that its answer is likely to be structurally variable. We shall examine a number of competing views and subject them to a critical assessment based on both a broad canvass of the available evidence and our own research. This is not to suggest that we fancy ourselves "value-free." In recent years there has been a noticeable shift in the ideological underpinnings of Latin American urban and developmental research. Highly generalized, evolutionary-functional approaches based on the *politics of development* are losing ground to theories based on analyses of international stratification and structural dependency. While our affinities are for the latter, we do not believe that they render impossible an honest examination of these competing views. Within the social scientific norms of fairness we shall attempt to assess these positions at close range and on the basis of our interpretive syntheses of the evidence. Moreover, our aim is less to settle these theoretical disputes than to extend the contemporary limits of what we regard as more viable lines of inquiry.

In light of these objectives, the essays attempt to formulate and address some of the key questions about the structure of urban politics in Latin America. Chapter two, "The Economy and Ecology of Urban Poverty," develops the historical argument based on the fact that the Latin American city was a creation of European colonialism. Accordingly, its present organization is to be understood in terms of how the heritage of colonial dependence has articulated with contemporary economic considerations to determine settlement patterns and the nature of the problem confronting the urban poor. Assuming this background, chapter three, "The Politics of Urban Poverty," examines the extent and nature of political behavior among the urban poor with central reference to system support and countersystem potential. Chapter four, "Elites and the Politics of Urban Development," provides material from a comparative study of four cities that addresses the question of variability in elite structures and consequences for policy making vis-à-vis urban development. Chapter five, "Structures of Power in Latin American Cities," attempts to summarize a large number of studies and to develop a theoretical interpretation of their collective results based on class structure and vertical integration.

The essays on elites and masses dovetail in a variety of ways that relate to our theoretical perspective. The historical interpretation of the impact of colonialism on Latin American cities (chapter two) is specified in concrete detail in the explanation of elite performance and urban development (chapter four). The origins of urban elitism (chapter two) are found to be persistent influences on contemporary power structures that articulate in specified ways with new influences from the national and international systems (chapter five). Similarly, the effects of both repression and rational adaptation among the urban poor (chapter three) are reflected in the mechanisms and patterns of elite control (chapter five). In addition to these and other substantive linkages, the essays are methodologically convergent in the sense that they attempt to synthesize the research literature and move from generalized patterns to more finely grained interpretations based on available original studies.

A concluding chapter follows these essays and endeavors to generalize their findings. Here again the interface between elite and mass politics is elaborated. We close with some prospective comments about changes that seem to loom on the horizon and those new research strategies that should and will address them.

2

The Economy and Ecology of Urban Poverty

Alejandro Portes

Historical Antecedents

The forces that have given rise to the current physical and
social divisions of the Latin American city must be sought,
beyond recent developments, in the early history of urban
growth in the region. An impressive continuity exists between
the organization and class divisions of the early colonial city
and the present situation. General orientations toward use of
the urban land, position and goals of the elite, role of government, and treatment accorded to the disenfranchised were crystallized early in the colonial period and, with amazing resilience, managed to persist despite the pressure of major external
events in ensuing years. Imported capitalism and the institutions of northern European bourgeois democracy never replaced
the basic corporatist orientation—the framework of empire—
built by Spain and Portugal in the New World cities. For this
reason, the study of determinants of the current forms of urban
poverty in Latin America must start with the colonial beginnings of present cities. No attempt will be made to cover in detail the history of Spanish and Portuguese urban settlements on
the continent, a task exhaustively accomplished by previous
writers,[1] but rather we shall try to isolate the basic structural
forms and cultural themes that provided the framework for
present patterns of development of these cities. In the attempt
to highlight such dominant trends, some violence will be done
to inevitable historical exceptions. The reader is referred to the
above general accounts for descriptions of the many nuances in
the colonial urbanization process.

Urban Dominance

Unlike "natural" forms of urban growth, where the city emerges as a service center for an already settled hinterland, the Spanish and Portuguese cities in the New World were established in unknown and often hostile territories as centers of conquest and political control. They were founded by fiat, projected on the land as branches of an imperial strategy rather than crystallized as necessary centers for expanding commerce. As several writers have noted, the Pirennean and Weberian accounts of classic emergence of cities in northern Europe fit the case of Spanish and Portuguese colonial foundations poorly. Here, the city was not the product of vigorous commercial rebellion against lordly authority but rather an instrument of the royal will to expand and solidify its power.[2]

A gradualistic strategy of colonization, such as the one employed by the British in North America, would have meant restricted coastal enclaves moving slowly inward after the initial territory had been settled. Casting away this model, the Spaniards moved directly inland in search of indigenous centers of political control and other points where immediate wealth could be found. In the cases of the Inca and Aztec empires, minuscule military forces subdued the leaders and capital cities to superimpose Spanish political institutions over a well-established administrative structure.[3] The Spaniards seldom destroyed to build on their own terms but rather adapted opportunistically to what they found in order to serve their immediate economic interests. Cuzco and Tenochtitlán thus became centers of the new empire as they had been of the old, and, from their inland locations, the conquest moved toward the coast and in several other directions.[4]

This pattern of colonization, the direct opposite of the British gradualistic model, permitted Spain to conquer and control an entire continent in a few years with a very small occupying force. It was, it is true, a tenuous and fragile control at first, but it covered the entire territory and tended to solidify as the years passed. Gradually, cities abandoned the role of military enclaves for imposing European authority and became integrated as the administrative, economic, and cultural centers of vast regions. This urban-centered strategy of colonization had two immediate consequences: First, it restricted, from the start, the possible emergence of a "frontier" in the North American sense. Especially in the case of Spanish America, the major part of the territory was immediately, albeit tenuously, controlled. Subsequent colonization was directed at filling in and solidifying juridically existing holdings, seldom at creating new ones via expansion from initial coastal settlements.[5]

Second, it established, from the start, the supremacy of city over countryside. The foundation of cities did not respond to the pressing need for urban services by established agricultural settlers or to the actions of an increasingly independent class of burghers concentrated around a marketplace. Rather it followed the strategic requirement of concentrating scarce human resources in a restricted, and therefore militarily defensible, perimeter. The city did not arise to serve, but to subdue. From it the Spaniards moved out to a hostile environment to conquer, control, and indoctrinate the surrounding populations. Conquerors lived, by and large, in the city, while conquered remained in the countryside.

This role of cities and the resulting power differential between rural and urban populations were immediately reflected in the judicial order. The *Ordenanzas de descubrimiento y población* of 1573 contained 148 articles, of which 44 were dedicated exclusively to the establishment of new cities and towns, selection of sites, designation of the form that cities should adopt, and distribution of land. Cities were entrusted with the mission of channeling and socializing the ambitions of an unruly European population. The careful attention given by Charles I and Philip II to urban foundations and the role assigned to them are also reflected in the detailed *Instrucciones* to Governors Nicolas de Ovando and Pedrarias Dávila and, in 1523, to Hernán Cortés.[6]

Unlike that of the city in Europe and North America, jurisdiction of the Latin American city was not restricted to a specific area and did not leave the countryside in the hands of rural proprietors. Chartered Spanish American cities "owned" their hinterlands, both in the sense of economic proprietorship— since lands were granted in the king's name by city authorities —and in the sense of politico-administrative control. It was the function of cities to ensconce early settlers on the land, as strategy for consolidating imperial control and as means for fulfilling personal ambitions. The royal or viceroyal authorization granting a settlement the status of *ciudad* carried with it effective control over its hinterland, frequently with no limitation other than the extension of the jurisdiction of another city.[7]

The urban scheme created by Spain and Portugal in the New World was remarkably comprehensive and resilient in time. Unlike the gradual pattern of urban foundations and growth in North America, the network of urban centers in Latin America emerged during the course of a single century. Between 1520 and 1580, almost all major Spanish cities on the continent were founded. The period between 1520 and 1540, following the conquest of Mexico, was especially noticeable for its feverish urbanizing activity. Cities founded during these years included Mexico City, superimposed on Tenochtitlán, and Lima, founded by Pizarro as the political center of the Peruvian viceroyalty. Also founded in this period were Puebla, Mérida, Oaxaca, Santiago de los Caballeros de Guatemala, and Quezaltenango in the viceroyalty of New Spain. Cuzco, Quito, Trujillo, Cajamarca, Tunja, Cali, Bogotá, and Arequipa were founded in the viceroyalty of Peru. Asunción and the first foundation of Buenos Aires in what was to be the viceroyalty of the Río de la Plata also date from this period.

Between 1540 and 1580, the creation of a continent-wide urban scheme was completed with the foundations of Monterrey, Guadalajara, Caracas, Maracaibo, La Paz, Santa Cruz, Cochabamba, Potosí, and Santiago de Chile. In the Argentine, Buenos Aires was firmly established as the major harbor and Santa Fe, Córdoba, Tucumán, Corrientes, and Mendoza were founded. Early primitive harbors, such as Veracruz, Piura, El Callao, Panama City, and Cartagena, developed into established city ports. Bahia was founded in the Portuguese territories, eventually becoming the first capital of colonial Brazil. Olinda-Recife on the northern coast, São Paulo in the south, and Rio de Janeiro were the other major Portuguese foundations dating from this period. Among major Spanish American cities, only Montevideo and Medellín were founded after the sixteenth century. In Brazil, the foundation of Porto Alegre in 1642 completed a basic urban system modified only in recent years.[8]

While many cities changed locations, some more than once, few casualties were registered among the early foundations. Cities struggled under adverse conditions and survived, leaving to republican Latin America a ready-made urban network. Early resilience implied, however, the rigidification of urban growth within the old colonial framework. With practically no exceptions, major cities in Latin America developed as enlarged and often distorted versions of those founded at the very start of the colonial period.

The data in table 1 illustrate the pattern of foundations of major Latin American cities as well as the remarkable contrast with the urban history of the United States during the same period. Fifteen out of twenty major Latin American cities were founded during a sixty-year period beginning in 1520. Only two date from the next century and only Montevideo (1726), Porto Alegre (1742), and the planned city of Belo Horizonte (1897) were founded afterward. No such ready-made urbanization took place in the United States: Ten years separated the founding of New York and Boston. An additional thirty went by before the chartering of Newark and twenty more before Philadelphia. In total, only five major cities emerged in the first colonial century. Five additional cities were founded in the eighteenth century, prior to the end of the colonial period. The remaining ten major cities were established gradually in the postrepublican period, with the last settlement, Seattle, chartered in 1851.

Economic Exploitation

While it is true that politico-administrative centers, such as Lima and Mexico City, acquired decisive importance in Spanish America, the major thrust of colonial foundations remained economic. For Crown and colonists alike, administrative centers and military enclaves were means for conquest and control of the wealth of the new countries. In the category of cities founded primarily for economic reasons, one must include mining and agricultural settlements, as well as harbors, such as Callao, Cartagena, Veracruz, and La Habana. Earlier foundations searched for both fertile land and significant concentrations of docile indigenous labor. As Jorge Hardoy has noted, Indian influences in the urbanization process of Spanish America had to do less with architecture and layout than with site selection.[9] Cities dedicated to the exploitation of surrounding land and labor included the original foundations by Nicolas de Ovan-

Table 1. Population and Year of Foundation of the Twenty
Largest Cities in Latin America and the United States

Latin American Cities

City and Country	Metropolitan Population, 1970 Estimate[a] (1,000s)	Year City Was Founded[b]	Rank
Buenos Aires, Argentina	9,400	1536	1
Mexico City, Mexico	9,000	1521	2
São Paulo, Brazil	8,405	1554	3
Rio de Janeiro, Brazil	7,213	1555	4
Santiago, Chile	2,600	1541	5
Bogotá, Colombia	2,500	1538	6
Lima-Callao, Peru	2,500	1535	7
Caracas, Venezuela	2,147	1567	8
Porto Alegre, Brazil	1,842	1742	9
Recife, Brazil	1,794	ca. 1550	10
Belo Horizonte, Brazil	1,728	1897	11
Havana, Cuba	1,700	1519	12
Montevideo, Uruguay	1,530*	1726	13
Guadalajara, Mexico	1,364*	1541	14
Salvador, Brazil	1,032*	1549	15
Medellín, Colombia	1,090*	1675	16
Monterrey, Mexico	1,009*	1560s	17
Fortaleza, Brazil	982	1609	18
Cali, Colombia	915*	1536	19
Córdoba, Argentina	814	1573	20

[a]Source: Kingsley Davis, World Urbanization 1950–1970, Table F, Part 3, "Projected Population and Rank of World's 100 Largest Cities in 1970," pp. 239–241.

[b]Source: New Encyclopedia Britannica; Leon E. Seltzer, ed., Columbia Lippincott Gazetteer of the World.

do in Española and the seven towns established by Diego Veláz-quez in Cuba, as well as the archetypal mainland examples of Puebla in Mexico and Cuzco in Peru.[10]

Later, discovery of mineral wealth and the concession of royalties for exploitation (reales de minas) became other power-ful economic incentives for urban growth. These incentives

| City | United States Cities | |
	Metropolitan Population, 1970 Census[c] (1,000s)	Year City Was Founded[c]
New York	11,572	1620s
Los Angeles	7,032	1781
Chicago	6,979	1796
Philadelphia	4,818	1680s
Detroit	4,200	1701
San Francisco	3,110	1769
Washington, D.C.	2,861	1790s
Boston	2,754	1630
Pittsburgh	2,401	1750s
St. Louis	2,363	1764
Cleveland	2,064	1796
Houston	1,985	1836
Newark	1,857	1666
Minneapolis	1,814	1849
Baltimore	1,729*	1729
Dallas	1,556	1841
Seattle	1,422	1851
Milwaukee	1,404	1818
Cincinnati	1,385	1789
Paterson	1,359	1680s

[c]Source: Demographic Yearbook, Table 9, "Population of Capital City and Cities of 100,000 and More Inhabitants," pp. 353–381.
*City proper estimates—Figures for the metropolitan area are not available.

were responsible for the founding of Guanajuato and Taxco in New Spain and Huancavelica and Potosí in Peru. By 1640, Potosí had 140,000 inhabitants and was by far the largest and most important city on the continent. Gold was also the cause behind the phenomenal urban growth in southern Brazil at the beginning of the eighteenth century. Gold was discovered by *paulis-*

tas in the territory of Minas Gerais. Villa Rica, or Ouro Preto, was the most notable of the instant cities that emerged from this discovery. Its wealth and growth were justified by the fact that between 1690 and 1770 half of the world's production of gold was extracted from Brazil. With depletion of the mines, this city and others in the region declined.[11]

While the importance of political centers reflected the centralization of the colonial administration and while the growth of harbors was a direct consequence of the external dependence of the colonies on the Spanish and Portuguese crowns, the economic characteristics of the rest of the foundations revealed the predatory nature of the colonial enterprise. An ad hoc typology of economic motivations for conquest of new lands could be constructed that divides such efforts into two categories: (1) Settlers may apply their skills to organize, implement, or otherwise put to use natural resources of a new territory. In this enterprise, the main ingredients are the knowledge and organized labor of the colonists themselves. Such settlements may be termed *developmental*. (2) New territories may be occupied for the purpose of plundering, taxing, or otherwise profiting from the available resources and native populations. Colonists are less interested in developing natural resources through their direct labor than in appropriating value produced by others. This type may be labeled *exploitative*.

Spanish and Portuguese urban foundations in the New World were, by and large, of a thoroughly exploitative nature. Some were superimposed on previously existing indigenous cities; others grew with the frenzied search for mineral wealth. Cities with an agricultural hinterland differed from similar settlements in other parts of the world in that they were established prior to organized agricultural production with the explicit purpose of subduing and appropriating the labor of the surrounding populations.[12]

The predatory nature of early urban settlements was closely linked with the interests of both the central governments and the colonists themselves. For the Spanish monarchy, the New World functioned primarily as a source of wealth, either in the form of gold and other precious metals or in the form of indirect revenues from agricultural production and commerce. While such monarchs as Charles I and Philip II made significant efforts to organize the new territories on a rational long-term basis, the main thrust from the central administration was toward maximization of immediate income from its American colonies. This effort was closely linked with the pressing need for financial resources to support the Court and army and to finance the European adventures of the kingdom.[13]

The emphasis on short-run acquisition of wealth was reinforced by motivations of those who traveled to the New World. The ambition of early conquerors and later colonists was not to secure land they could work but rather to exploit all available opportunities to amass a rapid fortune and return to Europe. New World settlements were thus viewed, not as final destinations, but as temporary means for attainment of economic goals. This pattern corresponded to, among other factors, the prevailing system for transmission of wealth in Spain. The rule of primogeniture relegated second or later sons in noble families to a search for alternative channels through which to secure a fortune commensurate with their social rank. It became institutionalized among these families that *segundones* would leave the homeland in search of opportunities in the New World.[14] While this source of emigration was not the only or most important one, it documents well the dominant motivations of America-bound colonists. Few in fact returned to Europe with wealth, but the original orientations persisted.

As noted by Ralph Gakenheimer,[15] Spaniards oriented themselves overwhelmingly toward the cities, regardless of whether their origins had been urban or rural. This was due in no small measure to the urban strategy of colonization of new territories, but, even in those settled areas where rural life and work were possible, few seemed disposed to move into the interior. Cities offered the only setting where an exploitative orientation could be implemented successfully. Ownership of land offered about the only effective opportunity for wealth and social position, and land was allocated by city authorities.

Founders of a new city received large tracts, with the remainder allocated among subsequent arrivals with the proper qualifications. The extensive tracts granted to early settlers were given in perpetuity and, with time, became the basis for emergence of an urban patriciate. In successful settlements, chartered land proprietors—the *vecinos*—became an elite that monopolized not only economic wealth but social prestige and access to political offices as well.

Exploitative colonization requires not only land but also subject labor. Cities also offered means for securing this resource via the royally established system of *encomiendas*. *Encomenderos* were urban settlers entrusted with a certain number of natives who, in theory, were to be protected, taught the Spanish language, and converted to the Catholic faith. In practice, the institution became an instrument for free allocation of indigenous labor.[16] Successful colonists thus received the necessary means of production: free land and free labor with which to satisfy their economic ambitions. Most did little more than take advantage of what was available without any systematic improvement of these resources.

The strategy of urban settlements of colonization and the system of *encomiendas* thus functioned as instruments for extending the Crown's possessions in the new continent and as means for satisfying dreams of enrichment and social position among the colonists. The result could not have been the growth of a dynamic urban bourgeoisie. Instead, a premature aristocracy, excessively preoccupied with reproducing European life styles in vastly different surroundings, evolved. The attempt of Diego Colón to establish a viceroyal court in Española at the very beginning of the conquest stood as a symbol of the orientations that were to dominate the next century and a half of colonization.

Three aspects of the process must be stressed for their influence on later urban developments: First, cities in Spanish America were established by men whose orientations toward the settlements themselves and their hinterlands were as mere means to the achievement of economic and social goals whose final locus was in Europe. Second, this exploitative attitude toward resources was legitimized by a social order that supported it via the widespread distortion of the original purpose of *encomiendas*. Third, goals of economic wealth and social position were based on private ownership of land, an institution held sacred by colonial society. Few limitations were imposed on exploitation of land for personal enrichment since its possession was defined as a quasi-absolute right.

Urban Elitism

As noted above, only landowners—the *vecinos*—had access to

positions of political authority. It is true that upon foundation, and for many years thereafter in the case of poor cities, the only inhabitants were the *vecinos*. In cases of important harbors, political centers, and cities in rich territories, however, the population swelled with new arrivals from Spain and natives from the interior. Spaniards of proper rank were also admitted into the landowning minority. The very size of tracts granted, however, accelerated the exhaustion of available land in the urban periphery. Without alternative channels for upward mobility, the social structure of many cities was at this point effectively closed.

Landowners remained for many years the only important city dwellers. They had the use of land and Indian labor, had the right to hold office, and bore most of the financial burdens of the municipality. In early years they were also the only source of military resources and personnel for the defense of the colonies. Thus, the first colonial censuses tended to be much more concerned with counting the number of *vecinos* than the total number of inhabitants of municipalities. In 1561, a report placed the number of *vecinos* in the entire viceroyalty of Peru at 427. In the same year the total population of the ten main municipalities of the viceroyalty was estimated to be 1,536,692. The municipality of Lima (city and hinterland) had 99,600 inhabitants of whom around 2,500 lived in the city proper. Of these, no more than 40 had the title of *vecino*. Similar figures for Cuzco were 267,000 inhabitants, 500 residents within the city, and 80 *vecinos*.[17]

By 1630 the number of *vecinos* in 165 cities throughout the continent was estimated to be 77,398, though the figure was probably inflated by counting all Spanish adult males, many of whom were not property owners. According to some official censuses, the population of the city of Lima was 25,434 in 1614. Of these, only 37.8 percent were Spaniards. The percentage of Spanish population in other cities was even lower. Spaniards represented 21.2 percent of the population of Panama City in 1610 and 16.2 percent of that of Santiago de Chile in 1613. Even these figures grossly overestimate the number of *vecinos* by including those without property (which were the majority) and their women and children.[18]

The markedly elitist character of the Spanish American city was thus defined by the superior positions of the few families of the founders and early arrivals who monopolized means for acquisition of wealth, governmental positions, and prestige. Later arrivals (of high rank) formed an inferior class, termed in many cities *soldiers*.[19] It formed a restless group in constant search of whatever opportunity became available to reach positions similar to those already occupied by the urban elite. Next came Spaniards of lower rank, foreigners, and the lower masses of mestizos and native Indians who came into cities as servants or in search of economic opportunities. To these were added, in time, imported black slaves and freed mulattoes.

Elites of rapidly growing cities governed them largely in their own interests with a measure of respect for the interests of Crown and Church, but without much concern for those of the new urban masses. Lower groups were allowed into the city, but few channels were provided for integrating them into the social structure. They had essentially the status of disenfranchised masses—permitted to fend for themselves in the city under the benign indifference of the authorities.

It is a fact seldom noted that major colonial cities quickly became acquainted with the phenomenon of internal migration. Destruction of preconquest patterns of agricultural production forced many natives, survivors of the *encomiendas*, to look for their livelihood in cities. Many were brought as servants; others gradually established themselves as small artisans and menial workers. These concentrated, like the Spanish population they served, in the largest cities, such as Mexico City, Lima, and Potosí, or, on a lesser scale, Cuzco and Guadalajara.

Though of much lesser magnitude than subsequent movements, early migrations confronted cities for the first time with the phenomenon of impoverished groups coming in search of whatever opportunities were available. The established city— early settlers now transformed into *señores* and political authorities—permitted the presence of disenfranchised masses and their efforts at economic survival but did not assume responsibility for their fate. Extreme cases had open to them the charity institutions of the Church, which offered the only, albeit feeble, link of aid from the powerful to the powerless.[20]

Urban reception of the poor thus crystallized from early years into a mixture of tolerance and indifference. As cities grew, the initial relative egalitarianism among founders changed into sharp separation of the classes, dividing established groups from the masses (formed by later European arrivals), freed blacks and mulattoes, and incipient native migrants from the interior. The elitist character of urban structure and the place that rural and other migrants occupied in it emerged, therefore, quite early in the Spanish American city. It need not be emphasized how these traits were destined to serve as precedents to later urban developments.

Spatial Patterns

The ecology of the early colonial city reflected well the centralized character of its social structure. The characteristic grid pattern of streets and blocks emerged from the central plaza, which, left empty except for minor adornments, was usually a square no larger than other city blocks. The main plaza served the multiple functions of marketplace on certain days, recreational center on others, and point of military concentration in times of danger. Around the plaza were concentrated the most important buildings, such as those housing political authorities from viceroys and *audiencias* to governors and municipalities. At the plaza was also located the cathedral or main church. In the style exemplified by Lima, the façade of the cathedral faced the main square. In the style of Puebla, the nave ran parallel to one of the sides of the plaza.[21]

The residences of the rich and powerful, the aristocracy formed by *vecinos* and political and religious authorities, were concentrated around the main plaza. This first concentric zone around the plaza contained the largest and best built houses and often had public lighting and street pavement. The convents of the most important orders were also located in this area; it was not uncommon to have small *plazoletas* facing their chapels. The next zone contained the homes of a rudimentary middle class of established artisans, government clerks, and small merchants and proprietors. Residences, which in the first zone were large one-story or even two-story buildings, became smaller and more primitive. The grid pattern persisted, but lighting and pavement disappeared. The third zone, the outskirts of the city, was a mixture of the poorest residences of artisans and menial workers with the beginnings of small farms. Beyond this area only an occasional chapel or country store at a crossroads could be found.[22]

With exceptions due to the terrain and the functional special-
ization of some streets and areas, this pattern seems to have
predominated in most colonial foundations. A regular layout
was first attempted in the second foundation of Santo Domingo
in 1504. Streets still did not form perfect parallelograms but
yielded a more regular distribution of residences than the camp-
like appearance of the first settlements. The model was improved in subsequent cases, such as that of Panama City, and
culminated in the foundations of Puebla in 1531 and Lima in
1535. City blocks in Puebla were rectangular; those in Lima,
square. With this difference, they formed the final urban
models, which, after two decades of experimentation and trial
and error, became adopted as the most efficient for the particular economic and social circumstances of the colonization.[23]

Exceptions to this model, besides earlier cities and instant
mining settlements, were those situated on difficult terrain. Harbors like Callao, Valparaíso, and Cartagena were the most common examples. In Brazil, the first important city, Bahia, followed an irregular layout of narrow, tortuous streets similar to
the medieval cities dominant in Portugal. The difficult topography of Rio de Janeiro made any attempt at regular development impossible.

For the most part, however, cities in the colonial period followed the simple, regular, highly cephalic pattern delineated
above. The city focused on its central plaza, and access to the
centers of economic, political, religious, and recreational activity, situated around the plaza, was the most prized aspect of
urban location. A rough but consistent positive correlation prevailed between the social and economic position of an individual and the physical distance of his residence from the central
square: the greater the distance, the lower the social status.
Elitism and centralization thus had in the colonial city their
ecological counterpart. As a small aristocracy controlled access
to legitimate wealth, power, and social prestige, it also came to
monopolize the most desirable urban locations—those at the
heart of urban life.

The Republican Period

From the early days of independence at the beginning of the
nineteenth century and until very recently, the urban scheme

that Latin American countries inherited from the colony remained essentially unchanged. A *criollo* elite reared during colonial days took the place of the Spanish and Portuguese authorities but continued to emphasize urban life and to govern cities largely in its own interest. The simple, cephalic pattern of urban settlement continued to reflect the simple, centralized character of urban structure: "Seen from the outside, the city was immediately understood; everything was revealed at first glance. The location of the cathedral and the main square, the parishes, the city gates, the fort when there was one; the rest were houses, the best ones near the center—the most simple ones, almost huts, on the outskirts."[24]

As seen above, only Belo Horizonte, among major Latin American cities, was founded during the republican period. The colonial urban scheme was maintained intact with its cities growing at different rates. The nineteenth and early twentieth centuries brought only two changes of importance to the existing order: First, the primacy of a few cities was accentuated during this period. Lima and Mexico City, the most important colonial cities, accelerated their pace of growth, outdistancing others in the area. La Habana, as the most important remaining Spanish city, came close behind. Caracas, Bogotá, and Santiago de Chile also grew rapidly. On the Río de la Plata, Buenos Aires and, to a lesser extent, Montevideo experienced rapid growth as a consequence of massive European immigration.[25]

The location of capitals of the new republics in the most important existing cities accentuated their predominance by superimposing central political functions on economic ones. Capitals and a few other cities benefited at the expense of others from the commercial policies followed by republican governments.

While Spanish and Portuguese colonial rules emphasized the city over the countryside, they provided existing cities with a measure of economic autonomy. Each served as a commercial center for a vast hinterland and maintained (legal or illegal) contacts with the outside. Concentration of urban development in a few cities gradually stripped the remaining ones of their economic autonomy.[26] While they continued to grow, they came to depend more and more on directives from primary cities. The economic and social orientation of most cities toward their own hinterland gradually changed as they became functional appendages of enterprises and authorities centered in the capital.

Gigantic heads of dwarfish bodies emerged and with them the basic conditions for the regional imbalances and internal dependence characteristic of the contemporary period.

Within major cities themselves, a second change during the republican period was the gradual displacement of elite families from the center to selected portions of the urban periphery. Three related factors seem to have promoted this trend. First, by mid-nineteenth century many large cities had become relatively crowded. As density around the city center increased, wealthy families began to look for residential environments that were both more pleasant and more isolated than other social sectors. Second, better roads and means of transportation made the center of the city more accessible from distant locations than it had been. Easy access to central locations remained a crucial consideration since the political, economic, religious, and recreational life of the city continued to be concentrated in them. Third, world demand for primary products of several countries suddenly enriched many families. Coffee, sugar, or beef became the basis for revitalizing old fortunes or creating new ones. Dominant patterns of high consumption dictated that part of this new wealth should be invested in larger and more luxurious residences.[27]

As Homer Hoyt has noted in the case of U.S. cities, upper-class displacement tended to occur consistently in a single direction.[28] In both North and South America, the movement invariably pointed to the most desirable areas of the urban periphery in terms of geographic, climatic, and aesthetic factors. Elite displacement was preceded or followed by the extension of the highest quality of urban services, infrastructure, and means of communication available to these areas. Elite control of the mechanisms of political authority allowed it to choose its residential settings while frequently placing the burden for extending necessary urban services on the entire community.

In Lima elite displacement started relatively early. By the second half of the nineteenth century, there was a visible front of upper-class residences moving west toward the Pacific Ocean. During the first decades of this century, elegant residences reached the ocean and bordered the new Arequipa Avenue, forming the suburb of Miraflores. In Santiago de Chile the trend also started early, moving northeast along Providencia Avenue toward the Andes. The search here was for higher ground, which provided better aesthetic and, especially, climatic conditions.[29]

In Mexico City, the movement was not visible until the late 1920s. Upper- and middle-class residences began to appear in the south, along Insurgentes Avenue and the road of Tacubaya. The residential colonies of Lomas de Chapultepec, Mixcoac, and Tacuba, among others, date from this period. In Buenos Aires elite families moved en masse from traditional locations in the southern portion of the central city toward the north. Fear of epidemics and the generally unhealthy conditions of the old sites near the harbor lay behind this move. Wealth from beef and wheat was soon translated into magnificent new residences, which formed the nucleus of the exclusive Barrio Norte.[30]

In Bogotá, a smaller city, elite displacement began later. During the first decades of the twentieth century, wealthy families began to move slowly toward the more desirable locations in the north of the city. The creation and growth of La Merced and La Magdalena, among other areas, date from this time. The continuous displacement of the elite toward northern locations and the growth of impoverished masses that settled in the south changed in a few years the social ecology of that city. From a simple cephalic pattern of successive concentric circles, Bogotá was transformed into a sharp physical dichotomy: the rich and powerful in the north, the poor and powerless in the south, and a feeble middle class of employees and small merchants occupying the center.[31]

Elite displacement in these and other major cities gradually reversed the traditional correlation between residential location and socioeconomic position. Social status, previously associated with nearness to the central city, became related to distance away from it, but only in those directions chosen by elite migration.

Regardless of its location, the urban upper stratum continued to maintain control of political and economic power and to exercise it authoritatively or paternalistically, as the occasion required. In the monolithic social structure of these cities, other groups existed by virtue of, and derived their social meaning from, their relationships with the elite.

The stability of this social order was not a mere function of the elite control of wealth and military resources but was based on belief among subordinate groups in the essential legitimacy

of existing arrangements. Positions of elite members were legitimized not only through their interests but also through the
values shared by the rest of the population. The generalized acceptance by subordinate groups of the existing distribution of
power and wealth prevented massive rebellions and permitted
institutions of urban government to adopt the facile role of cus-
todians of a consensually supported order.[32] While serving in
reality the interests of the elite, they were manifestly defined,
by themselves and others, as representative of the entire city.

Summary

The above outline of the early urban history of Latin America
aims not at exhaustive coverage but rather at isolating those aspects that laid the groundwork for contemporary developments.
The phenomenon that will serve as focus of ensuing chapters—
contemporary urban poverty—can be properly understood only
against the background provided by the birth and later evolution
of these cities. The argument will not be made that early historical occurrences "caused" the present situation. While direct
causal links between the historical past and the present can be
found, the crucial point is that the colonial urban framework
provided logical continuity for later structural developments.

The economic and social evolution of Latin American cities
never deviated markedly from the general directions set in
colonial days. It is this inertial force of early events that permitted the natural acceptance of subsequent chains of events,
an almost imperceptible evolution that led, by gradual steps, to
present patterns of massive poverty and structural polarization.

Present cities served as loci for the Iberian conquest, gaining
from the start a dominance over the countryside, which they
never lost. They were settled by men who defined the city and
rural hinterland as means for social position and rapid enrichment. Their orientations promoted an exploitative culture that
legitimized unregulated use of land and labor for private profit.
The juridical order reflected these values by upholding the
quasi-absolute character of property rights. Those who were
successful within this order joined the ranks of land proprietors,
which soon evolved into a self-regulating aristocracy. Their

control of economic and political resources and the absence of resistance from lower groups, especially nonwhite working masses, allowed them to mold cities largely in their own image. Urban ecology reflected this elitist social order in its simple, highly focused pattern of settlement.

Independence from Spain and Portugal brought few changes except those that accentuated structural imbalances between urban and rural areas and between primary and other cities. The urban upper stratum maintained its social position but displaced itself gradually from an increasingly crowded center into more desirable locations.

Acquainted since colonial days with urban poverty and the migration of impoverished groups in search of economic opportunity, this elite permitted continuation of an inertial trend. The eventual fate of the poor, allowed to enter the city as sources of cheap labor, remained an object of total unconcern to the official and wealthy city, except perhaps as objects of Catholic charity.

It is within this general portrait of legitimized elitism, adherence to canons of private property, growing structural imbalances, and official disregard for their consequences on popular sectors that origins of urban poverty and forms adopted by it in recent years must be understood.

Economic Factors

The peculiar features of contemporary urban poverty in Latin America are directly linked to the evolution of national economies in the region and to the structural hierarchy of power that guides them. Perhaps one of the closest similarities among Latin American countries is the manner in which they effected the transition of their economies from the colonial to the republican (or imperial) period. The close and self-serving control of commerce exercised by Spain and Portugal gave way, after independence, to a brief economic vacuum. The victorious *criollo* elites had no inclination to implement a vigorous developmental strategy of their own, preferring to spend their energies on internal political struggles or on the acquisition of refinement in the civilized lands of Europe.

The profound influence of a predatory orientation, crystallized during early colonial days, was shown throughout this period with utmost clarity. Land, wealth, and cheap labor were regarded rather passively, not as elements for dynamic entrepreneurship and expansion, but as sources of rent to be spent on noneconomic pursuits. Such an orientation found its concrete reflection in the life style of elites—wealthy landowners for the most part—who used their rents to live away from their rural sources, either in major cities or in Europe.[33]

This exploitative economic order was easy prey to the capitalist currents branching out from the industrialized nations. Without exception, the new republics entered into the spheres of influence of one or another of the major capitalist powers, with Britain as the most important of the group. International commercial-industrial interests forged a pattern of constrained capitalism for the region as producer of primary commodities and market for surplus manufactures.

The point to be stressed, however, is that this dependent role was not particularly resisted by local establishments since it fitted in well with the economic order legitimized from early colonial days. The goal of these elites was not to compete with but rather to adapt to the new international order. A symbiotic relationship was established between the interests of capitalist centers and those of local elites: the former acquired new markets and economic expansion; the latter, untroubled flow of rents for consumption and the financing of political causes. The new commercial capitalism, moreover, did not do violence to a traditional social structure endorsing the rights of private property and ownership for profit.

Latin American economies, structured without exception around dependent capitalism, continued to evolve during the nineteenth and twentieth centuries under the increasing domination of the United States. Foreign tutelage and the pressures of internal differentiation and growth have led to two highly visible developments in recent years: First, industrialization, mostly of the import-substitution variety, has gained a visible foothold in the region. While industry has reached some maturity in the larger countries, it remains in an incipient stage in most. In all cases it concentrates in the larger cities and is controlled, to a large extent, by foreign corporations.

Second, massive processes of internal migration from rural to urban areas, and from smaller cities and towns to primary cities, have occurred during the last four decades. To a large degree, this has been a migration of the poor and destitute and has resulted in the emergence of shantytown belts around the larger cities.

The two trends—industrial concentration and rural-urban migration—form the intervening links through which the economics of external dependency has been seen to affect development of cities in Latin America.[34] Specific implications of this economic order for patterns of city growth are the subject of the following sections.

Capitalism and Urbanization

Massive urban poverty, the type characterized by emergence of fringe squatter settlements, occurs only under capitalism.[35] Not all capitalist countries exhibit this pattern, however. Though extensive poverty is present even in the most developed nations, it tends to occur in them under less precarious conditions. Even then, the presence of numerous shantytowns—*bidonvilles*— around a developed capital like Paris gives testimony to the persistence of the phenomenon.

With the sole exception of Cuba, urban poverty, which finds its physical expression in thousands of individuals living in shacks on illegally occupied land, is found throughout Latin America. It is important to examine in great detail the concatenation of events leading from the particular forms of capitalist organization in the region to their specific urban impact. The development of capitalism in Latin America can be characterized in this regard by four main aspects: (1) it occurs under, and tends to perpetuate, conditions of chronic material scarcity; (2) it is superimposed on a social structure centered around cities where the political role and economic evolution of rural areas were, until recently, primitive; (3) industrial capital is controlled to a large extent by foreign-owned corporations, which have a major say in the direction of national development; and (4) economic growth remains tied to foreign trade and, hence, is affected by the conditions of external markets over which the country has little control. Persistent deterioration of the prices of many primary products and the growing demand for imports either for direct consumption or for industrial development lead to chronic deficits in the balance of payments. This situation, plus the internal scarcity of governmental resources and agricultural-supply bottlenecks, leads to persistent inflationary pressures.

The economic pattern of foreign and domestic investments can be depicted as a rational adaptation to these general conditions. In particular, two consequences deserve emphasis: First, a scarcity of capital, investment resources, and trained personnel leads to concentration of the little that is available in a few centers. This tendency is reinforced by a historical pattern of centralizing economic functions in major cities. Concentration of the larger markets, facilities of infrastructure, better transportation systems, skilled personnel, and cheap unskilled labor in a few metropolitan centers has, in turn, led foreign-sponsored industrial ventures to center in the same areas, thus aggravating regional imbalances. Second, chronic inflation and control of major industrial development by large, usually foreign-owned corporations have led a large portion of domestic capital to be invested in the urban land market. Land investment is the most secure defense against a deteriorating currency, and the pattern of rapid urban growth has resulted in sharp increases in the real value of land. Land speculation thus offers the possibility of augmenting wealth without excessive risks and without the complexities of industrial investment. The passive nature of this investment fits in well with the traditional exploitative orientation of economic activity in the region.

Intensive capital investment in urban land and a traditional respect for property rights resulted in the growth of many cities almost exclusively shaped by private interests. Feeble government regulation has allowed the price of land to be established by market forces that pushed it steadily upward in response to high demand and speculation.[36]

The final step in the concatenate events consists in the response of popular sectors to the above patterns of capital investment and resource concentration. Two trends are especially important: (1) in response to the concentration of industry, resources, and opportunities in a few cities, rural and small-town lower-class groups have tended to migrate with increasing rapidity and in increasing numbers to the larger centers, and

(2) in response to capitalist speculation in urban land values and a land market that automatically prices the poor out, migrant sectors have tended to generate their own "reception centers" in the city.[37] The poor have bypassed established market procedures by settling unoccupied land illegally. The result has been the large-scale emergence of squatter or "uncontrolled"[38] settlements and the forced partition of the system of urban land allocation into a dual structure: one formal and governed by capitalist market forces, the other informal and ruled by popular demand.

The first trend, lower-class rural-urban migration, has been discussed above and constitutes, perhaps, the topic most exhaustively examined in the literature on Latin American urbanization. Population migration obviously stimulates trends toward centralization and concentration in a few overexpanded centers. These trends are illustrated by compelling demographic data, such as the ones presented in tables 2 and 3.

In table 2, recent available data on the largest city of each Latin American country are presented. The proportion of the total population concentrated in the primary city seldom falls below 10 percent of the national population, and in fourteen out of twenty cases it reaches or exceeds 15 percent. Buenos Aires contains 39 percent and Montevideo 46 percent of their respective national populations. Santiago, San José, and Panamá all exceed 25 percent.

More importantly, perhaps, figures on population growth point to an acceleration of this trend. With the notable exception of Cuba, where the primary city grows at a much slower rate than the total population, and Panama, where growth rates are identical, the annual population increase of the largest city considerably exceeds that of the nation as a whole. Ratios of urban primate to national growth rates exceed 1.5 in fourteen out of twenty cases; in five countries—Brazil, Colombia, Haiti, Peru, and Uruguay—the growth of the largest city more than doubles the total growth rate.

The pattern of interurban centralization is perhaps best depicted by the index of urban primacy. This is the ratio of the largest urban concentration to the sum of the population in the next three largest cities. In all but two cases, the index exceeds 1.0, indicating that the primary city is larger than the next three cities put together. The index reaches such implausibly high

Table 2. Population Characteristics of Largest Cities in Latin American Countries

Country[a] Total Population (1,000s)	Largest City[b] Metropolitan Population (1,000s) (A)	Year of Census or Estimate	% of Total Population Concentrated in Largest City	% of Total Urban Population Concentrated in Largest City[a]
Argentina (24,089)	Buenos Aires (9,400)	1970	39.0	63.8
Bolivia (3,956)	La Paz (500)	1970	12.0	83.3
Brazil (93,545)	São Paulo (8,405)	1970	8.9	26.5
Chile (9,510)	Santiago (2,600)	1970	27.3	73.8
Colombia (21,168)	Bogotá (2,500)	1970	11.8	30.6
Costa Rica (1,767)	San José (435)	1970	25.6	100.0

Next Three Largest Cities[c] Metropolitan Population (1,000s) (B)	Index of Urban Primacy (A/B)	Annual Rate of Growth of Largest City[b] 1960–1970 (C) (%)	Total Rate of Growth of Population (D) (%)	Ratio of Urban Primate to Total Population Rates of Growth (C/D)
Córdoba (814) Rosario (806) Mendoza (712)	4.03	3.0	1.9	1.58
Cochabamba* (158) Santa Cruz* (109) Oruro* (91)	1.40	2.3	1.4	1.64
Rio de Janeiro (7,231) Porto Alégre (1,842) Recife (1,794)	.77	6.4	2.8	2.29
Valparaíso-Viña del Mar (455) Concepción-Talcahuano (325) Antofagasta (140)	2.83	3.1	2.0	1.55
Medellín (1,090) Cali (915) Barranquilla (645)	.94	7.3	3.2	2.28
Puerto Limón (24) Alajuela (29) Puntarenas (24)	5.65	5.4	4.2	1.29

Table 2—Continued

Country[a] Total Population (1,000s)	Largest City[b] Metropolitan Population (1,000s) (A)	Year of Census or Estimate	% of Total Population Concentrated in Largest City	% of Total Urban Population Concentrated in Largest City[a]
Cuba (8,663)	La Habana (1,700)	1970	19.6	64.2
Dominican Republic (4,324)	Santo Domingo (650)	1970	15.0	85.5
Ecuador (6,089)	Guayaquil (800)	1970	13.1	61.5
El Salvador (3,499)	San Salvador (375)	1969 1970	10.7	78.9
Guatemala (5,172)	Guatemala City (770)	1970	14.8	100.0
Haiti (4,856)	Port-au-Prince (400)	1970	8.2	100.0

Next Three Largest Cities[c] Metropolitan Population (1,000s) (B)	Index of Urban Primacy (A/B)	Annual Rate of Growth of Largest City[b] 1960–1970 (C) (%)	Total Rate of Growth of Population (D) (%)	Ratio of Urban Primate to Total Population Rates of Growth (C/D)
Santiago de Cuba (280) Camaguey (225) Santa Clara (180)	2.48	.9	2.4	.38
Santiago de los Caballeros (155) San Francisco de Macorís (44) San Pedro de Macorís (44)	2.67	5.9	3.6	1.64
Quito* (528) Cuenca* (77) Ambato* (75)	1.18	5.9	3.4	1.74
Santa Ana* (168) San Miguel* (108) Zacatecoluca* (55)	1.13	4.6	3.6	1.28
Quezaltenango* (54) Escuintla* (32) Puerto Barrios* (29)	6.7	5.0	3.1	1.61
Cap-Haiten* (44) Pétionville* (30) Gonaïves* (26)	4.0	5.2	2.0	2.60

Table 2—Continued

Country[a] Total Population (1,000s)	Largest City[b] Metropolitan Population (1,000s) (A)	Year of Census or Estimate	% of Total Population Concentrated in Largest City	% of Total Urban Population Concentrated in Largest City[a]
Honduras (2,703)	Tegucigalpa (281)	1968 1970	10.3	74.0
Mexico (50,624)	Mexico City (9,000)	1970	17.7	52.4
Nicaragua (1,989)	Managua (350)	1967 1970	17.5	100.0
Panama (1,465)	Panama City (440)	1970	30.0	100.0
Paraguay (2,378)	Asunción (445)	1970	18.7	100.0
Peru (13,581)	Lima-Callao (2,500)	1970	18.4	78.6

Next Three Largest Cities[c] Metropolitan Population (1,000s) (B)	Index of Urban Primacy (A/B)	Annual Rate of Growth of Largest City[b] 1960–1970 (C) (%)	Total Rate of Growth of Population (D) (%)	Ratio of Urban Primate to Total Population Rates of Growth (C/D)
San Pedro** (102) La Ceiba*** (34) Puerto Cortés*** (21)	1.79	5.9	3.4	1.74
Guadalajara (1,364) Monterrey (1,009) Ciudad Juárez (532)	3.1	4.9	3.8	1.29
León* (89) Matagalpa* (76) Chinandega* (53)	1.61	5.9	3.5	1.69
San Miguelito* (70) Colón* (68) David* (36) Santiago* (14)	3.96	4.9	3.1	1.0
Encarnación**** (27) Concepción**** (25) Villarrica**** (22)	6.01	3.6	3.1	1.16
Arequipa (190) Chiclayo (140) Trujillo (140)	5.32	5.1	2.1	2.43

Table 2—Continued

Country[a] Total Population (1,000s)	Largest City[b] Metropolitan Population (1,000s) (A)	Year of Census or Estimate	% of Total Population Concentrated in Largest City	% of Total Urban Population Concentrated in Largest City[a]
Uruguay (2,889)	Montevideo (1,350)	1970	46.7	88.2
Venezuela (10,390)	Caracas (2,147)	1970	20.6	56.0

[a]Source: Kingsley Davis, *World Urbanization 1950–1970*, Table A, "Total, Rural, Urban and City Populations," pp. 57–82. Urban population includes large urban centers with populations over 100,000 and towns with populations of less than 100,000 that have urban characteristics.

[b]Source: Ibid., Table E, "Population of Cities of 100,000 or more in 1950, 1960, and (Estimated) 1970, with Growth Rates," pp. 163–233.

[c]In the endeavor toward comparability, figures for largest cities populations were taken from Table E in Davis, *World Urbanization*, whenever they were given. Figures from sources other than Davis are indicated by asterisks.

América en cifras 1972, Table 201–207, "Población de la capital y ciudades principales, 1962–1971," pp. 31–36.

values as 5.65 for Costa Rica, 6.7 for Guatemala, 5.32 for Peru, and 8.88 for Uruguay. One of the two exceptions, Brazil, is a notable case of urban bicephalism, leaving only Colombia as an example of a nonatrophied, acceptably balanced urban system.

Table 3 provides additional data by countries, further documenting the trend toward urban concentration. National populations are more than 70 percent urban in Argentina, Chile, Uruguay, and Venezuela, and more than 50 percent in Brazil, Colombia, Cuba, and Mexico. Only in the case of Haiti does this figure fall below 25 percent. The rate of urban population growth is, without exception, higher than that of the nation as a whole. The growth of large cities (100,000+) exceeds, in all

Next Three Largest Cities[c] Metropolitan Population (1,000s) (B)	Index of Urban Primacy (A/B)	Annual Rate of Growth of Largest City[b] 1960–1970 (C) (%)	Total Rate of Growth of Population (D) (%)	Ratio of Urban Primate to Total Population Rates of Growth (C/D)
Salto*** (58) Paysandú*** (52) Piedras*** (42)	8.38	4.7	1.3	3.62
Maracaibo (682) Barquisimeto (281) Valencia (222)	1.81	5.3	3.5	1.51

**Demographic Yearbook, Table 9, "Population of Capital City and Cities of 100,000 and More Inhabitants," pp. 353–381.

***Figures for the third and fourth largest cities of Honduras and the second, third, and fourth largest cities in Uruguay are not given in any of the above sources. The Honduran figures are taken from the Honduran National Census (1968) and the Uruguayan figures from the Uruguayan Census (1963).

****In the case of Paraguay there is a large gap between the date of the figure for the largest city (1970) and the date of the figure for the next largest cities (1962). The final estimates are based on 1962 figures adjusted upward by a factor equal to the primary city's annual rate of growth.

but three cases, one and a half times the national figure. In seven countries the growth rate of large cities more than doubles the national rate, and in two, Uruguay and Peru, it triples this figure.

What the demographic literature accompanying such data has not stressed sufficiently is that the massive movements giving rise to these trends are not determinants but largely consequences of previous historical and economic imbalances. It is not excessive ambition or perverse instinct that makes masses stream into cities, as so many journalistic reports have suggested.[39] Rather, it is the absence of alternate channels for survival in the existing economic structure. This structure is not a product of the poor but has been framed for them by the re-

Table 3. Size and Growth of Urban Population in Latin American Countries

Country	Total Population^a (1,000s) (A)	Total Urban* Population^a (1,000s) (B)	% of Urban Population	Total Population in Centers over 100,000^a (1,000s) (C)	% of Population in Centers over 100,000	Total Population in Four Largest Cities** (1,000s) (D)	% of Total Population in Four Largest Cities	Annual Rate of Growth of Population^b (E) (%)
Argentina	24,089	16,978	70	14,726	61	11,732	49	1.9
Bolivia	3,956	1,002	25	600	15	858	22	1.4
Brazil	93,545	50,025	53	31,662	34	19,254	21	2.8
Chile	9,510	7,007	74	3,520	37	3,520	37	2.0
Colombia	21,168	11,748	56	8,157	39	5,150	24	3.2
Costa Rica	1,767	640	36	435	25	512	29	4.2
Cuba	8,663	5,058	58	2,645	31	2,385	28	2.4
Dominican Republic	4,324	1,601	37	760	18	893	21	3.6
Ecuador	6,089	2,283	37	1,300	22	1,480	24	3.4
El Salvador	3,449	1,392	40	475	14	706	20	3.6
Guatemala	5,172	1,892	37	770	15	885	17	3.1
Haiti	4,856	857	18	400	8	500	10	2.0
Honduras	2,703	700	26	281	10	438	16	3.4
Mexico	50,624	29,468	58	17,158	34	11,905	24	3.8
Nicaragua	1,989	869	44	350	18	568	29	3.5
Panama	1,465	685	47	440	30	614	42	3.1
Paraguay	2,378	852	36	445	19	519	22	3.1
Peru	13,581	6,256	56	3,180	23	2,970	22	2.1
Uruguay	2,889	2,433	84	1,530	53	1,502	52	1.3
Venezuela	10,390	7,934	76	3,830	37	3,332	32	3.5

Country	1960–1970 Rate of Growth of Urban Population[b] (F) (%)	Ratio of Urban to Total Population Rate of Growth (F/E)	Rate of Growth of Large Urban Centers (100,000+)[b] (G) (%)	Ratio of Large Urban Centers to Total Population Rate of Growth (G/E)
Argentina	2.4	1.26	3.2	1.68
Bolivia	2.4	1.71	4.1	2.92
Brazil	4.6	1.64	5.7	2.03
Chile	3.4	1.70	3.7	1.85
Colombia	5.0	1.56	8.1	2.53
Costa Rica	4.6	1.09	5.4	1.28
Cuba	2.6	1.08	3.5	1.45
Ecuador	4.7	1.38	5.5	1.61
El Salvador	4.0	1.11	7.1	1.97
Guatemala	4.9	1.58	5.0	1.61
Haiti	3.8	1.90	5.2	2.60
Honduras	5.2	1.52	5.9	1.73
Mexico	5.2	1.36	6.4	1.68
Nicaragua	4.6	1.31	5.9	1.68
Panama	4.4	1.41	4.9	1.58
Paraguay	3.5	1.12	3.6	1.16
Peru	3.3	1.57	6.8	3.23
Dominican Republic	5.7	1.58	7.6	2.11
Uruguay	2.9	2.23	4.9	3.61
Venezuela	5.6	1.60	5.9	1.68

[a]Source: Kingsley Davis, World Urbanization 1950–1970, Table A, "Total, Rural, Urban and City Populations," pp. 57–82.
[b]Source: Ibid., Table D, "Annual Growth Rate of Population, 1950–1960 and 1960 to 1970," pp. 141–160.
*Urban population includes large urban centers with populations over 100,000 and towns with populations of less than 100,000 but considered urban.
**Total population in the four largest cities is computed from figures given in table 2 and its accompanying footnotes.
***Rate of growth of urban population and rate of growth of large urban centers (100,000) are rates of change in the combined population living in places of the specified size at each date.

Table 4. Estimates of the Numerical Importance of the Urban Marginal Population in Latin America

Source	City or Country	Year	Relevant Figures
ECLA (I)	Arequipa	1961	40% of the city's population living in *barriadas*
Labadia Caufriez	Brasília	1969	200,000 persons or 50% of the city's population living in *favelas*
ECLA (I)	Buenaventura	—	80% of the city's population living in *tugurios*
Rosenbluth	Buenos Aires	1956	100,000 persons or 2% of the metropolitan population living in *villas miseria*
Ministry of Public Health	Buenos Aires	1965	423,824 persons in the metropolitan area (central city excluded) living in *villas miseria*
Abrams	Cali	1962	30% of the city's population living in *barrios de invasión*
ECLA (I)	Caracas	1950	17.4% of dwellings classified by the census as *ranchos* or equivalents
Rosenbluth	Caracas	1953	311,000 or 38.5% of the city's population living in *cerros* and *quebradas*
Abrams	Caracas	1962	*Rancho* inhabitants numbered 263,000 according to official figures. Unofficial estimates put the number at 400,000 or 35% of the city's population
DESAL (I)	Chile	1960	400,000 persons or 8% of the population living in *callampas*
ECLA (II)	Chile	1960	321,863 dwellings with a total population of 1,507,841 in urban marginal areas; figures represent 34.3% of the dwellings and 31.1% of the urban population

Source	City	Year	Description
ECLA (I)	Chimbote	1961	70% of the city's population living in *barriadas*
Cuevas	Guatemala City	1965	10% of the metropolitan population living in *barrios de invasión*
Presidency of the Republic	Iquitos	1968	64.7% of the city's population living in *barriadas*
Rosenbluth	Lima	1957	108,988 persons or 10% of the population living in 56 *barriadas*
Abrams	Lima	1960	958,000 persons living in *barriadas* in the metropolitan area
Rosenbluth	Lima	1960	394,263 persons or 24.43% of the city's population living in 154 *barriadas*
ECLA (I)	Lima	1961	21% of the metropolitan population living in *barriadas*
DESAL (I)	Lima	1961	21% of the metropolitan population living in *barriadas*
Abrams	Maracaibo	1962	50% of the city's population living in marginal settlements
ECLA (I)	Mexico City	1952	14% of the population of the Federal District living in *colonias proletarias*
Rosenbluth	Mexico City	1952	993,000 persons or 33.6% of the population living in *tugurios* and dilapidated central city tenements; 315,000 or 10.7% of the population living in *jacales* and other illegal peripheral settlements
Turner	Mexico City	1965 (approx)	1.5 million people or approximately one-third of the city's population living in *colonias proletarias* or *barrios paracaidistas*
Harth Deneke	Mexico City	1966	2 million people living in *colonias proletarias*. By 1970, the *colonias* would cover 40% of the area of the Federal District

Table 4—Continued

Source	City or Country	Year	Relevant Figures
Presidency of the Republic	Peru	1967	804,878 persons or 24.1% of the population in eleven major cities living in barriadas
ECLA (I)	Recife	1961	50% of the city's population living in favelas
Rosenbluth	Rio de Janeiro	1950	14.3% of the metropolitan population living in favelas
ECLA (I)	Rio de Janeiro	1961	900,000 or 38% of the city's population living in favelas
ECLA (III)	Santiago	1960	135,150 "irregular" or marginal dwellings with a total population of 633,856; figures represent 33% of dwellings in the metropolitan area and 29.8% of its population
Rosenbluth	Santiago	1961	5% of the metropolitan population living in callampas, the worst type of peripheral settlement; an additional 20% living in conventillos or central city tenements
Abrams	Santiago	1962	25% of the metropolitan population living in marginal settlements
Rosenbluth	Santiago	1962	120,000 persons or 18% of Santiago's municipal population living in a single settlement: the José María Caro area

DESAL (II)	Santiago	1966	18,142 adult women living in central city tenements; 46,709 in callampas; 93,705 in other peripheral marginal settlements
ECLA (I)	Uruguay	1963	30,000 urban dwellings in conventillos, cantegriles, and rancherías with a total of 100,000 inhabitants
ECLA (II)	Venezuela	1960	34.6% of the urban population living in ranchos

Sources: Charles Abrams, Squatter Settlements; Marco Antonio Cuevas, Análisis de tres áreas marginales de la Ciudad de Guatemala; DESAL I, Marginalidad en América Latina; DESAL II, "Encuesta sobre familia y fecundidad en poblaciones marginales del Gran Santiago," vol. 1; ECLA I, report to the First Pan-American Conference on Population, Cali, 1965, reported in Luis M. Morea, "Vivienda y equipamiento urbano," in La urbanización en América Latina, edited by Jorge Hardoy and Carlos Tobar, pp. 87–112; ECLA II, "La participación de las poblaciones marginales en el crecimiento urbano"; ECLA III, "Los servicios públicos en una población de erradicación"; Jorge Harth Deneke, "The Colonias Proletarias of Mexico City: Low Income Settlements on the Urban Fringe"; Antonio Labadia Caufriez, "Operación sitio: A Housing Solution for Progressive Growth," in Latin American Urban Research, vol. 2, edited by Guillermo Geisse and Jorge Hardoy, p. 203; Ministry of Public Health, Diagnóstico sanitario aglomerado bonaerense, quoted in Carlos Tobar, "The Argentine National Plan for Eradicating Villas de Emergencia," in Latin American Urban Research, vol. 2, edited by Guillermo Geisse and Jorge Hardoy, p. 226; Presidency of the Republic, Oficina Nacional de Desarrollo de Pueblos Jovenes, Incidencia de la urbanización acelerada en ciudades con poblaciones de 25,000 y mas habitantes, quoted in Jorge Hardoy, "Urbanization Policies and Urban Reform in Latin America," in Latin American Urban Research, vol. 2, edited by Guillermo Geisse and Jorge Hardoy, p. 35; Guillermo Rosenbluth, "Problemas socio-económicos de la marginalidad y la integración urbana"; John F. C. Turner, "Uncontrolled Urban Settlement: Problems and Policies," International Social Development Review, no. 1 (1968), pp. 107–130.

sults of industrial and commercial investments, which, in turn, fit the particular characteristics of capitalism in the region. The image of "circular causality" fits the interplay of economic forces and demographic movements as they compound each other in generating ever greater regional imbalances. Yet the primary forces initiating and sustaining the circle must be sought, not in demography, but rather in the history and economy of dependent capitalism.[40]

Similarly, the growth of squatter and other uncontrolled lower-class settlements does not obey the aberrant dictates of a "culture of poverty" or come from the cultural inertia of marginal groups.[41] It constitutes instead a rational response to unregulated manipulation of urban land for profit to the exclusion of immediate demands for shelter.

Table 4 documents the extent of the trend toward illegal urban settlement with numerical estimates from sixteen different cities. Marginal settlements are said to comprise up to 80 percent of the urban population in Buenaventura, Peru, 70 percent in Chimbote, and 50 percent in Maracaibo, Venezuela. They extend over 40 percent of the metropolitan area in Mexico City. A U.N. study estimates that 34 percent of the urban dwellings and 31 percent of the urban population of Chile exist in precarious settlements. For Venezuela, 34 percent of the urban population is said to live in marginal *ranchos*. In Lima, all estimates put the current *barriada* population at over 20 percent of the total metropolitan figure.

The two popular responses to the constrained conditions of economic development in the region are, in turn, interrelated: massive migration accelerates city growth and promotes a constant increase in the price of land in the established market.[42] Greater numbers of the urban poor and higher land values lead to an increasing shift toward illegal means for securing shelter and, hence, an increasing frequency of land invasions. This massive popular initiative and its eventual institutionalization effectively destroy the monopoly of capitalist practices of land allocation. The success of previous migrants in obtaining even minimal land and shelter and the new opportunities opened by an informal popular land market serve as potential stimulants to further migration.[43] Once again, the image of circular causality provides an adequate summary of forces promoting uncontrolled urban expansion.

The Urban Land Market

It is by now well established that the unrestricted operation of market forces produces distortions in a developing economy.[44] Domination of modern expansion of Latin American cities almost exclusively by private interests has created a series of such consequences. While social scientists generally recognize this situation, few have explored in detail the specific physical and economic impact of market forces as they impinge upon urban growth. Planners, who must deal directly with the phenomenon, have contributed a body of literature more concrete and far more instructive in this area.[45] It is their lead that we will follow in emphasizing three major aspects of capitalist regulation of the urban land.

Excessive land subdivision. The pressures of inflation, the opportunities to profit without restrictions from the surplus value created by urbanization, and the absence of alternate channels for investment have led to a frenzied concentration of low- and middle-level capital in land speculation. Urban land is bought and sold on the established market less for its residential value than for its profit value. Land as preferred investment, aided by the weaknesses of regulatory agencies, has encouraged overextension of city perimeters and excessive subdivision of the urban soil.

The middle- and upper-class areas of Lima expand toward the west, occupying fertile agricultural land that has been shifted from productive to speculative use. In Buenos Aires planners estimate that there are more than three subdivided vacant lots for each lot with construction on it. Even without further extension of its metropolitan area, privately held unused land would furnish adequate construction space for a city of twenty-eight million, a figure that, at the present rate of metropolitan population growth, would not be reached for fifty years.[46]

While appropriate for their functions and size in colonial times, the locations of many cities have become inadequate for their contemporary pace of growth. Level land in Caracas, Quito, Cali, and Medellín, to cite only a few cities, has become increasingly scarce, and cities have had to expand on hills at increasing costs of construction and urban services. The difficult topography of harbors like Guayaquil, Valparaíso, and Rio creates similar problems. The scarcity of available physical space in major cities aggravates the competition and the tendency toward subdivision of land.

The problem of excessive land subdivision is that it compounds the difficulties of providing an adequate urban-services infrastructure and of implementing a rational strategy of growth. Land subdivision for profit represents a distorting factor because it multiplies the number of juridical units to be dealt with in the city, it increases the costs of public land acquisition for community services or planning purposes, and it pushes the growth of cities in irrational directions. In this distortion, as in other aspects, unrestricted forces of supply and demand tend to develop cities for the exclusive benefit of profit-oriented owners to the detriment of broader community goals.

Low densities. Contrary to commonly held stereotypes, major cities in Latin America, especially those situated on vast open terrain, have very low densities. Crowded conditions do exist in central areas and in many of those areas occupied by lower-class groups. The overall metropolitan densities remain, however, at levels lower than those in many European cities. Central Buenos Aires has areas with more than 3,000 inhabitants per hectare while the overall metropolitan density is 8.8 inhabitants per hectare. Within the metropolitan perimeter zones exist where cattle and poultry are raised and where intensive agriculture takes place. While the area of Copacabana in Rio de Janeiro has 5,000 inhabitants per hectare, the state of Guanabara, occupied almost entirely by the metropolitan city, drops to 27.4 inhabitants per hectare. Mexico City, which is now coterminous with the Federal District, has vast rural and quasi-rural areas, especially in the *delegaciones* of Tlalpan, Thahuac, and Milpa Alta.[47]

As in the case of the United States, urban hyperexpansion occurs in an erratic fashion following accidents of the terrain and the major arteries of transportation, which furnish relatively rapid access to the central city. This trend gives the suburban areas of cities a radial shape, with blots of urbanized land along main avenues and highways and huge, unused expanses in between. The similarity between U.S. and Latin American cities in this respect is more than coincidental since growth has been largely governed in both areas by consideration to private interests, convenience for the wealthier sectors, and rapid realization of profits from investment capital.

Another problem of excessive urban expansion is that it strains the capacity of public agencies to provide adequate services. It requires extension of the networks of energy, water, and transportation, among others, often across huge portions of unused land. The movement of elites away from central areas spearheaded, and still constitutes, a major demand factor in the expansion of cities.[48]

Wealthy sectors select living areas solely on the basis of their convenience, privacy, and attractive environments. In a market-regulated economy, their purchasing power has been a powerful propellant for a continuous supply of luxury developments, each farther away from the central city and each built without regard for the overall needs and resources of the city. Pressure on centers of political authority by elite members or by commercial developers has generally ensured a smooth supply of public services in the new areas at the expense of other urban sectors.[49]

While movement of the wealthy toward peripheral zones has not been the only cause of excessive urban expansion, they have been the ones freer to choose their locations. Lower-class settlements in the less desirable sectors of the periphery are, to a large extent, not a matter of choice but of necessity.

Caught between disenfranchised masses and elite sectors, agencies of urban government are faced with the impossible task of maintaining the urban infrastructure with minimal resources. The city confronts the paradox that, while in the central zone and other areas excessive overcrowding prevents adequate provision and renovation of urban services, in the periphery, excessive sparseness of settlements makes extension of such services unbearably costly.

Inflated land prices. Demand for urban land in Latin America is governed not only by need but also by its use as a safeguard against inflation and as secure investment. Such speculation exercises a constant pressure on the price of soil. Surplus values produced by continuous urban concentration and growth should quite properly revert to the entire community. However, the absence of an adequate tax structure allows land speculators to appropriate this social product without reciprocation.

Even in situations of rapid urban growth, prices are artificially inflated beyond their "natural" increases by deliberate manipulation. It is this aspect of the urban economy that impinges most directly on the situation and needs of the poor.[50]

In one of the very few studies of land values in the region, prices in ninety-two sectors of Cali were monitored from 1959 to 1963. It was found that fifty-five sectors experienced increases of over 40 percent in the four-year period. The value of land in nine sectors increased over 30 percent; six had increases of over 20 percent; twelve increased over 10 percent; and the other ten remained stationary. Among the high-demand sectors, twenty-one doubled their value in a three-year period and two increased it over 800 percent.[51]

In Lima, the fertile lands of the Rímac Valley, located in the areas of upper- and middle-class urbanization, command the highest prices. Seven years ago land adjacent to the major highway in the area brought prices of over US $55,000 per hectare out to a distance of three miles from the limits of the city. The value gradient was found to decrease from there on in a linear fashion.

In Caracas, the value of land in the central districts increased 400 percent from 1938 to 1951. However, the true explosion in prices occurred after that in response to accelerated urban growth, industrialization, and the scarcity of suitable land for further urbanization.

In Mexico City, prestigious residential districts, such as Lomas de Chapultepec, registered spectacular price increases. From 1930 to 1950 the value of a square meter grew from eighty cents to US $48, a 6,000 percent increase. The figure in adjacent residential colonias approached 50,000 percent.

Even in a poor country like Bolivia and under circumstances of more restricted urban growth, land speculation has forced prices to a level bearing no relation to the real income of the majority of the population. In residential areas of high demand in La Paz, land sold in recent years for US $40 a square meter. This figure descended, following a status gradient, to US $20 in middle-class areas and US $12 in working-class districts. In the commercial downtown area, the value was over US $200 a meter.[52]

The price of land is, of course, not the only cost incurred in securing urban shelter. Lower-middle groups, "established" working classes, and marginal sectors must contend also with the costs of construction, materials, extended urban services, and taxes. A wage structure governed by high supply and restricted demand for menial and lower nonmenial occupations and affected by perennial inflation makes it impossible for all but the upper levels of these groups to even start considering the housing market.[53] At lower income levels, the price of land alone forms an impassable barrier to securing minimal housing through conventional means.

Government Regulation

A final aspect is the specific role of urban authorities in a capitalist-regulated economy. Since colonial days, the role of institutions of urban government has been that of custodian of a consensually established order. A monolithic social structure operated without conflict in favor of a landed elite with which public authority cooperated and from which it recruited its major dignitaries. The advent of intense land capital speculation during this century did not change this basic orientation. The function of government in most countries has remained that of guaranteeing public order (keeping outbursts and demands from the less privileged in check) and ensuring the exercise of private initiative (permitting the improvement of the economic and social position of the more powerful).

With market forces shaping the form of urban growth, the consequences of excessive subdivision of property, low metropolitan densities, and inflated land prices have become increasingly apparent. The dominant role of contemporary public institutions has not been to prevent capitalist distortions of urban development but rather to adapt the city, as well as possible, to the new and difficult conditions. It has been, by and large, an alleviating, "patching up" function, not a regulatory or preventive one.[54]

A privately regulated economy, legitimized and promoted since the early history of the region, has always employed public institutions at both national and local levels in a secondary supportive role. This support consists at present of a mixture of suppression—of possible protests and militant opposition—and alleviative efforts at moderating the distorted consequences of capitalist expansion. The alleviating function occurs for the most part as a sequel to private initiative, not parallel or prior to it. This "cleaning up" function cushions the impact of land speculation in the city and allows it to go on unheeded.

Effective governmental control over urban land use and patterns of city growth can follow three strategies: external regulation of the land market and intended subdivisions (a tax structure that ensures a return to the community of value increases generated by the process of urbanization); actual participation of public agencies in the land market and, thus, internal regulation of prices and profit via supply and demand; and elimination of a capitalist system of land use and its replacement by government-controlled central planning.

Among Latin American countries, only Cuba has adopted the third radical alternative. In most cities the regulatory function of public bodies is limited to a few poorly enforced zoning laws and/or the strictly physical conception of delimiting plans (planos reguladores).[55] Only a few cities have been able to approach the first alternative with any degree of supervision and control over trends of urban expansion. In chapter 4, the relative successes of urban planning bodies in the cases of Medellín and Guadalajara are analyzed and compared with the more common situations of private-elite control.

Montevideo has managed to preserve a measure of continuity in its development, thanks to continuous reactualization of regulations and at least partially effective enforcement. In Caracas, new laws offer the possibility of taxing profits from land transactions, thus permitting a partial return to the public of community-produced surplus. In most cities, however, increases in land values stimulated by a growing population and demand are allowed to go almost entirely into the hands of speculators. Even in the exceptional cases above, control is only partial and does not alter the basic distorting tendencies of the market.[56]

Chile is the only country that has implemented to any degree the second alternative of active state participation in the land market. Even prior to the advent of the leftist coalition to power, the urban land market was much more controlled there than in other Latin American countries. The strategy that was followed combined relatively effective regulation, implemented at the national level by the Ministry of Housing and Urbanism

(MINVU), and large purchases of urban land by the state. The latter function was the task of the Corporation of Urban Improvement (CORMU), an autonomous body charged with buying land for public use and planning and selling it when necessary for regulation of the market.[57]

The concept of the state as active participant and even entrepreneur is so foreign to the history of urbanization in Latin America that similar attempts have not been made in other countries or have been so feeble as to make no real difference. Even in Chile, the plight of the most deprived urban sectors was not solved since the value of the land still remained clearly above their economic possibilities and public resettlement plans, such as the well-publicized Operación Sitio,[58] were insufficient to meet the demand.

Summary

Development of cities and the framework within which urban poverty occurs in Latin America are the products of forces deep within the history and economic structure of the area. This section has attempted to outline the basic concatenation of events leading to the present situation. Capitalism in Latin America has been characterized by a situation of material scarcity, traditional domination of cities over the countryside, dominant foreign influence in the process of industrialization, and chronic inflation due to structural economic imbalances. In this context, the tendency of both public and private investments has been to increase urban concentration. A foreign-directed process of industrialization has taken advantage of centralized facilities, resources, and large markets to establish its plants in the same metropolitan areas, thus aggravating the trend toward regional imbalance. Domestic capital, often excluded by large foreign corporations from control of industry, finds in rapid urban growth a unique opportunity to safeguard its own resources against inflation and to increase them rapidly.

The passive role of the government allows these interests to take full advantage of the economic surplus produced by urban expansion without reciprocal benefits for the total community. Heavy capital investments in the urban land market effect a series of irrationalities and distortions in urban development: excessive subdivision of property, low densities due to unused land held for speculative purposes, and ever-rising costs of land and housing. Faced with the present uncontrolled expansion of cities, the efforts of public authorities have seldom been directed toward wresting the initiative from private interests but rather toward alleviating the chaos created by them. This meliorative function becomes increasingly inefficient as cities grow and relative scarcity of public resources becomes more pronounced.

Responses of popular masses in Latin America bear a logical relation to the situation created for them by a constrained economy. To urban concentration of facilities, opportunities, and resources, there correspond massive processes of rural-urban migration. To inflated land prices in the cities and the absence of adequate programs of public housing and credit, there corresponds an extensive pattern of illegal settlements and land invasions.

The city thus becomes an arena where the long-term consequences of dependent capitalism turn dialectically upon itself. The growing scarcity of urban land casts into sharp relief the competition between the profit interests of the few and the basic need for shelter of the many. Massive urban migration has brought to light the intrinsic contradiction between the two functions and forced a change in the structure of capitalist land control.

Concrete patterns of adaptation by the poor to the established economic order and the changes wrought in the ecology of these cities are the topic of the following section.

The Ecology of Poverty

Mechanisms developed by traditional Latin American cities to deal with impoverished newcomers were effective as long as the flow was kept within certain numerical bounds. Solutions to the problem of shelter for the poor were embedded in a well-structured order that quickly showed the migrant his "proper" place in the social hierarchy. An official attitude of unconcern for migrants shifted the burden of their care to religious institutions and private citizens. Together with whatever material care they received, poor migrants were also socialized into the values and norms dominant in the city.

The key point is that, in the absence of formal institutions dedicated to this purpose, the task of assimilating the new urban poor was accomplished through informal channels. While no clear data are available on this point, one may speculate that migrants' needs for permanent shelter were handled through the primary, cliental relations so common in other areas of the Latin American social structure.[59]

Employers and patrons, together with churches and convents, probably found ways to accommodate the "deserving" poor who had come into their confidence. When shelter was not available within their households or on their property, cheap rental housing or other alternatives could be found through an informal network of relations. Such highly personal mechanisms tended to promote feelings of gratitude and bondage and thus were probably effective in assimilating individuals into an authoritarian social order.[60]

Massive rural-urban migration broke down these particular mechanisms. Their importance depended on bringing to the surface the problems of work and shelter for the poor and on finding the means for their solutions. Confronted with a closed land-and-housing market, urban masses could no longer turn to the spontaneous relations of trust and deference and the individual emergence of friendship as effective solutions. Thus, the problem of land use for shelter shifted from a primary, and hence structurally irrelevant issue, to a secondary phenomenon.[61]

It was not the massive anger of the poor or their deliberate political intentions that challenged the sacredness of private property and the capitalist land market.[62] Rather, it was simply the impact of massive numbers, confronted with the same basic problem, that spontaneously broke the defenses of the previous order. New urban poverty, a result of broader structural imbalances, forced the collapse of a monopolistic land market and, in the process, radically altered the ecology of the city.

Migration and Urban Poverty

One of the most common assumptions made about squatter settlements and other areas housing the urban poor is that they constitute ad hoc centers for rural migrants who create them and live in them as long as they cannot move into the city

proper.[63] Such a view contains an implicit definition of these
settlements as temporary locations, places of ultimate destitu-
tion to be abandoned as soon as minimal economic improvement permits.[64]

More importantly, definition of peripheral settlements as exclusively migrant formed and inhabited suggests the existence
of a fundamental division in the city between urban-born and
migrant newcomer. The former, even at the most modest levels,
would be more integrated with the urban economic structure,
which would be reflected in his living within the city proper and
abiding by the housing regulations. Migrants, on the contrary,
would have to find ways to improvise their shelter and circumvent regulations; squatter and other illegal settlements would
thus represent the direct ecological reflection of their poverty
and lack of recognized position in the urban system.

Contrary to these views, empirical research has consistently
negated the existence of a sharp division between urban-born
and migrant in the ecological distribution of the city. Not all
migrants move into improvised or illegal settlements, nor do all
inhabitants of the latter come exclusively from a migrant background. While the majority of urban migrants undoubtedly
come from very low economic and educational levels, a significant minority arrives in the city with the necessary means and
connections to avoid settlements altogether and move into the
city proper. This fact accounts, in part, for the empirical finding that migrants are dispersed throughout the city, living both
in precarious settlements and in established urban areas.[65]

Migration studies, however, have failed to stress the point
that the heterogeneity of the migrant population prevents identifying the migrant with the urban marginal or the urban poor.
While most migrants belong to these categories, others do not.
More importantly, neither these social categories nor their physical manifestations are composed entirely of migrants. Empirical studies of squatter and other illegal settlements have consistently reported that a sizable number of their inhabitants are
urban-born.

Table 5 presents relevant data from fifteen studies in different cities. Neither these results nor any others I am aware of
indicate that significant numbers of settlers in lower-class
peripheral areas are not natives of the city itself. The implication of these data is that the basic cleavage between established

city dwellers and the periphery of precarious settlements occurs not along the residential axis, migrant vs. urban-born, but rather along a class hierarchy separating different locations in the economic structure. Migrants with sufficient resources are spared the need to circumvent the legal market in precarious dwellings while a sizable proportion of the urban poor are forced into them.

The temporal coincidence and obvious causal relationship between vast rural-urban migration and the massive emergence of squatter and other lower-class settlements have led incautious theorists to posit a one-to-one relation between the two phenomena: slums, shantytowns, and so forth are created and inhabited by migrants as way stations in their economic and social assault on the city. The fact that up to 50 percent of dwellers in these areas were born in the city itself has failed to impress many with the obvious incorrectness of this interpretation. In part, this failure is due to the fact that no alternative explanation has been advanced. Interpretations of these data have not attempted, to my knowledge, to account for this significant departure from conventional wisdom.

The view advanced above about the origins of urban poverty provides a suitable framework for interpreting this phenomenon. The surplus value generated by concentrating resources in large urban areas and the subsequent waves of migration, in addition to continuous speculation in urban land, result in a housing market closed to both poor migrants and large sectors of the urban lower classes. The capitalist market system provides no special mechanisms for the defense of the urban-born vis-à-vis migrants.

To the inexorable climb of land and housing prices, one must add the breakdown of traditional primary arrangements through which many of the native poor were able to secure shelter from the wealthy and established. Not only does this mechanism become insufficient when faced with vast numbers, but also the atmosphere of impersonality and the new pace of rapid urbanization discourage the establishment of such ties.[66] In this situation, both migrants and urban poor are forced to look for alternate means of securing shelter. Both are subjects and victims of the same economic order.

A chainlike mechanism, which begins with regional imbalances, promotes migration of the less privileged to the few centers where opportunities concentrate. The massive presence of opportunities in the cities reinforces market tendencies that aggravate the situation of the urban poor. Class differences, not residential ones, become important as both migrant and native groups are forced to engage in illegal actions to meet a basic housing need.

The impact of urban growth on the "uncontrolled" expansion of marginal settlements is thus not direct, as conventional descriptions indicate, but indirect through the formal pressure that increasing numbers exercise on the housing market. The breakdown of traditional mechanisms for assimilation of the poor by the city and the inability of a profit-oriented system to absorb impoverished masses force the opening of new, unconventional channels. Effects of rural-urban migration are, therefore, not individual and accretive—through gradual accumulation of migrant dwellings at the fringes of the cities—but structural and collective, forcing drastic actions on the part of both migrant and native urban poor.

Types of Settlements

Strategies followed by the lower urban groups in circumventing official regulations and the housing market are not identical everywhere. No one has attempted a systematic survey of the determinants and specific forms of illegal urban settlement throughout the continent. That different forms exist, however, is abundantly clear from the results of empirical research.

William Flinn and James Converse[67] distinguish three types of lower-class peripheral areas in Bogotá: (1) *barrios piratas o clandestinos*—illegal "pirate" subdivisions in which parcels of land without basic services are sold against official regulations, (2) *invasiones o tugurios*—squatter settlements on private or public land, and (3) *urbanizaciones* and other public housing projects. Bryan Roberts[68] differentiates between planned and spontaneous or unplanned *colonias* in Guatemala City. The same distinction was adopted in the Central American Population Center study, which comprised a large number of *colonias* in the metropolitan area, including the well-known La Limonada settlement. The rather unique case of Rio de Janeiro's *favelas* and their varying types has been studied by several researchers, especially Anthony and Elizabeth Leeds.[69]

Table 5. Percentage Native-Born in Studies of Peripheral Lower-Class Settlements in Latin American Cities

Source	City	Year	Sample	% Born in the City
Usandizaga and Havens	Barranquilla	1966	Random sample of adult dwellers in 3 barrios de invasión; N = 243	30.4
Cardona	Bogotá	1968	Population of adult dwellers in 2 barrios de invasión; N = 727	8.0
Flinn and Converse	Bogotá	1970	Random sample of household heads in 2 clandestine settlements and 1 invasion settlement; N = 319	11.4
National Housing Commission	Buenos Aires	1957	Sample of household heads in villas miserias; N = 1,500	51.0
Roberts	Guatemala City	1970	Random sample of household heads in 2 lower-class colonias; N = 229	21.3
UNESCO and ECLA	Lima	1957	Census of household heads in 56 barriadas; N = 21,033 (approx.)	11.0
Ministry of Public Health	Lima	1960	Census of household heads in 154 barriadas	23.0
Goldrich et al.	Lima	1967	Random sample of adult dwellers in 2 barriadas; N = 260	11.0
Tefel	Managua	1972	Multistage probability sample of the entire marginal settlement population; N = 450	29.3
Lomnitz	Mexico City	1970	Population of adult settlers in 1 shantytown; N = 244	30.0
ECLA	Rio de Janeiro	1950	Census of adult dwellers in all favelas in the metropolitan area	39.0
ECLA	Santiago	1962	Population of household heads & their wives in 122 callampas	29.0
Goldrich et al.	Santiago	1967	Random sample of household heads in 2 poblaciones; N = 289	35.0
DESAL	Santiago	1967	Random sample of adult women in all poblaciones in the metropolitan area; N = 1,114	51.0
Portes	Santiago	1969	Random sample of household heads in 4 poblaciones; N = 382	42.0

Sources: Ramiro Cardona, Dos barrios de invasión; Comisión Nacional de la Vivienda, ed., Informe sobre su actuación y plan integral, vol. 2; DESAL, "Encuesta sobre la familia y la fecundidad en poblaciones marginales del Gran Santiago 1966/67," vol. 2; ECLA, Condiciones mundiales de la habitación y calculo de la demanda de viviendas, 1962, reported in Guillermo Rosenbluth, "Problemas socio-económicos de la marginalidad y la integración urbana"; ECLA, Encuesta realizada por CEPAL (ECLA) y la Escuela de Servicio Social de la Universidad de Chile a 122 poblaciones callampa en Octubre de 1962, reported in Rosenbluth, "Problemas socio-económicos"; William L. Flinn and James W. Converse, "Eight Assumptions concerning Rural-Urban Migration in Colombia: A Three Shantytowns Test," Land Economics 46 (November 1970): 456–464; Daniel Goldrich, Raymond B. Pratt, and Charles R. Schuller, "The Political Integration of Lower-Class Urban Settlements in Chile and Peru," Studies in Comparative International Development 3 (1967–1968): 3–22; Larissa Lomnitz, "The Social and Economic Organization of a Mexican Shantytown," in Latin American Urban Research, vol. 4, edited by Wayne A. Cornelius and Felicity M. Trueblood; Ministerio de Salud Pública, Censo de las barriadas limeñas, reported in Rosenbluth, "Problemas socio-económicos"; Alejandro Portes, Cuatro poblaciones; Bryan Roberts, "The Social Organization of Low-Income Urban Families," in Crucifixion by Power, by Richard Newbold Adams, pp. 479-514; Reynaldo A. Tefel, El infierno de los pobres; UNESCO and ECLA, La urbanización en América Latina, joint seminar conducted in Santiago, Chile, in July 1959, reported in Rosenbluth, "Problemas socio-económicos"; Elsa Usandizaga and A. Eugene Havens, Tres barrios de invasión.

Alejandro Portes[70] distinguishes four main types of peripheral *poblaciones* in Santiago de Chile: (1) spontaneous slum settlements, the older variety, represented by areas like Nueva Matucana and the now extinct Colo-Colo; (2) squatter settlements, the product of organized land invasions; (3) decaying housing projects, represented by the well-known case of the José María Caro area; and (4) new resettlement areas, predominantly created under the Operación Sitio Program, which followed guidelines suggested by the experience of successful squatter invasions.

Public housing projects have not had until recently a significant impact on land and housing needs of the urban poor. This is directly linked to traditional limitations on the role of urban public agencies vis-à-vis private initiative. In cities where major public projects have been attempted, they have not always had positive consequences.[71] Effective programs have emerged only in reaction to the widespread institutionalization of popular initiatives and have followed their natural characteristics rather than oppose them.[72] For this reason, types of settlements created by popular initiative, rather than belated official imitations, will be the focus of attention below.

Past empirical research suggests that popular efforts to bypass land market prices have taken three main forms: 1. "Spontaneous" settlements, formed illegally on unoccupied land by accretion. No deliberate collective decision precedes the emergence of these areas. They develop gradually with a few families setting up rustic shacks and tents at the start. If not expelled, they are soon joined by others until the whole area is covered by precarious dwellings. Absence of initial planning prevents development of a rational layout of streets and homesites. Pressing need forces the use of land to a maximum, leaving little or no space between one dwelling and the next.

2. Land invasions, established on private or public land by the deliberate decision of a group of homeless families. Homesites are usually allocated in advance and the entire layout of the settlement is planned. Invasions usually involve a large number of participants, a pattern designed to increase chances of success when confronted with government reaction.

3. Clandestine subdivisions, established by landowners who sell cheap homesites to poor families. These settlements constitute, in essence, an extension to the poor sectors of the capitalist pattern of land manipulation for profit. "Coyotes," as these

speculators are called in Mexico and Central America, are able to offer low prices by failing to meet minimal public regulations for the provision of services. In most cases, buyers receive bare land and a dubious title without access to water, electricity, transportation or minimal social services.

The tendency in many metropolitan areas throughout Latin America is for all three types to be present, offering a range of possibilities for the needs of different groups. The three have in common two basic characteristics: First, they are illegal and thus subject to the threat of expulsion. Second, they provide land either free or for very small payments. "Owners" in spontaneous settlements pay no rent, and those in land invasions begin payments only when an agreement has been reached with the government or the legal owners. Clandestine subdivisions involve higher payments, but they are usually far below those of the legal land market or conventional public housing.[73]

The pattern of spontaneous settlements with gradual accretion is dominant among Rio's *favelas* and common among the *villas miseria* of Buenos Aires.[74] The pattern is also found, though with decreasing frequency, among the older Santiago *poblaciones*.[75]

Land invasions are the most vigorous and most distinctly popular strategy for coping with the housing problem. They have long been dominant in Lima and grew rapidly to be so in Santiago.[76] They have been reported in Bogotá, Barranquilla, Panama City, and most large Central American cities, among others.[77]

Clandestine subdivisions are usually an alternative available only to those with a relatively stable income. They exist in Santiago de Chile under the name of *loteos brujos*, occupying, for example, the huge Peñalolen area at the foot of the Andes.[78] They appear to be the dominant form of illegal settlement in Bogotá, San Salvador, and Guatemala City, and are present in the rest of the major Central American cities, as well as in Mexico.[79]

Spontaneous settlements represent the older and more primitive form of popular initiative. They do not evidence the long-term perspective and planning present in land invasions but rather an immediate urgency for shelter. Their timid and unplanned pattern of settlement gives rise to an irrational layout that prevents further development.[80]

Because they are the oldest form of popularly initiated housing and the city grows around them, spontaneous settlements tend to be the least "peripheral" of the three forms. In this situation, the value of land where they are situated tends to increase, becoming the object of conventional land speculation. The survival of the settlement then depends on the race between the position of the land in the urban value gradient and the effectiveness of the dwellers' organization in legalizing their occupancy.[81] That they do not always succeed is vividly demonstrated in the example of Rio's *favelas,* many of which have been razed and their dwellers resettled against their will in the outskirts of the city.[82]

While no empirical research has explored the problem systematically, it is possible to hypothesize that the predominance of each type of settlement is the result of two factors: the balance between rewards and costs involved in each alternative and the inertial force of the alternative institutionalized in the past.[83]

If the general orientation of the urban poor toward nonconventional housing could be described as fundamentally rational, the specific choice between one or another strategy also appears to follow a rational assessment of opportunities.[84] Violent and successful police actions against invaders discourage spontaneous settlements or, at least, force invaders to search for new tactics in order to ensure success.[85] Unscrupulous dealings by clandestine land manipulators discourage lower-class groups from following this path. Finally, the dead-end situation that spontaneous settlements represent deters families from seeking permanent shelter in them. Crucial considerations in all cases are the amount of money to be saved in rents or payments, the distance of an area from places of work, and the security of tenure or, conversely, the likelihood of expulsion.

Rational assessment of alternatives occurs in a context heavily influenced by the past history of each city. If elite residences move along a particular geographic axis, partially from sheer inertia,[86] so too the success of earlier settlements encourages similar strategies in later settlements. Following the established road is, in most cases, less costly than attempting new alternatives. Inertial forces are effective, however, only as long as the economic and political framework remains unaltered. When overwhelming force is employed against illegal settlements, as has been the case in Brazil, settlers must look quickly for different alternatives. Conversely, when police repression is limited by a popularly oriented government, as it was during the Allende government in Chile, the alternative of massive land invasions is encouraged.

Intraurban Migration

Competition for urban land takes place between the demand for profit and the popular need for shelter. The latter, however, is not homogeneous. A distinction must be introduced between an early "survival" stage, which merely seeks temporary shelter, and a later stage of search for a permanent home.

A vast proportion of lower-class migrants do not move directly into a given settlement but rather change residences one or more times within the city.[87] These changes generally correspond to advances in the economic and social position of the individual. New lower-class migrants give primary attention to securing a stable job. The tendency at this stage is for migrants to minimize rents while looking for dwellings as near as possible to places of work. In this initial period, labeled the "bridge-heading" stage,[88] economic survival and not security of land tenure is the crucial consideration.

After a period of several months to several years, many migrants do succeed in reaching minimal economic security. At this point, attention is shifted to the problem of residence, and here the varying meaning of "shelter" comes into sharp focus. Quite apart from purely physical needs, landownership represents the establishment of definite roots in the city.[89] It is the culmination of a successful urban career and offers the certainty that, with time, a home can be built as a refuge for old age and a defense against economic uncertainty.

When asked, for example, for their most important aspiration, 70 percent of the lower-class respondents in a study of peripheral settlements in Santiago de Chile named housing, landownership, or securing legal title to their present land as their major goal for the future.[90] It is during this "consolidator" stage[91] that migrants are joined by groups of the native urban poor in the struggle to obtain land outside the conventional market. The outskirts of the city—unoccupied and cheap land—offer the only alternative available to most.[92] It is there they move in search of permanent shelter.

Table 6. Length of Urban Residence of Migrants Living in Peripheral Urban Settlements

Source	City	Year	Sample	Relevant Figures
Usandizaga and Havens	Barranquilla	1966	Random sample of adult dwellers in 3 barrios de invasión; N (migrants) = 169	Migrants living in the city: Less than a year 3% 1–5 years 21% 5–10 years 21% 10 years or more 55%
Cardona	Bogotá	1968	Population of adult dwellers in 2 barrios de invasión; N (migrants) = 632	Migrants living in the city: Less than 8 years 42% 8 years or more 58% Migrants' first residence in the city: Present barrio only 11% Central city or other areas 89%
Flinn and Converse	Bogotá	1970	Random sample of household heads in 2 clandestine settlements and 1 invasion settlement; N (migrants) = 283	Migrants' first residence in the city: Present barrio only 18% Other peripheral settlements 36% Central City 46%

Flinn	Bogotá	1971	Random sample of household heads in 2 clandestine settlements; N (migrants) = 193	Migrants living in the city: Less than one year 35%, 1–5 years 30%, 6 years or more 35%
Ray	Caracas	1969	Participant observation study of rancho dwellers	Almost 100% of rancho dwellers came from other areas of the city, despite the fact that most were migrants
Ugalde	Ciudad Juárez	1969	Population of household heads in 1 barrio; N (migrants) = 115	88% of dwellers came from other areas of the city. Migrants living in the city: Up to 3 years 6%, 4–6 years 6%, 7–12 years 19%, 12 years or more 69%
Cuevas	Guatemala City	1965	Study of the population of three peripheral settlements	73% of adult migrant dwellers came to settlements from other areas of the city
Roberts	Guatemala City	1970	Random sample of household heads in 2 lower class colonias; N (migrants) = 180	Migrants living in the city: Less than 10 years 29%, 10 years or more 71%

Table 6—Continued

Source	City	Year	Sample	Relevant Figures
Goldrich et al.	Lima	1967	Random sample of adult dwellers in 2 *barriadas*; N (migrants) = 221	Migrants living in the city: Less than 3 years 7% 3–5 years 16% 5–12 years 24% 12 years or more 53%
ECLA	Santiago	1962	Population of household heads and their wives in 122 *callampas*	64% of adult migrant dwellers moved to the settlements after having lived in other areas of the city
Goldrich et al.	Santiago	1967	Random sample of household heads in 2 *poblaciones*; N (migrants) = 188	Migrants living in the city: Less than 3 years 3% 3–5 years 10% 5–12 years 27% 12 years or more 60%
DESAL	Santiago	1967	Random sample of adult women in all *poblaciones* in the metropolitan area; N (migrants from small towns or rural areas) = 334	Migrants living in the city: Less than 1 year 3% 1–4 years 7% 5–9 years 10% 10 years or more 80%

| Portes | Santiago | 1969 | Random sample of household heads in 4 *poblaciones*; N (migrants) = 222 | Migrants living in the city:
Less than 1 year 0%
1–4 years 8%
5–9 years 19%
10 years or more 73% |
| Corten | Santo Domingo | 1965 | Sample of adult dwellers in squatter settlements | 100% of migrant dwellers came to settlements from previous residences in other areas of the city |

Sources: Ramiro Cardona, *Dos barrios de invasión*; Andre Corten, "Como vive la otra mitad de Santo Domingo: Estudio de dualismo estructural," *Caribbean Studies* 4 (1965): 3–19; Marco Antonio Cuevas, *Análisis de tres áreas marginales de la Ciudad de Guatemala*; DESAL, "Encuesta sobre la familia y la fecundidad en poblaciones marginales del Gran Santiago 1966/67," vol. 2; ECLA, *Encuesta realizada por CEPAL (ECLA) y la Escuela de Servicio Social de la Universidad de Chile a 122 poblaciones callampa en Octubre de 1962*, reported in Guillermo Rosenbluth, "Problemas socio-económicos de la marginalidad y la integración urbana"; William L. Flinn, "Rural and Intra-Urban Migration in Colombia: Two Case Studies in Bogotá," in *Latin American Urban Research*, vol. 1, edited by Francine F. Rabinovitz and Felicity M. Trueblood, pp. 89–93; William L. Flinn and James W. Converse, "Eight Assumptions concerning Rural-Urban Migration in Colombia: A Three Shantytowns Test," *Land Economics* 46 (1970): 456–464; Daniel Goldrich, Raymond B. Pratt, and Charles R. Schuller, "The Political Integration of Lower-Class Urban Settlements in Chile and Peru," *Studies in Comparative International Development* 3 (1967–1968): 3–22; Alejandro Portes, *Cuatro poblaciones*; Talton F. Ray, *The Politics of the Barrios of Venezuela*; Bryan Roberts, "The Social Organization of Low-Income Urban Families," in *Crucifixion by Power*, by Richard Newbold Adams, pp. 479–514; Antonio Ugalde, *The Urbanization Process of a Poor Mexican Neighborhood*; Elsa Usandizaga and A. Eugene Havens, *Tres barrios de invasión*.

The data in table 6 illustrate that peripheral settlers are not, by and large, new migrants but individuals with extensive urban experience. The studies summarized in the table indicate that the vast majority of migrant settlers have come to these areas from other parts of the city and have had five or more years of urban residence. Such results cannot be harmonized with a traditional view of peripheral settlements as staging areas for the recently arrived poor.[93]

The crucial point is that the pressure on urban land by the poor is differentiated. Needs vary according to the stage of economic advancement and stability reached by individuals. While for some, bare shelter is sufficient, others demand the security of landownership and the possibility of expansion and improvement of their dwellings.[94] For the latter, it is residential rather than occupational goals that shape their patterns of action in the city. The dilemma of these individuals is that a stable menial position permits survival and even small savings but, because salaries are still too low, does not permit entry into the conventional housing market. "Consolidators" must thus turn to public housing projects—seldom available or adequate—or defy official regulations in illegal settlements.

Geographic Location

Combined with the movement of elites away from the central city, the pattern of settlement of the urban poor has dramatically altered the ecology of the Latin American city. This alteration represents in essence the final breakdown of the old, cephalic pattern of urban distribution and the substitution of a sharp ecological polarization.[95] By contrast, clandestine subdivisions and land invasions have moved toward the less desirable portions of the urban periphery. Common sense dictates that illegal settlements would have greater chance of success if established in land of little speculative value. These are areas where geographical accidents or the proximity of industry and so forth make living undesirable for wealthier groups. Generally, they are in the periphery of the poorer sectors of the city.

Lower-class settlements have grown predominantly toward the south in Bogotá and Quito, and toward the the north, west, and southwest in Santiago. In Lima, they have occupied the desert alluvial pampas emerging from the eastern mountains,

and in Mexico City their fastest growth has occurred in the
eastern districts of Ixtapalapa, Ixtacalco, and Gustavo A. Ma-
dero, as well as in the south.[96]

While in both U.S. and Latin American cities elite groups
have followed an identical pattern of flight toward the suburbs,
the fate of the zone surrounding the commercial center has been
altogether different.[97] The fill-in pattern of elite replacement in
this zone has been carried out by different social groups: In
Latin America, it has been predominantly used by the growing
middle and lower-middle urban strata. Thus, the rapid transformation of core cities into abysmal slums, characteristic of
the United States, has not occurred in most of Latin America.

In Santiago, Mexico City, Lima, and other cities, the central
city does contain large numbers of *conventillos, pasajes, cités,
solares,* and other tenements.[98] None of these areas possesses,
however, the massive character and the atmosphere of despair
of U.S. slums.[99] In this sense, they do not encircle the commercial district but rather constitute part of a diversified central
area, sometimes diffused in several directions, as in Santiago, or
concentrated in an identifiable sector, such as the *zona negra* in
Bogotá.[100]

Central zones of Latin American cities have evolved from an
aristocratic past to the position of transitional areas separating
a periphery of residential districts from the periphery of illegal
settlements. As both the poor and the wealthy leave the city,
the commercial center and its surrounding perimeter acquire
the double role of linkage and buffer between two divergent
populations.[101]

The current trend of urban expansion is one in which elite
and marginal areas not only grow physically apart but also tend
to become increasingly self-sufficient. Stores, elegant shops,
food markets, and places of recreation have begun to move in
recent years toward suburbs occupied by wealthier groups.
These groups find it increasingly easier to live their lives within
a privileged quarter, avoiding contact with the lower classes in
the transitional center. The poor, as seen above, have also
shown a definite preference to abandon the central city for
stable homesites in the urban periphery. As marginal settlements grow and mature, they, too, develop commercial and
recreational facilities of their own: a surprisingly diversified
gamut of food and clothing stores, canteens and bars, small

restaurants, pharmacies, and small variety shops.[102] These conveniences in lower-class quarters also render transportation to the center unnecessary.

The physical distribution of space in major cities of Latin America reflects the triadic pattern of their present social structures: extreme status groups occupy rapidly growing, but opposing, poles of urban expansion; different levels of middle-class population occupy the in-between zones, with their proximity to one or the other pole in rough agreement with their economic position. If the homogeneous social order of traditional cities found its physical expression in a concentric distribution, the forces shaping current urban growth have produced this new ecological triad. Growth and differentiation of the economy have resulted in the expansion of elite and middle zones in the city. Massive processes of migration and illegal occupation—consequences of the impact of the same economic order on the more deprived classes—have produced the periphery of marginal settlements. The ecology of the city thus comes to mirror the limited dynamism and the basic distortions imposed by a particular economic order—dependent capitalism—on the continent.

Conclusion

Historical writings on the process of urbanization in Latin America have tended to emphasize the absolute dominance of city over countryside and the elitist character of urban social structure. Empirical studies of present-day urban structure have stressed, on the other hand, the massive character of these cities and the growing impact of the migrant poor on the urban social order. On the surface, these phenomena do not follow logically from one another. This is because their relation is not linear but dialectical. The city offers one of the most visible arenas where consequences of a particular sequence of historical and economic developments turn upon themselves.

Early history provided a framework within which later economic and social trends could occur without undue violence to the existing social order. Conquering cities established a pattern of dominance over rural populations. Within the city, the Iberic corporate order favored the growth of elitism and a tolerant but indifferent attitude toward masses. Landownership emerged for both instrumental and consummatory reasons as the main factor in elite formation. This social structure offered no serious opposition to the penetration of economic currents emanating from the capitalist centers. Local elites were historically more adept at the role of *rentiers* than at that of competing entrepreneurs. They were thus universally agreed in permitting the transfer of economic initiative to foreign hands while using their share of the product in consummatory pursuits.

External control superimposed on a structure of economic scarcity aggravated urban concentration by investing in those few cities where resources, facilities, and markets were available. Growing urban concentration and inflationary pressures stimulated in turn investment in urban land for both security and profit.

A rational orientation among popular masses has finally dictated urban migration in response to resource concentration, and illegal invasions and settlements in response to land speculation and government inertia. Like most major historical processes, these phenomena arise not from deliberate ideology, but from the simple formal pressure of basic needs common to very large numbers. In response to them, the urban social structure has changed from a homogeneous, unchallenged order into a de facto plurality of interests. The highly centralized city of the past has given way to a triadic arrangement formed by enclaves of the established, a growing and amorphous middle sector, and the marginal city of the poor.

The fascination that the city has always held for its students, from Pirenne and Weber to contemporary researchers, is closely linked to the way in which its physical structure comes to mirror social patterns and change. In the case of the Latin American city, the abrupt transformation of a simple, centripetal ecology accurately reflects the termination of a monolithic social order and the emergence of a massive popular antithesis, which is its own creation. This dialectic development further spells the latent tension between elite and marginal groups—the two growing components of urban society. In unobvious and probably surprising ways, such contradiction is likely to furnish the basis for major structural transformations. Though specifics are unknown, the trends toward synthesis and change in the Latin American city are almost palpable to every careful observer.

3

The Politics of
Urban Poverty

Alejandro Portes

In this chapter, I wish to examine the logical complement of the economic and ecological framework presented in chapter 2: the political reactions of the urban poor to the forces conditioning their situation.

Impressionistic observation gave rise to and supported for many years a wide assortment of myths on this topic. Most common, perhaps, was the imputation of seething fury and radicalism to shantytown dwellers and other marginal groups.[1] This view emerged, in part, from the introspective reaction of middle-class observers asking themselves what they would do were they forced to live under such conditions. Vicarious rebellion was then projected onto marginal settlers, who were pictured as potential destroyers of the bourgeois urban order. Such views raised unnecessary alarm among defenders of the status quo and equally vain hopes among revolutionary minorities.

At the opposite extreme, observations by anthropologists and others of the relative passivity of marginal groups gave rise to the notion of "subculture of poverty." These groups were then characterized as apathetic, fatalistic, without aspirations, acting on emotional impulse, and without the minimal cultural and psychic skills necessary for rational action.[2] By this new myth, blame for the situation of the urban poor was shifted from structural factors to the poor themselves. The culture of poverty thus became the cause of poverty since it impeded the dynamic, calculated efforts necessary to overcome this situation.

While at apparent extremes, the two mythologies of urban

poverty supported each other in subtle ways. Perhaps without deliberate intention on the part of their proponents, both points of view became establishmentarian ideologies. "Marginal radicalism" came to embody the distrust by urban middle-classes of the disenfranchised poor; "subculture of poverty" became popular as an interpretation of marginality that lifted the responsibility from the social order and placed it on the qualitative inferiority of the poor.

Empirical research in lower-class settlements of Latin American cities has caused, as its major consequence, the demise of these two mythologies. The works of Anthony and Elizabeth Leeds in Brazil, William Mangin and John Turner in Peru, Daniel Goldrich in Peru and Chile, Bryan Roberts in Guatemala, Talton Ray in Venezuela, and Wayne Cornelius in Mexico City, among others, have convincingly shown the untenability of conventional (and convenient) views of urban poverty.[3] The following sections summarize the main findings of these studies as they provide definite evidence against traditional viewpoints and, more importantly, as they define the actual profile of political action by the most deprived of urban sectors.

If neither apathy nor destructive anger characterizes the political orientations of the poor, what is their distinctive response to the strains of their situation? The answer is made difficult by the very heterogeneity of the urban lower classes. There are about twenty thousand urban squatter settlements in Latin America; this figure does not take into account central-city tenements and other marginal areas.[4] The socio-political context in which the poor live and from which marginal settlements emerge varies greatly from country to country. Within each country, as Anthony Leeds also notes, there are significant differences among cities along the gradients of size and relative economic and political importance.[5] Finally, in each city, areas housing the poor vary by origin, age, size, security of tenure, leadership and internal solidarity, and particular problems affecting the community.

Such differences must be considered in any attempt to generalize a new interpretation for all marginal groups. Yet, as the remainder of this chapter will attempt to show, differences in situation among the urban poor basically account for different manifestations of a similar underlying syndrome. In characterizing such a syndrome, I do not pretend to interpret what the actors themselves think or to reproduce exactly their own explanations of their behavior. Here, as elsewhere, Max Weber's statement that "in the great majority of cases actual action goes on in a state of inarticulate half-consciousness or actual unconsciousness of its subjective meaning" holds.[6] Positing a basic underlying orientation is justified by its usefulness in interpreting and bringing together a large number of isolated empirical instances.

This syndrome is one of rational adaptation to the existing social situation. By "rational," I mean a strategy of calculated pursuit of social and economic goals through available means. This strategy adapts to the existing situation by taking it as a given to be coped with and not as a contingency to be challenged. Patterns of political behavior exhibited by the urban poor in Latin America can more easily be characterized as deliberate manipulations of available channels for survival and mobility than as either careless abandon (subculture of poverty) or militant opposition (radical potential). This orientation remains dominant despite the structural imbalances of a situation of dependency, the growing conflict between need for shelter and demand for profit, and the increasing ecological polarization of these cities.

The analysis of political reactions by the urban poor proceeds in the following sections by asking three interrelated questions: (1) What is the *nature* of political activities by the poor? (2) What is the *extent* of such activities? (3) What is the *impact* of these actions on the urban social order?

These questions provide a simple and useful framework for the material in this chapter. Under the first question, an attempt is made to portray the qualitative character of political organization among the poor. Under the second, current knowledge of the quantitative aspect of these organizations is summarized. Under the third, finally, a linkage is established between the preceding two aspects and the structural situation summarized in chapter 2.

As in any attempt at generalization, specific instances and deviant cases must receive little attention. The reader is thus forewarned against seeking in the following pages a comprehensive summary of all available nuances of research in this

area. The pages represent, instead, my own attempt at synthe-
sizing what seem to be the dominant trends and lessons emerging from political studies of the urban poor in Latin America.

The Nature of Popular Participation

Settlements as Settings for Political Action

The study of political participation by the poor can be approached from different perspectives. From the discussion
above, however, it should be clear that I have chosen the residential context—the highly visible and generally organized
lower-class settlements—as point of entry for the topic. Some
criticism has been leveled against identifying "marginality"
with squatter and other forms of lower-class precarious settlements in the city.[7] If marginal means only the unemployed and
those employed in menial services, it is true that the population
of settlements is not formed exclusively by these sectors. A
major advantage of employing a residential perspective in this
context is precisely the heterogeneity of the population of these
areas.

As seen in the preceding chapter, both migrants and urban-
born are found in peripheral settlements. In occupational terms,
there are significant contingents of unemployed workers and
domestic servants, street vendors, and workers at odd jobs and
other menial services. Together with them, however, one finds
semiskilled and skilled industrial workers, artisans, and even
white-collar and minor professionals, such as government
bureaucrats, teachers, secretaries, and bookkeepers. In a representative survey of the entire *barriada* population of Lima,
10 percent of male family heads were found to be unemployed;
45 percent were blue-collar workers; 25 percent were independent salesmen and petty vendors; and 20 percent were office employees. Commenting on this heterogeneity, the survey authors
observe that "the considerable variation in jobs is indicative of
the wide range of people from Lima's working and lower-middle
classes who have taken up residence in the *barriadas*. These are
not specialized, one-occupation communities."[8]

The cross section of urban population offered by squatter and
other settlements can be compared to advantage with that pro-

vided, for example, by trade unions. In the context of the transitional economies of Latin America, established industrial, construction, and transportation workers—especially those belonging to unions—represent a much more restricted sector. Their level of income and occupational security puts them clearly above urban marginal masses; many live not in settlements but in regular areas of the city.[9]

Lower-class settlements not only represent the most varied and highly focalized cross-section of the urban poor but also, and perhaps most importantly, embody the most vital manifestations of their political action. Organized land invasions, to cite only the best known case, represent visible instances of the political struggle against the existing land tenure system. As will be seen below, rather than occupational or income needs, it is the demand for housing that has most effectively politicized the poor. Through it, disjointed masses have been transformed into purposeful, organized forces. Such needs and the forms taken by demands are illustrated in the following section.

Two Petitions

After several public meetings with officials of the Chilean Housing Corporation (CORHABIT), officers of the Junta de Vecinos (Neighborhood Council) of the La Faena settlement decided to address a petition to the minister of housing. La Faena is a government project in the southeastern fringes of Santiago; it was built under the Operación Sitio Program to provide minimally urbanized sites at the lowest possible price. Residents were thus drawn from the poorest layers of the marginal population. The main point of contention between government and *pobladores* (settlers) was the refusal of the former to quote a firm total price and monthly payments for the sites. The government argued that the "necessary studies" had not been completed. The *pobladores,* on the other hand, stressed the uncertainty produced by ignorance of the total price. Rumors circulated about enormous total sums and payments impossible to meet.

This demand for certainty stems from an essentially middle-class preoccupation with investment and allocation of a limited budget. A subculture-of-poverty orientation could not produce this concern since lack of mobility goals and inability to articulate means and ends would prevent any such long-term calculation. Along the same lines, the remaining requests in the petition are not for money, food, clothing, or any other "gifts" for immediate consumption but rather for public services that would permit long-term development of the area. Neither those trapped in a subculture of poverty nor those seething with radical fury would ask the government for increased police vigilance in their settlement.

Santiago de Chile, November 20, 1968

Mr. Minister:

We take the liberty of addressing ourselves to you to present you with some of the problems affecting our settlement.

We have at present 3,350 inhabitants (472 families), who have formed a Junta de Vecinos with which they aim to solve their housing problems and others.

1) Socio-economic Problems:

People in our settlement are seriously worried by the economic problem that affects a great majority of land purchasers (Operación Sitio), and which is the following:

A great proportion of our neighbors declared to COR-HABIT that they earn 10 escudos [approximately U.S. $1.05] daily, which adds up to 300 escudos per month. There are even some unemployed who, wishing to have a place to live, committed themselves to pay the dividends. Yet, Mr. Minister, in a public meeting in which a functionnaire of COR-HABIT took part, it was emphasized that a decent house, plus the urbanized lot, would cost around 27,000 escudos.

The present worry lies in the fact that, having declared a daily salary of 10 escudos, it would be very difficult for us to pay such an amount regardless of how decent the house is; some calculations that ratify this point follow.

Of the 10 escudos declared we must discount the following percentages:

8.25%	Social security
3.25%	Dividend or rent
5.00%	Electricity
1.00%	Water
3.50%	Electric cable and meter
13.00%	Credits for wood and roofing materials
34.00%	

With this, a margin of 62.1 percent is left for food; that is, 6.21 escudos.

It is of vital importance for us to know the real value of our sites, urbanized and semiurbanized.

Thus, we plead with you, Mr. Minister, to proceed, if you find it convenient, to study and help us attain our socio-economic aspirations.

2) Water:

In our settlement, there are at present ten spigots, which are insufficient, given the number of settlers that live in it.

These spigots are placed at a distance of 150 meters from each other. We believe that an expansion of this system with twenty new spigots would help to solve our problems.

3) Street Lights:

It so happens that we do not have this element and that it is very indispensable because delinquents take advantage of the darkness to perpetrate their crimes and deprivations, and they are terrorizing the settlement, which, unfortunately, has no police protection. We would appreciate it if, through your mediation, they speed up the work of the public street lights, especially in the alleys, which are the ones that suffer most from these consequences.

4) Police Protection:

We also ask your intervention for the building of a small police station, since this settlement is so large and police protection is nil.

5) Provisional Medical Center:

Due to the scarcity of water and lack of cleanliness in the streets, contagious diseases are appearing and accidents suffered by our children who, sometimes, cannot be taken to a hospital or first aid station.

We would like, with your cooperation, which for us is invaluable, to obtain a Provisional First Aid Medical Center, both of medicine and healing.

6) Pavement:

We ask from you to find it convenient to intervene in the construction of pavement of the streets and sidewalks; that they be of solid material, definitive, and constructed as soon as possible; since, before, they were of cement and they have proven until now a failure, as they are totally deteriorated. Because of this, we are about to be victims of not having public transportation.

7) Schools:

We also ask your valuable cooperation with respect to primary schools that are insufficient and, because of this, more than five hundred children of our settlement are being deprived of admission to schools so they have to go to faraway places, filling public transportation, which is very scarce.

8) Public Telephone:

Another grave problem is that in many circumstances our children and women become sick late at night without having any means of transportation or of calling the public assistance services.

We find ourselves completely isolated from society since, even for making an urgent call, we have to walk about forty blocks. We would like to have about five telephones in our settlement, given the great number of inhabitants who live here and many will be the needs for night assistance met by these services.

Mr. Minister, before taking leave, we do not hope that all these be attained right away but we do, as workers and fathers and that our salaries are low, plead with you to make our problems your own.

Sincerely,

The Junta de Vecinos of La Faena
[Signatures of junta officers
follow; translation from my
original copy]

Something came out of this petition in the form of improved public transportation and additional water spigots. The basic demand for a fixed final price for the sites was not satisfied, however, for many more months.

The squatter settlement of Los Arroyos is situated on a steep hillside on the outskirts of Bogotá. It emerged from an organized land invasion. Most of its inhabitants are migrants from the interior who came to Bogotá to escape la violencia, the rampant banditry in the Colombian rural zones. Not finding a place to live, some of them set up organizations to take over unused land. Los Arroyos is the major settlement to emerge from such efforts.

As a solution to the precarious legal situation of settlers, the Colombian Housing Agency bought the occupied land and planned to sell it back to the inhabitants for a flat price per lot, which included the cost of minimal urbanization and sanitary services. Some of the settlers, however, were dissatisfied with the terms offered by the government. About 15 percent of the inhabitants, grouped in the Committee for the Defense and Possession of Los Arroyos, addressed the following letter in 1968 to the Housing Agency. To be noticed is the level of legal information displayed by settlers. Once again, demands have nothing to do with immediate rewards and gratifications but rather with security of land tenure at prices deemed reasonable. The style of the letter is deferential, though less so than the previous one:

SECOND OPEN LETTER OF THE INHABITANTS
OF THE SETTLEMENT LOS ARROYOS TO THE
POPULAR HOUSING ADMINISTRATION

Director of the Popular Housing Administration
Bogotá, D.E.

In the most courteous manner we address ourselves to you to present the opinion of the inhabitants of the settlement Los Arroyos about the financial aspects of the so-called Plan for Development of Los Arroyos, which is under the control of the agency you represent.

1) We consider that if the sum paid by the agency for the purchase of the land was of $291,856.20 [one Colombian peso was approximately US $0.92] with a total area of 1,216 square hectares (121,600 square meters), it corresponds to the settlers to pay the amount of $2.40, two pesos and forty centavos, per square meter of land and if the average size per family is 90 square meters, *its total would be of $216.00* and NOT of $355.92, as quoted by you.

2) If for urbanization the maximum cost per square meter is $44.05, the part of urbanization corresponding to each lot, assuming that this is from the beginning of the sidewalk to

the middle of the street for the corresponding front, indicates that for those lots in front of the widest streets the total of urbanizable square meters WOULD NOT EXCEED 20, *that is, for this rubric, maximum cost would reach the amount of $881.00.*

3) The so-called sanitary unit consisting of a laundry tub, sink, water tank, toilet, shower with their corresponding connections of water and sewage and also their brick divisions, *the price of the above materials does not exceed the sum of $2,500.00.*

4) If it is attempted, as you say, "to sell an urbanized lot with sanitary unit," if the above-mentioned aspects that compose it are added up, *its total price would be $3,597.00 maximum* and NOT $6,000.00 as established by that agency and above this sum we must add the 4 percent yearly interests plus life and fire insurance demanded as backing for the acquired debt, which increases the cost by more than $3,000.00, totalling a real price of $9,000.00 for that site.

Thus, as the amount of land is not equal for all, the price must be fixed for each one individually according to the amount of land he possesses, the urbanizable meters of front, and the sanitary unit for those who have it, but departing from these prices: $2.40 per square meter of land used for the dwelling; $44.05 per square meter of the urbanizable part of its front (beginning of the sidewalk to middle of the corresponding street), as maximum price for those adjacent to the main street and with corresponding reductions for the others.

5) As the plan is subsidized by the District Administration [refers to the Special District of Bogotá] for which the District Council allocated a sum of seven and a half million pesos. If we divide that sum among the 940 families that live in the settlement, it would correspond to an "aid" of $6,861.00 for each PLUS THE SOCIAL CENTER FOR THE COMMUNITY. But as WE DO NOT PRETEND THAT EVERYTHING BE FREE, we do demand that at least 50 percent of the price accepted by us be subsidized with this sum given by our people through the District Administration. That the beneficiaries not be burdened with the debt-backing in-

surance and that the urbanized plot, with sanitary unit that is, be handed with the corresponding property tax exemption as well as exemptions from any future tax imposed over this type of property. The quoted prices as the result of contracts calculated or made with private entities, could be reduced if the Administration implements article 3 of the Municipal Resolution #27 of the year 1966 which authorizes it to use, without any costs, the transportation and construction equipment of the Special District.

6) The serious economic situation in which most of the inhabitants of our settlement find themselves requires that the so well advertised "social sensitivity" be implemented in such a way that in each concrete instance a "promise to sell" be elaborated, taking into account that greater facilities should be given to those families suffering most from low salaries and large numbers, in the prices and the installments.
Sincerely,

> Comité Pro-Defensa y Posesión del
> Barrios Los Arroyos
> [Signatures of officers follow;
> emphases in original; translation
> from my copy]

Alternatives for Political Action

The demand for housing and landownership among the poor has both an objective component of need for shelter and a subjective component of desire to establish definite roots in the city. Ownership of a plot of land and a roof, no matter how modest at the start, has the symbolic value of chartering the individual as a permanent member of the community. Homeownership provides respectability, the possibility of improvement and expansion, and a measure of protection against economic hardships and inflation.

It is important to consider the alternatives open to lower-class groups for fulfillment of these goals. One alternative is to proceed individually, attempting to accumulate enough resources to enter the conventional housing market or the programs offered by the government. Lack of resources close this alternative to most, especially in those countries lacking extensive public housing programs or having them at prices unreachable by the poor.

A second alternative is to enter the political arena by joining a party. Within this option there are two possible choices: The first is to attempt to build contacts with influential politicians so as to receive individually dispensed favors. This option is open only to the politically gifted. Isolated individuals count for little in the electoral game unless they are influential in attracting the votes of others. This role, therefore, does not provide a meaningful option for the vast majority of the poor.

The second choice is to join populist or leftist movements aiming at a drastic transformation of the society. Problems of marginal and impoverished masses, from this viewpoint, will not be solved until the existing social order is abolished. Massive support of this alternative by the poor has been a rare occurrence. Even at the electoral level, studies in Peru, Venezuela, Chile, and Brazil, among others, indicate that the vote of lower-class settlements tends to be moderate and in no way dominated by extreme leftist parties: "Because organizational potential is greater in the urban setting than in rural areas, some form of radical political behavior may be expected . . . This behavior may take the form of demand aggregation by ideologically leftist parties, or by strong political organizations acting independently of political parties and using either the electoral process or tactics of limited violence. The research has shown that neither of these forms of behavior exists in the *barriadas* to any great degree."[10]

The last alternative for marginal groups is to organize themselves into associations, either for invading and holding unoccupied land, or for attaining public service improvements, credit, and/or security of land tenure. This alternative brings together lower-class settlements to act as interest groups within the existing political order. The associational alternative thus sets a middle course between the atomistic path of individual achievement and the national revolutionary strategy of leftist affiliations.

This third alternative has been by far the most common instrument in the popular struggle for land and housing. Goldrich and others report levels of participation in *juntas de vecinos* of up to 21 percent in Lima and Santiago. In Goldrich's study of

Santiago in 1969, *junta* membership reached 42 percent.[11] This figure must be compared with the minimal participation of the same groups in all other noncommunal organizations. In a recent study in Managua, where organizational participation of marginal settlers is practically zero, Reynaldo Tefel notes "the encouraging finding that 25.6 percent of the settlers place their hopes to resolve their major problems in the communal associations."

Antonio Ugalde finds that in Ciudad Juárez, Mexico, up to 57 percent of family heads in a marginal settlement take part in community-oriented organizations, while only 15 percent belong to labor unions. In Mexico City, Cornelius reports, levels of participation in community self-help activities reach 95 percent of inhabitants in a lower-class *colonia*.[12]

The dominance of this alternative is manifested not in formal membership in associations, but in the collective mobilizations preceding and following a land invasion and the assemblies (*asambleas*) and rallies for petition and protest at crucial junctures in the development of a settlement.

In most instances, the associational strategy is guided by conditions dominant in the political system. It is instructive to compare the menacing picture of slum radicalism with the general adaptation of the urban poor to "rules of the game" set by the existing political order. The associational alternative and its orientations are exemplified by recent urban history in several countries. Two illustrations follow.

Urban History in Chile and Brazil

During the last fifteen years and up to the overthrow of Salvador Allende, the Chilean political system experienced a continuous turn toward the Left and, with it, an increasing receptivity toward popular demands. During the conservative government of Jorge Alessandri (1958–1964), the official policy toward the "*callampa* problem" was massive eradication of those in existence coupled with decisive repression of any attempt at illegal land takeover. The passivity of settlement dwellers during this period reflected their logical adaptation to conditions that did not permit anything beyond deferential petitioning.

The advent of the Christian Democrats to power in 1964 marked the beginning of an era of reformism and strong concern with promotion of marginal settlements. Conventional housing programs were replaced by the new Operación Sitio program, which provided sites and minimal urbanization at affordable prices. The response to the new program was so overwhelming that the government found itself unable to meet the demand. By 1969, twenty-three thousand "housing solutions" were planned, more than the total number provided during the entire Alessandri period; yet the demand more than doubled this figure.[13]

Ironically, the very atmosphere created by a reformist government stimulated a parallel increase in land invasions. The reluctance of the government to use force against the most deprived groups opened a channel of land acquisition closed in the past. Parties of the extreme Left also saw an opportunity to build support among the poor while, at the same time, embarrassing the government. They supported and even organized "committees of the homeless" (comités de los sin casa), which pressured the government for rapid attention to their housing needs and organized invasions when their demands were not met.

According to Goldrich, major Santiago-area land invasions "increased from a rate of single large-scale seizures in 1947, 1957, 1960, 1961, 1965 to two in 1967, and six major and several minor ones in 1969."[14] During this last year, I personally visited two "invasions" of public roads under construction. Their purpose was not to occupy that land but rather to pressure the government to resettle invaders in an Operación Sitio project. In another instance, I witnessed a "preventive invasion" by legal occupants of a project to discourage a planned illegal invasion by a los sin casa committee. Such instances give an idea of the complexity of the situation.

The framework created by the Christian Democratic government permitted the poor to vigorously pursue new alternatives for attainment of housing aspirations. Although the official sites-and-services program was well received and gained support for the party in power, the extreme Left also capitalized on opportunities to sponsor and support illegal invasions.

The election of Salvador Allende in 1970 marked the effective end of governmental repression of popularly organized invasions. In speeches and personal exchanges, President Allende repeatedly indicated that since his was the government of the people, it would not repress popular initiatives, even if they ran against official planning. Stimulated by MIR (Movimiento Izquierda Revolucionaria) and other militant groups, land invasions multiplied, and demands from lower-class settlements became more assertive. This was the time in which radical *campamentos* (encampments), such as Nueva Habana, emerged.[15]

The enthusiasm produced by the socialist experiment moved some writers to overemphasize the radicalism of the *pobladores* during this period.[16] It is true that long-term socialization of objective needs by the Marxist parties had produced a core of leftist radicals in the settlements. The error, however, consists in generalizing this situation to include the urban marginal population as a whole. Evidence from empirical research and from the history of political action by *pobladores* indicates the previous absence of a dominant radical orientation in these areas. The growing participation during the Unidad Popular government is a function not only of the long-held radicalism of the few but also of the adaptive capacity of the many. The latter responded to conditions created by a nonrepressive and sympathetic government. This is not to say that participation in land invasions and the experience of a more dignified existence during the socialist period did not increase militant beliefs. What it does say is that the rapid change in patterns of political behavior among *pobladores* followed closely the modification in structural power arrangements brought about by a populist government. The same rational orientation that prevented political action during the Alessandri period and encouraged response to specific housing programs during the Christian Democratic government found expression in broader and more assertive demands in the three years of democratic socialism.

The *favelas* of Rio de Janeiro differ from most *poblaciones* in Chile in having grown by accretion rather than by organized invasions and in occupying relatively central hillside areas rather than peripheral locations.[17] Before the military coup of 1964, an intense political exchange took place between *favela* dwellers and *políticos* interested in municipal or legislative office. Prior to 1964, Brazil had a multiparty political system that lacked, however, the ideological overtones of the Chilean parties. Although party platforms were formally presented to *favelados,* what really counted was the personal relation, the machinelike exchange of favors for votes in *favela* settlements.

Such was the option that the political system offered, and *favela* dwellers attempted to make the best of it: No organized invasions, no radical postures, and, at the same time, no apathy were characteristic of these areas. Instead, *favelas* employed their considerable electoral strength as weapon and resource. This electoral power had a double function: "on the one hand, to reward or punish government performance in general, and on the other, to reciprocate for specific individual favors."[18]

Before the present government's mass removal program, close to one million *favela* voters exercised a decisive influence in Rio's politics. Large *favelas,* especially, carried considerable weight both with elected politicians and with government bureaucrats. In the words of a *favela* leader, quoted by Elizabeth Leeds, "politics in the *favela* is called a business."[19] At election times, "business" became particularly intense as candidates wooed *favela* voters with promises and displays of past performance and as *favelados* played one candidate against another for advantage. Benefits sought, once again, were protection against eviction, surety of titles to the land, and improvement of collective services, such as electricity, water, and public transportation.

This situation changed drastically with the 1964 military coup. The permanent elimination of elections as vehicles for popular expression and the imposition of authoritarian rule deprived the urban poor of their only effective political resource. Without it, they were left helpless vis-à-vis government policies. As it turned out, such policies amounted to the elimination of the *favela* as a social entity without provision for a functional substitute. The "eradication" program of the military government called for the razing of existing *favelas* and transportation of their inhabitants to new housing projects (Vila Kennedy, Aliança) on the extreme outskirts of the city.

For government agencies and sympathetic entrepreneurs, the eradication program had major advantages: It freed valuable, scenic areas from *favela* eyesores and left them free for construction of tourist hotels and upper-middle-class housing. Tourism was supposed to benefit from this strategy, as was the construction industry. The latter also profited from construction of massive, cheaply built housing projects into which the poor were forced to move and whose amortizations they were forced to pay.

For the *favelados*, the eradication program had numerous disadvantages. The central-city location of most *favelas* permitted easy access to places of work and made possible a second job or odd jobs for extra income after hours. *Favelados* paid no rent and made only small payments to the government once title to the land had been secured. Savings in transportation and rent allowed investment in durable household goods or in home expansion and improvement whenever there was some security of tenure.

Forced removal to housing projects in the urban periphery means a one- or two-hour bus trip to central-city work. Added to the substantial cost of transportation is the impossibility of supplementing the major source of income by secondary jobs. Construction materials in the new houses are cheap, and there is little possibility of expansion. For this unsatisfactory housing situation, the poor are forced to pay monthly quotas comparable to rents in many apartments in the city. Those who cannot meet these payments are expelled and left with no place to go. Early attempts by *favela* organizations to prevent eradication were met with military force; leaders were jailed or deprived of political rights; and the organizations, dissolved.

Closure of channels for demand and petition and lack of receptivity by authorities are conditions conventionally expected to lead to radicalization and antiregime violence. Absence of such actions among *favelados* is not a reflection of apathy; it is the result of a rational assessment of structural conditions: A powerful, repressive government renders any such attempt by the most deprived of urban groups futile. Instead, the poor have attempted to adapt, as far as possible, to the new conditions. Some have attempted to brave the housing project "solutions"; others have returned to live in still existing *favelas;* still others may have moved into cheap, cramped rooming houses in the city or returned to their places of origin.

Situations as radically different as the militant assertiveness of *pobladores* during the Allende years, the intense and astute manipulation of Brazilian electoral politics by *favelados,* and their current inaction thus emerge as manifestations, under different structural conditions, of the same basic syndrome. Rational adaptation and instrumental organization to cope with the existing social order have been the trademarks of the politics of urban poverty in Latin America.

Sources of Political Adaptation

What are the causes of the absence of lower-class radicalism in Latin American cities? For Horowitz and others, a basic cleavage exists between city and countryside in potentiality for rebellion.[20] The city is said to offer greater possibilities for the integration of the poor. Rural areas, on the other hand, maintain sharp class barriers, patterns of traditionalism and deference to authority, and open exploitation of the masses. The city thus becomes the locus of the politics of cooptation, while the countryside remains the arena for revolutionary confrontation.

This interpretation of the "reformist" character of urban politics is based on the view that involvement of the poor in the urban system provides a modicum of upward mobility and, hence, prevents frustration from reaching threatening levels. At the core, this interpretation rests on the same frustration-aggression mechanism employed by previously dominant theories. If, before, a high potentiality for rebellion was predicated on the basis of frustration among marginal masses, at present the empirical findings of the general absence of such tendencies is explained by simply turning the theory around: there is no radicalism, because there is not enough frustration and/or there are sufficient opportunities for attainment of aspirations.

The peculiar attachment of political theorists to the frustration-aggression hypothesis reveals their ignorance of important facts. First, as the case of socialist Chile demonstrates, there can be political militance and radicalism among the poor under certain structural circumstances. Second, and more important, substantial levels of subjective deprivation and frustration prevail among these sectors. The point is vividly illustrated by anthropological and case studies.[21] Survey data also provide evidence in this direction.

Table 7 presents data from my study of four lower-class settlements in Santiago. Items appearing in the table are components of a Subjective Frustration Index (SFI). As can be seen, proportions of respondents reporting their present situation to

Table 7. Frustration in Lower-Class Settlements of Santiago

Item	Categories	Percentages (N = 382)
Comparison between present and past occupations	Better now than before; best occupation R has ever had	40
	Better now than before; not best occupation R has had	5
	Same as before	29
	Worse than before; unemployed	26
Comparison between present occupation and initial occupational aspirations	Better than aspired	16
	Same as aspired	22
	Worse than aspired	24
	Much worse than aspired; unemployed	26
	No initial aspirations; does not know	12
Comparison between present income and initial income aspirations	Better than aspired	14
	Same as aspired	7
	Worse than aspired	23
	Much worse than aspired; does not earn anything	47
	No initial aspirations; does not know	9
Comparison between present situation in general and initial life aspirations	Better than aspired	26
	Same as aspired	18
	Worse than aspired	36
	Much worse than aspired	20
Evaluation of present income in relation to family needs	Earns enough; can save	5
	Earns just enough	30
	Does not earn enough; has difficulties	48
	Does not earn enough; suffers serious deprivations	17

Source: My research in four lower-class settlements in Santiago, 1968–1969.

be worse than that aspired to at the beginning of adulthood are, without exception, significantly higher than those reporting having attained or exceeded initial aspirations. Similarly, those evaluating their present income as inadequate in relation to family needs far exceed those satisfied with their income level. Finally, while respondents reporting that present occupation is the best they have had amount to a sizable 40 percent of the sample, they still represent a minority in comparison with those experiencing no absolute occupational progress or those believing they have moved downward.

Similar findings are apparent in studies by Ramiro Cardona in Bogotá, Elsa Usandizaga and Eugene Havens in Barranquilla, and Goldrich in Lima and Santiago, among others.[22] The unique value of the ethnographic study of conditions in Rio's *favelas* by Elizabeth Leeds lies precisely in documenting the absence of any significant increase in radical violence among groups severely penalized by the military regime. The etiology of political orientations and, specifically, political radicalism among urban lower classes is considerably more complex than the frustration-aggression and other such simple mechanisms would lead us to believe.

Two distinct but related factors seem to be crucial for the explanation of this political phenomenon. One has to do with the structural context in which frustrations occur; the other, with the socio-psychological framework in which frustrations are interpreted.

1. Concerning structural conditions, the basic point is the lack of viability of revolutionary initiatives in most concrete instances. Vis-à-vis relatively efficient military establishments, the more numerous but weakest of urban sectors stand very little chance. Classical interpretations speak of "pent-up" radicalism, which accumulates within impoverished masses waiting for the opportune moment to thrust itself against the existing order. Such interpretations essentially assume that attitudes can remain unchanged for long periods of time despite a clearly adverse reality. As a substantial body of evidence on cognitive balance processes has shown, objective reality has, in turn, a decisive impact on what individuals come to believe. In most concrete instances, attitudes and objective situation interact until reaching a minimum of balance.[23] In the case of Latin America, the less the vulnerability of the existing order to organized challenges is and the longer this situation has been maintained, the more removed "rebellion" is from the field of practical alternatives among the masses. The frustrations of poverty must still be coped with, but overt political aggression

loses salience as a possible alternative. In this manner, the threat of swift repression is transformed into cognitive acceptance of the existing order, and the narrowing of concerns to more "practical" issues.

Urban poverty in Latin America occurs in a historical context that has often witnessed interelite struggles but seldom any meaningful threat to the class structure itself: Lines of hierarchy and authority have been institutionalized for generations, and, from the standpoint of marginal masses, the political and military machinery that support them appears truly awesome.[24] For migrant and native urban families in search of economic survival and a minimum of security, the prospect of prolonged violent struggles and drastic replacement of old elites by new ones seems both farfetched and undesirable.

Acceptance of radical beliefs carries with it the perennial difficulty of harmonizing thought and action, ideology and reality. As such, it is left for those willing to risk life and opportunities for the sake of ideals. The examples of the post-Allende military regime in Chile and others document the willingness of governments to use force against the poor. However, the historical legitimacy and institutional strength of the existing political order are manifest less in its ability to repress radicalism, than in its ability to remove it from the field of meaningful, practical alternatives for the urban poor. This alternative acquires a quality too remote to deserve serious consideration by those who must carefully weigh the use of very scarce resources.

2. Interpretation of the situation by the poor is as important a factor as the inhibiting potential of the political structure. Frustration-radicalism theories do not consider that deprivation anger need not be directed against the social order. In the absence of mediating cognitive factors, the emotional energy that frustration unleashes can be easily deflected into alternate channels.[25] Perceived causes of permanent social inequality and, more importantly, factors to which responsibility for frustrations are imputed form crucial intervening variables that mediate effects of frustration on political attitudes. In the case of Latin American cities, they help to explain the apparent contradiction of having high levels of frustration among the poor but relatively weak tendencies toward radicalism.

All things being equal, blame for frustrations placed on

social injustice, class privileges, and selfishness of powerful groups ought to channel the potential frustration into political militance. On the other hand, blame focused on the self, parental neglect, fate, or transcendental forces will deflect lower-class frustration into politically irrelevant paths.[26] The ethic predominant in lower-class settlements in urban Latin America has not been conducive to imputing responsibility for frustrations to the class structure. Governmental policies or specific government authorities may be held responsible for an undesirable situation, but blame is rarely placed on the existing social structure as a whole. Although this situation can be altered at times by political socialization, at present the dominant cognitive orientation is to adapt to existing structural arrangement: "The dominant ideology of most of the active *barriada* people can be summed up in the familiar and accepted maxims: Work hard, save your money, outwit the state, vote conservatively if possible, but always in your economic self-interest, educate your children for the future and as old age insurance for yourself."[27]

In my study of four *poblaciones* in Santiago, 90 percent of the households visited had radios and 30 percent had television sets; installment payments on these and other appliances seemed to play a far more important role in the hierarchy of the families' preoccupations than the social structure of which they were a part. Economic successes and setbacks were consistently interpreted in terms of occurrences within the individual's own circle of activity: illness, lack of education, vices, low pay in his present job. Speculations about the relation of personal happenings to the broader social order were definitely less vital and often brought about only by the artificial prodding of the interview. The government, as Ray also notes,[28] certainly plays an important role as donor of facilities for individual advancement but seldom as instrument or target of the class struggle.

Evidence in support of this general interpretation is presented in table 8. An item in the four-settlement study in Santiago asked respondents with unfulfilled initial aspirations who was to blame for this. A second item asked a similar question of respondents who stated they deserved a better situation. Table 8 presents the frequency distributions of responses.

"Nonstructural" responses—fate, parents, accidental happenings, own fault, and so on—are most frequently named in both items: 68 percent in the first and 63 percent in the second. "Structural" blame for frustrations—exploitation of the poor, social injustice, and so forth—accounts for only 15 and 7 percent of responses, respectively. The percentage of structure blamers in the second item is, in fact, lower than that of respondents declaring themselves satisfied with their present situation. "Quasi-structural" blame—imputation of responsibility to objective national conditions, such as inflation or unemployment but not to specific agents or centers of power—is hardly more frequent, amounting to 4 and 18 percent, respectively. Thus, the combined percentages of those placing responsibility, directly or indirectly, on the social order amounts to only one-fourth of the sample in one item and less than one-fifth in the other.

The study of two lower-class settlements in Lima and two in Santiago by Goldrich contains two items also relevant to the problem of imputation of blame to the social order.[29] One is a Likert-type question asking respondents' opinions about the statement: "In general our system of government and politics is good for the country." The second asks whether the present government has been more or less helpful toward the poor. Though these items are more indirect measures of the concept of structural blame, a similar pattern of response emerges. In both, the percentage of structure blamers (those opposing the existing political system or believing in a worsening orientation of governments toward the poor) is a minority. In Lima, proportions range from 42 percent in the first item to 11 percent in the second. In Santiago, proportions are only 12 and 2 percent, respectively.

The cognitive framework in which the existence of frustration is interpreted in Latin American cities emphasizes individual responsibility. It notes proximate causes and consequences and, hence, interprets failures more as unique occurrences than as systematic derivations from broader social arrangements. If the inhibiting potential of the existing power structure renders radicalism impractical, the individual ethic in which lower-class groups have been socialized renders it cognitively remote from their situation. Neither determinant is independent: to the extent that the existing order is perceived as an im-

Table 8. Blame for Economic Frustrations in Lower-Class Settlements of Santiago

Focus of Blame	Item	
	Who Is Responsible for Non-attainment of Initial Aspirations? (%)	Who Is Responsible for Non-attainment of a Better Life Situation, if Deserved? (%)
Nonstructural (fate, bad luck, happenings in past personal life: got sick, too little education, started to work too soon, abandoned by husband)	68	63
Quasi-structural (objective aspects of national situation: inflation, unemployment)	4	18
Structural (government indifference, exploitation of the poor, selfishness of the rich)	15	7
Satisfied with Present Situation	12	12
No Information	1	0
Total	100	100
	(N = 382)	(N = 382)

Source: My research in four lower-class settlements in Santiago, 1968–1969.

mutable framework, a "fact of life" as unquestionable as basic human needs, the plausibility of making it responsible for everyday frustrations is reduced.

Thus, the conspiratorial view that interprets each deprivation and failure as caused by a societally unjust order is discouraged. Absence of structural blame for frustrations, rather than absence of frustration, lies at the very core of the weakness of radicalism among the urban poor.

The Extent of Participation

The Evolution of Organizations

The preceding sections have shown that the need for housing and land furnishes the single most powerful motive for political action by the urban lower classes and that this action takes the form of organizations that adapt to dominant political conditions. What follows concerns the resilience of this form of collective action. Many writers have focused on participation in organizations and, more broadly, on "politicization" as crucial indicators of a dynamic and modern population.[30] From this standpoint, lower participation is defined as "depoliticization," or an absolute loss of political dynamism. In these writings, participation often acquires an absolute value: no matter what the purpose or circumstances, it is automatically preferred to nonparticipation. The participant is modern and integrated; the nonparticipant, traditional and marginal. And the obvious lesson is the need to increase participation.

The pattern encountered in most lower-class settlements in Latin America is one not of sustained or increasing participation in political activities, but of sharp ups and downs, with upsurges of interest and collective spirit followed by periods of individualism and apathy. In a theory that assumes only traumatic experiences can turn the process back, once individuals begin modernizing, the erratic behavior of these groups is puzzling indeed. In the effort to match theory with empirical reality, recourse has been found in depoliticizing experiences—such as police repression of squatters—which are said to turn back ongoing processes of increased participation.[31] In the most uncompromising versions, the organizational capacity of lower-class groups is altogether denied: "Marginality within the groups inhabiting peripheral settlements is defined by the concept of disintegration. That is, as a lack of internal cohesiveness that makes them appear atomized and dispersed . . . Dominant in these areas are isolationism and dispersion; these make them appear as disorganized groups, without internal links or coherent social expression to define them positively in front of the society as a whole."[32]

Such a view fails to consider the very crucial question of the purpose of organizational participation. The same adaptive syndrome that served above for interpreting the nature of political action by the poor offers here an alternate perspective on the extent of such action. In contrast with the politicization-modernization viewpoint, it notes that taking part in political meetings and activities consumes considerable time and effort. From a rational perspective, its utility must be weighed against the economic or psychological profits derived from other activities, such as work, home improvement, family life, interaction with friends, and so on. Individuals in lower-class settlements, like inhabitants of the better parts of the city, can rationally allocate time and effort in accordance with expected returns.

Some problems and aspirations do require collective action. Utilitarian considerations dictate that, when such problems become relevant, participation in collective organizations ought to increase. On the other hand, solution of problems, fulfillment of aspirations, and absence in general of socially relevant issues result in decreasing participation. Organizations at such times lie dormant. They remain, however, latent as potential instruments to be employed in future confrontations.

From the point of view of the poor, communal organizations are not artificial entities to be maintained for their own sake but instruments to be employed when necessary. In the same fashion that these groups adapt their political action to external social conditions, they also adapt organizational efforts to fit their varying internal needs. Considerable data are available in support of this interpretation.

1. A study by the Chilean government[33] among a random sample of participants in communal organizations (juntas de vecinos) in seventeen lower-class settlements measured the level of communal participation by an index of three moderately correlated items: frequency of attendance at meetings, degree of collaboration in junta activities, and amount of participation in junta decisions. This index was cross-tabulated with

Table 9. Participation in Juntas de Vecinos in Santiago de Chile and Selected Determinants

Variable	Category	Percentage Having High Level of Participation in the Local Junta (%)	(N)
Evaluation of present dwelling by respondent	Insufficient	31.82	(088)*
	Regular	24.47	(094)
	Sufficient	12.04	(108)
Legal ownership of dwelling	Nonproprietor	35.37	(082)
	Proprietor	16.83	(208)
Time of residence in area	1 month to 7 years	32.86	(070)
	8 years to 15 years	21.55	(116)
	16 years or more	15.38	(104)

Source: Promoción Popular, "Estudio sobre participación en un tipo de asociación voluntaria: Junta de Vecinos," 1968.
*Figures in parentheses represent the total number of cases in each row.

quality of dwelling, as evaluated by respondents; with report of being or not being a legal proprietor of the homesite; and with time of residence in the settlement.

Housing improvements in lower-class settlements in Santiago are, by and large, a collective enterprise. If participation in communal associations is in fact a function of their perceived utility for attainment of basic goals, it is to be expected that those in the worse housing conditions should participate more than those in better dwellings. Results in table 9 support this conclusion.

Writings on political modernization have generally predicted positive relations between proprietorship and stability of residence, on the one hand, and participation in voluntary associations, on the other.[34] Proprietorship is associated with characteristics of success and responsibility. The proprietor better fits

Table 10. Perceived Effectiveness of Juntas de Vecinos in Promoting Interests of Slum Dwellers and Level of Participation in Them

Participation	Effectiveness		
	Not Effective (%)	Effective (%)	Very Effective (%)
Low	46.59	32.94	30.00
Medium	43.18	38.82	23.33
High	10.23	28.24	46.67
Total	100.00 (88)*	100.00 (85)*	100.00 (88)*

Source: Promoción Popular, "Estudio sobre participación en un tipo de asociación voluntaria: Junta de Vecinos," 1968.
*Figures in parentheses are raw marginal frequencies.

the image of "responsible citizen" and "informed individual" than the nonproprietor. Therefore, proprietors should have higher levels of social participation, a behavior characterized as modern and responsible. Similarly, individuals with longer residence spans in an area are commonly the most settled and responsible inhabitants, according to this viewpoint. Thus, higher participation should also be expected of them. Results in table 9 contradict these predictions.

From the point of view of rational self-interest, proprietors and long-term residents, precisely because of being better established—that is, having solved their most pressing housing problems—have less interest in employing the communal organization to attain these goals. Thus, participation among them should be lower than among nonproprietors and newcomers to the area. This is what the data indicate.

2. If participation in communal organizations is mainly determined by rational considerations, it can be expected that, the more efficient the organization is perceived to be in promoting the interest of settlers, the greater will be the participation in it. Table 10, based on the same Santiago data, strongly supports this expectation. Results are highly significant statistically with percentages running in the predicted direction.

3. The comparative study by Goldrich[35] covered two marginal settlements in Santiago and two in Lima. Two of these—a

Table 11. Participation in Communal Organizations in Lima and Santiago

	Established Settlements		Precarious Settlements	
	Pampa Seca (Lima)	Santo Domingo (Santiago)	El Espíritu (Lima)	3 de Mayo (Santiago)
Percentage of Membership in Communal Organization	10	6	22	21
	(127)*	(191)	(119)	(98)

Source: Daniel Goldrich, Raymond B. Pratt, and Charles R. Schuller, "The Political Integration of Lower-Class Urban Settlements in Chile and Peru," Studies in Comparative International Development 3 (1967–1968): 3–22.
*Figures in parentheses are total sample sizes for each settlement.

squatter settlement in Lima and a government-sponsored project in Santiago—were more developed, approaching the characteristics of the established city in quality of dwellings and services. The others, one in each city, were in much more precarious situations, lacking legal title to the land and confronting other serious problems.

According to the view advanced above, it is not the more integrated, advanced settlements but rather the ones in difficult conditions that should exhibit highest levels of participation in communal organizations. In established settlements, further progress is largely a matter of individual initiative; for those in which legal proprietorship and basic services are lacking, collective action is still a vital necessity. Results in table 11 confirm such suppositions. Participation in advanced settlements reaches 10 percent in Lima and only 6 percent in Santiago. In contrast, participation in the less developed areas of both cities surpasses 20 percent.

4. More recent studies in Mexico City, Santiago, Lima, and other cities report essentially the same pattern uncovered by Goldrich. In Mexico City, Wayne Cornelius[36] conducted a survey among samples of residents in six lower-class colonias. Two

Table 12. Participation in Communal Organizations in Mexico City

	Recent Squatter Settlements			More Established Settlements				
	Colonia Nueva (%)	Colonia Periferico (%)	Total (%)	Colonia Militar (%)	Colonia Unidad Popular (%)	Colonia Texcoco (%)	Colonia Esfuerzo Propio (%)	Total (%)
Participation in communal self-help activities	96	76	87	42	31	53	38	42
Overall political participation	80	57	70	44	27	38	49	41
	[130]*	[101]	[231]	[116]	[77]	[124]	[131]	(448)

Source: Wayne A. Cornelius, Political Learning among the Migrant Poor.
*Figures in cells are rounded percentages; sample sizes are in parentheses.

of these were new squatter settlements created by illegal occupation of vacant land. Despite some assistance by the government, the two areas still had serious problems with services and land allocation. A third settlement was the product of an older land invasion, which was conducted in a highly organized fashion by low-ranking military personnel. At the time of the study, it was the most highly urbanized of all areas. The three remaining settlements were an older commercial subdivision and two conventional government projects. Though each settlement had problems of its own, the two new squatter settlements confronted the most precarious situation. In these, therefore, higher levels of communal organization and participation should be expected. Data in table 12 again support this expectation. Not only does participation in communal self-help activities in the two new settlements far exceed those in the other areas but also overall political participation (a composite of several different political activities) is significantly higher in them than in all other areas.

My study in Santiago comprised four different types of marginal settlements. Villa Norte, a poor, very deteriorated slum, was perceived by its inhabitants as an unsuitable place to live. Escape from it was defined, however, as an individual rather than a collective venture. The second area, Villa Sur-Oeste, an established government project, had dwellings and services of better quality than those in all other areas. The third settlement, Villa Oeste, emerged as a result of an organized squatter invasion. Though legal title to the land had been obtained, the settlement was still plagued by numerous problems. The last area, government-sponsored Villa Sur-Este, was part of the Operación Sitio Program of the Frei government. Though sites had been assigned, settlers had not been given final legal title to their land, and this insecurity was compounded by many other problems, such as lack of basic services.

Once again, settlements in which the communal *juntas de vecinos* performed the greatest function of meeting the needs and promoting the interests of settlers should yield the highest rates of participation. On the other hand, the most developed area, the one in which *junta* participation was not relevant to meeting settlers' needs, should exhibit much lower levels. Results in table 13 strongly support this supposition.

On the basis of extensive, observable experience, William

Table 13. Participation in Communal Organizations in Santiago, 1969

Settlement	Major Problem	Participation in Communal Organization (%)
Villa Oeste (113)*	Basic Public Services	54
Villa Sur-Este (114)	Security of Land Tenure	72
Villa Norte (84)	Individual Flight from Area	39
Villa Sur-Oeste (71)	Established Area; No Major Problem	46

Source: My research, 1968–1969.
*Sample sizes for each settlement are in parentheses.

Mangin concluded several years ago that, in Lima's *barriadas*, organizations reach the peak of their importance at the time of the land invasion and tend to decline thereafter as settlements become established. In a pioneer study of marginal settlements in Managua, Reynaldo Tefel found that reports of the existence of communal organizations were inversely related to the level of socioeconomic development of the area. In the more developed occidental zone, only 4 percent reported the existence of Juntas Comunales. The percentage increased in proportion to the precariousness of the area until it reached 24.3 percent in the most marginal southern zone. The author thus observes that "the poorest seem to feel more strongly the need for social solidarity."[37]

Summarizing findings from his study, Cornelius states: "In Latin American cities, communities characterized by insecurity of land tenure place highest priority on securing officially recognized title to the land. Next in importance is the installation of basic urban services such as water and electricity, followed by the construction of schools, public markets, health care centers, and other community facilities. While such problems exist, they provide a focus for internal self-help efforts . . . But once the most acute developmental problems are resolved, rates of participation in community associational activity and all other forms of political action tend to decline sharply."[38]

The extent of political participation by the urban poor in Latin America is equal to the extent of political provision for basic collective needs. That these needs are seen as limited to housing and urban services and not to other aspects of poverty is a reflection of the individually centered ethic of these groups. Housing and landownership are regarded as needs for which collective action is both necessary and possible. Thus, political participation is tailored to fit these needs. It is for this reason that communal organizations, not political parties, have become the main vehicles for collective action. It is for the same reason that politicization gathers considerable strength in the most deprived and insecure settlements but loses it again as they become integrated with the city.

Socialization Effects

Under which conditions will radicalism and sustained political activism occur? Answers to the question are similar, for they imply a viewpoint that transcends a purely individualistic orientation. One hypothesis is that with increasing education the structural roots of poverty and the need to struggle for goals beyond immediate housing become apparent. However, though education may promote greater awareness, it is also an instrument for individual mobility into the social system. Available data indicate that it is the promotional aspect of education, not its clarification of structural forces, that has the greatest importance. Summarizing findings of a study of youth in the José María Caro settlement, the largest in Santiago, Adolfo Gurrieri states: "In general, as the educational level increases so does the trichotomous perception of society. Even when they continue living in the marginal settlement, individuals of higher education will tend to identify themselves with the middle class."[39] A similar pattern is reported by Goldrich in Santiago and Lima: "The significance of this lies in its indication that the most educated (also both scarce and potentially most socially effective) *pobladores* may become increasingly individualistic in pursuit of their goals once the housing-urbanization needs are close to being met."[40]

Those among the urban poor that become politically militant or extend their collective demands beyond housing are not necessarily among the most educated. Rather, they seem products of direct political socialization. The structural origins of frustration and poverty are not self-evident and, hence, must be learned. Direct determinants of radicalism and sustained political participation do not inhere as much in situations of poverty as in forces of political socialization that act on those situations.

Evidence from different cities suggests, for example, that the experience of a land invasion itself is a politically socializing experience. Land invasions give participants a sense of their own collective strength and bring them into direct confrontation with the police, press, legislators, and government officials. During the period following the invasion, what before was a purely individual concern becomes a public matter and, hence, the target of forces previously unclear to the invaders themselves. Under certain circumstances, such experiences can be transformed into attitudes and concerns quite different from those that gave rise to the invasion in the first place.

Table 14 summarizes evidence from Mexico City, Lima, and Santiago documenting the political importance of land invasions. In all cases, invaders exhibit higher levels of political militance and activism than noninvaders. It can be argued that such results may be the consequence of self-selection by invaders among the politically active rather than the consequence of the invasion experience itself. While the point is methodologically sound (and may better fit the agitator image with which respectable classes and officials associate the invaders), it does not fit observed accounts of these events. Ray in Venezuela; Turner, Mangin, and Dietz in Lima; and Goldrich in Santiago have provided vivid accounts of the formation of "committees of the homeless" and similar organizations oriented toward acquisition of land by legal or illegal means. Without exception, they conclude that recruitment into these organizations is not limited to radical minorities but draws from a broad and fairly representative cross section of the urban poor.[41]

More to the point, perhaps, are the purposive intervention and socialization by political agents, usually members of a populist party. It should be noted, however, that their form of intervention and the response they solicit from the poor vary

Table 14. Political Activism and Political Militance among Land Invaders and Noninvaders

City	Variable	Invaders	Noninvaders
Mexico City[a]	% of complete political activists	76	24
	% of complete nonparticipants	24	89
Lima[b]	% belonging to communal organization	19 (106)*	5 (59)
Santiago, 1966[c]	% belonging to communal organization	17	1
	% affiliated with extreme Left parties	25 (157)	16 (79)
Santiago, 1969[d]	% affiliated with any political party	18	7
	% favoring violent means when necessary to achieve community goals	27	20
	% believing that most of the rich attained their positions exploiting the poor	81 (113)	58 (269)

Sources: [a]Wayne A. Cornelius, "Political Involvement among Low-Income Migrants to Mexico City," in Poverty and Politics in Urban Mexico, ed. Wayne A. Cornelius. "Political activism" is defined as a composite measure of different activities, scaled into six categories. "Invaders" in this case are those exposed to squatter eviction attempts; "noninvaders" are those not so exposed.

[b]Computed from Daniel Goldrich, Raymond B. Pratt, and Charles R. Schuller, "The Political Integration of Lower-Class Urban Settlements in Chile and Peru," Studies in Comparative International Development 3 (1967–1968): 3–22.

[c]Ibid.; also from Daniel Goldrich, "Political Organization and the Politicization of the Poblador," Comparative Political Studies 3 (July 1970): 176–202.

[d]My research, 1968–1969.

*Figures in parentheses are raw marginal frequencies.

widely across countries and historical periods. External political agents that merely request electoral support in exchange for favors, such as in pre-1964 Brazil, tend to reinforce the individualistic ethic common in these settlements. In Mexico, alternatively, the ruling party pursues a populist policy of integration and participation by all sectors in a vertically structured order. Favors and support for *colonia* dwellers are granted less in exchange for electoral votes—an essentially symbolic act in Mexico anyway—than as attempts to convert these groups into loyal supporters of the official ideology and the PRI (Revolutionary Institutional Party). This form of socialization leads the poor away from class consciousness and militance and encourages participation within the parameters set by the ruling party. In this instance, those who choose to transcend the purely instrumental view of politics and become converted to a broader-looking ideology do so in terms favorable to the existing order.[42]

Socialization for political militance is exemplified, on the other hand, by the action in Chilean *poblaciones* of the Marxist parties—especially the Communist—in the pre-Allende period. This frequently took place at or immediately after a land invasion, thus combining the "spontaneous" learning produced by the experience with deliberate political indoctrination. Communist socialization attempted to present the invasion and subsequent confrontations with government and landowners as practical lessons in the class struggle. The effective help provided by the Party on these occasions was aimed neither at purely electoral support nor at participation within the existing order but rather at drastically changing the dominant ethic among these groups. Its goal was to effect a transformation of basic needs into a clear understanding of the structural origins of poverty and the necessity of class solidarity. When successful, such strategy produced individuals who were not only politically active but also militantly opposed to the existing order and willing to make more radical demands on behalf of the poor.

Available data provide support for this conclusion. In his 1965 study in Santiago, Goldrich reported a consistent trend among those affiliated with the parties of the extreme Left to remain politically active after housing demands had been met and to support extension of collective action to demands for

Table 15. Political Radicalism in Lower-Class Settlements of Santiago, 1968–1969

Variable	Settlements	
	Intensive Communist Party Influence	Christian Democratic Influence or Other
% Supporting the elimination of private property	48	20
% Believing that the revolution was good for Cuba	55	33
% Believing that a revolution would be good for Chile	44	26
% Believing that authentic social changes should only include the poor and go against the rich	39	27
% Believing that authentic social changes can only be attained through a revolution	34	22
% Endorsing the use of force as the only means to attain authentic changes	39	28
% Supporting extreme Left parties (Communist or Socialist)	64	24

Source: My research, 1968–1969.

better incomes and occupational conditions. This is in clear contrast with the Christian Democratic supporters, who tended to return to personal concerns once housing demands had been satisfied.[43]

In my study in Santiago in 1969, two areas—a squatter settlement and a section of a new government project—had been more effectively exposed to Communist party influences and had, at the time of the study, *juntas* dominated by Party members. Table 15 compares respondents in these areas with those in other settlements along indicators of political radicalism. Respondents in communist-influenced areas are distinct in their support of radical measures and even of force for the attainment of social changes and in their sympathy for the Cuban Revolution. Against the objection that such findings could be the result of self-selection, one may note that selection and location of inhabitants in government projects were made by the official agency and not by the settlers themselves, thus barring any deliberate concentration of agitators. The evidence also indicates that radicalism among inhabitants in both communist-influenced settlements increased with greater time of residence in the area, a finding that could not occur if self-selection were the only factor in operation.[44]

Political activism among the poor that transcends a purely instrumental orientation is the result of forces that do not inhere exclusively to their objective situation. Rather, it results from combination of that situation with the direct influence of socializing agents and events. The conditions and results of such processes vary with the country and the specific historical circumstances. Thus, similar socialization mechanisms have given rise, in some instances, to reinforcement of a utilitarian view of politics; in others, to limited participation in support of the existing order; and, in still others, to class consciousness and a coherent radical orientation.

Conclusion: The Political Impact of the Poor

This chapter has attempted to examine, at close range, the patterns of collective action with which the poor respond to the conditions of urban capitalism in Latin America. This has been based on illustrations from the considerable body of evidence accumulated in recent years. Major trends identified differ significantly from what was conventionally believed a few years ago. Such trends can be summarized under six categories:

1. The political behavior of the poor is governed not by anger or by apathy but by rational adaptation to what structural circumstances permit and encourage.

2. Housing and landownership are the issues around which marginal groups coalesce politically. This is a function of the urgency of the problem and of the impossibility of defying the capitalist land market on an individual basis.

3. Communal organizations—centered on local problems—rather than political parties—concerned with national issues—have been the preferred vehicles for political action.

4. "Politicization" is not a constant or increasing factor but rather a function of perceived relevance of politics to basic needs. Collective organizations grow, mature, and decline depending on their changing instrumental value.

5. Relative absence of political radicalism is a consequence not of absence of frustration but of the perceived impracticality of challenging the existing order. More generally, it is determined by the weakness of a structural interpretation of frustrations.

6. Political action that departs from conventional means and goals requires decisive external intervention. The content and results of these processes of political socialization vary with the setting and the historical circumstances. This point clarifies the fact that the minority of political activists among urban lower classes is no less dependent on external circumstances than the majority, which adapts to existing conditions.

In relation to the political impact of marginal groups in the city, the above findings yield several important lessons. Despite much rhetoric to the contrary, the political role of the poor appears to be limited. It is never insignificant since the sheer formal impact of numbers renders it crucial at times of election and as a source of support for populist (or demagogic) leaders. It is, however, a politics of audiences and followers, not one of initiators.

Urban society in Latin America conducts a process of cooptation by which the most capable and best educated among the poor are most rapidly assimilated by the existing order. Socialization of a minority in consummatory political doctrines is as dependent on external efforts and influences as on objective circumstances. More than seed and source of a new social order, urban lower classes follow the initiatives of different political elites. Depending on them, their political actions can be permeated by the varying shades of populism represented by Odría in Peru, Rojas Pinilla in Colombia, and Perón in Argentina; by militant Marxism under Allende in Chile; by the corporate paternalism of the PRI in Mexico; and by disorganization and apathy under military rule in Brazil.

The political importance of urban marginal groups is limited, not by their enormous potential impact at certain historical junctures, but by the fact that such circumstances are largely made for them and not by them. The extent and form of their political participation are dependent variables adapting and, perhaps, reinforcing but not initiating structural processes of change. It is, therefore, not surprising that recent revolutionary violence in Latin American cities—such as the Tupamaro movement in Uruguay, Peronist and Marxist guerrilla activity in Argentina and the FAR (Fuerzas Armadas Revolucionarias) in Guatemala—seldom had its base in the lower-class periphery.[45] Such challenges to the capitalist order are the acts of middle-class intellectuals, white-collar employees, and certain proletarian elites, not of the marginal poor. If the movement approaches victory, the latter may again adapt to the changed conditions and provide revolutionaries with crucial support. This shift, however, only occurs during the last stages of the process.[46]

The above conclusions would seem to contradict previously noted tendencies toward structural polarization and obvious social tension in the Latin American city. In the preceding chapter, it was pointed out that syntheses emerging from the growing contradictions between established and marginal cities would probably occur in nonobvious and surprising ways. It is, perhaps, time to return to that statement.

Dialectical thought in its application to processes of social change has often been flawed by the simplistic expectation of a final, decisive confrontation.[47] Progressive and regressive classes would engage in apocalyptic war until the victory of the former. Applied to Latin America, this translates into the expectation that the historical synthesis would be accomplished by the rebellion of marginal masses against an oppressive social order. Processes of structural change have, however, seldom followed such simple schemes. In the concrete case of Latin American societies, they depend on complex interactions between elites, counterelites and the poor, rather than on a one-sided initiative by the latter. The juncture of the politics of poverty with that of elites acquires from this perspective a crucial importance.

It is beyond the scope of this work to examine in detail such interactions. Yet one important, though seldom noted, aspect deserves mention. This concerns the enormous symbolic impact that the lower-class periphery has acquired for elite groups. If organized challenges by marginal masses have been nil, their sheer existence stands as a vivid denunciation of the distortions of the socioeconomic order. As such, they have been the source of concern, anger, and inspiration to others. Platforms and manifestoes of leftist parties and radical guerrilla movements rarely omit references to the plight of the marginal poor in the cities. The lower-class settlement comes to embody and represent to them all that is unjust and stagnant in the ongoing society.

Thus, for the strategy of initiating and legitimizing rebellion, it has often been the presence rather than the actions of marginal groups that has become crucial. The complex dialectics of political opposition have made vicarious suffering for the poor more important than the actual suffering, a symbolic injunction against the existing order more vital than their own beliefs. Carried by the enthusiasm to synthetize this dialectic of symbol and reality, many have described the peripheral settlement as a radical school from which the "builders of tomorrow" would emerge. As seen above, these views are not supported by facts. For the poor, it is enough to struggle with their poverty. Understanding its origins and acting on its causes are tasks for the more fortunate groups, those who can act and think without the immediate demands of everyday survival.

Elites and the Politics of Urban Development: A Comparative Study of Four Cities

John Walton

"The strategy of urban development is just as necessary to determine the future course of politics in Latin America as the strategy of industrial development. Urbanism can be viewed as coincidental and parallel with the growth of industrialization, rather than as a stage on the road to industrialization."[1]

Introduction

Contemporary thinking about major social changes and attendant social problems typically proceeds from certain fundamental axioms. One of the most common of these is the notion that accelerated urbanization is a worldwide phenomenon. The figures available across nations describe an exponential curve indicating that even in the short run most of the world's population will dwell in large cities.[2] On a comparative basis we also have suggestions of what sorts of consequences may be expected to follow from urbanization. Deficiencies in employment, housing, services, recreation, and unpolluted life space are predictable. An "evolutionary" trend may be in motion leading to greater spatial segregation of class, status, and ethnic groups.[3] An extended amount of social and economic interdependence can be anticipated.[4] Certainly, life styles will change though few agree whether urban living leads to a segmented and anomic condition or a new style of communalism.[5] Nevertheless, each of these aspects of urbanization has been and will continue to be examined as we grope for the means with which to make urban life livable. Given the compelling nature of this question, it is curious that so little investigation has been devoted to comparative appraisals of more or less successful efforts to cope with urban problems. For years we have been producing a sociology of urban problems but have done little in the area of a sociology of urban development.

In what follows I will attempt to provide the outlines of a comparative study of urban development. The term *urban development* is used here in a broad sense to refer to the formulation and implementation of policies that extend urban services, for example, communications, housing, sanitation, economic infrastructure, environmental control, and so forth. The analysis is comparative in two senses. First, it deals with cities outside the United States and, thus, adds some balance to our ethnocentric literature. Second, it compares four cities, in Mexico and Colombia, whose urban development experiences have been quite different. By looking into the explanation of those differences, it is hoped that we will arrive at some working hypotheses, if not policy implications, concerning a strategy of urban development.

For those who regard urban planning as the exclusive province of North American and European cities, the Latin American urban scene is typically conceived of as a sprawling slum that encircles a few luxurious enclaves of the politically powerful and the economically dominant. This is certainly the picture provided by the available literature, and quite rightly so, since a good deal of the reality corresponds to this image. Like any stereotype, however, this overlooks some notable exceptions, which can be profitably examined. Two cities in Mexico and two in Colombia provide an unusual natural laboratory for the study of more or less successful experiences of urban development. These are Monterrey and Guadalajara in Mexico—both close to a million and a quarter in population and the third and second largest cities, respectively, of the Republic—and Medellín and Cali in Colombia—each close to one million and the second and third largest cities.

Four Urban Worlds

Strategically located in the northeast scarcely one hundred

miles below the Texas border and equidistant from gulf coast seaports, Monterrey became a commercial and industrial center in the late nineteenth century. For many years its proximity to the United States and major communication arteries gave it a distinct commercial advantage. Toward the end of the nineteenth century these advantages were nullified by the establishment of rail communications between Monterrey's hinterland and Mexico City and by changing trade arrangements with the United States. These circumstances precipitated what is by now Monterrey's legendary industrial development. Several families with small fortunes acquired in commerce founded a brewing industry. Its success snowballed as many of the same investors developed satellite industries; glass for the beer bottles, steel for the caps, wooden and cardboard cartons for packing the bottles, and so forth.[6] In subsequent years these derivative industries expanded and developed their own autonomy, although their ownership remained in the hands of a small circle of family capitalists. Monterrey is currently second only to Mexico City in terms of capital investment and industrial productivity, and, unlike the situation in most cities in Latin America, the bulk of its industry is locally owned.

Guadalajara's development represents something less than a Horatio Alger story. Located in the west-central part of the Republic, it has historically been the commercial and distribution center of a large agricultural region. Until recently its industry, devoted principally to artisan crafts, textiles, construction, and food processing, was small in scale. In the last two decades, industrialization has been noticeably on the upswing, mainly in the area of light manufacturing and under the impetus of nonlocal investment. Commerce and services, however, continue to make the largest contribution to the region's gross product with manufacturing and agriculture almost equal in importance. Possessing several universities and an influential segment of Mexico's Roman Catholic church he'rarchy, Guadalajara has come to be regarded as something of a cultural center.

Although Medellín's developmental history differs in many ways from that of Monterrey, these two cities share equal renown among the few cases of pre–twentieth century industrial development in Latin America. Located in a mountainous and physically isolated area of northwestern Colombia, Medellín prospered initially as a center of gold mining. Interestingly, the early impetus to development tapered off rapidly as the low-level mining technology then in use encountered fewer easily exploited deposits. Added to this setback was a crisis in food production that required costly imports and, thus, restrained any economic "take-off." The secret of Medellín's contemporary development was its economic and political response to crisis. Large-scale migrations proceeded from central Antioquia in search of new mines and agricultural properties. New towns were established under laws that ensured political autonomy and small-scale landownership. Many new mines were operated by individual or small-scale proprietors. A decisive step was taken with the introduction of coffee, which could be raised as a cash crop on these small properties, thus fostering a rural middle class. The export trade helped to promote Medellín's entrepreneurs, particularly the brokers in coffee and gold, who channeled investment into industries producing farm implements, household goods, and mining equipment. Ultimately, however, textiles became Medellín's major industry. Originally prompted by a desire to reduce European imports, Medellín textiles flourished in the regional market and, due to advances in transportation, soon dominated markets in Colombia and several countries to the south.

Cali, in southwestern Colombia, is located in a fertile valley that lent itself well to the sedentary ways of the colonial *latifundia*. From the appearance of the Spanish *conquistadores* in the 1530s until at least the mid-twentieth century, the Cauca Valley witnessed a pattern of increased concentration of large landholdings among a rural aristocracy engaged in extensive, inefficient land use, such as cattle raising. Recent advances in sugar production and pressure for land reform have altered this pattern to some extent; more productive uses of land have been adopted, although the structure of ownership has changed very little. Like Medellín, Cali benefited from advances in transportation to become a commercial and distribution center between the west coast seaport of Buenaventura and the rest of the interior. Local industry, primarily controlled by foreign firms, grew in the post–World War II period, mainly in agricultural and raw material processing.

Parallel to these differences in the economic and social structures of the four cities are dramatic contrasts in the urban ambience—or *ambiente* as the Spanish would have it.

Approaching Monterrey from the north, one has the discon-
certing feeling that he is actually on the outskirts of Los An-
geles. The smog thickens long before the city comes into view.
From the vantage point of a small hill on the edge of town, the
sources of this pollution are apparent. Within the perimeter of
the city proper, a number of factories, including two large steel
mills, pour industrial waste into the already hot and dusty air.
Most of these factories were established before zoning laws
were ever conceived, and subsequent efforts to locate new industry in an industrial park area to the west of town have met
with little success.

Irrespective of where one is in the city, another ever present
sight is the slums and substandard housing. Shacks made of
wood and concrete block spread out from the center of the city
and climb the nearby hillsides. Most of these are without electricity, plumbing, or piped-in water. One of Monterrey's few
wide avenues passes in front of the large brewery so important
in the industrialization of the city. Driving down that street
early in the morning it is not uncommon to see women crossing
with large pots, which they fill with water at a gas station and
carry to their makeshift abodes located on the dirt alleys that
surround the home of Mexico's finest beer.

Yet, not only the poor are deprived of urban services. Most of
Monterrey's streets are narrow, congested, and in ill repair. The
drainage is so poor that a brief cloudburst usually floods the
major arteries. Public transportation is inadequate in passenger
capacity and areas of the city served. The plazas and public
parks so characteristic of other Mexican cities are conspicuously few in number and hopelessly overcrowded on a weekend
evening. Similar deficiencies are notable in middle-class housing and recreational facilities despite the efforts of several large
industrial firms to provide such services for their own employees. Finally, because Monterrey is located in a semiarid
zone, it is chronically subject to water shortages. Whereas this
problem is geographical in origin, local authorities have done
little to improve the situation by, for example, providing water
reclamation systems.

Guadalajara provides a striking contrast and, indeed, is widely renowned as one of Mexico's most beautiful cities. Perhaps
its most compelling feature is the absence of anything resembling a slum or shantytown. To be sure, occasional wooden

shacks, hurriedly erected, are on vacant suburban lots or on the outskirts of town. Also, areas of clearly lower-class housing exist. Nevertheless, these neighborhoods usually have paved streets, electricity, indoor plumbing, and community centers. Furthermore, numerous public housing projects, rather than forming one large ghetto, are dispersed throughout the city. Middle-class housing is abundant and is the source of a flourishing construction industry.

The sheer layout of Guadalajara's civic center reveals a great deal about the city. Four large plazas surround the main cathedral and form the shape of a cross. On one arm of this cross is the state government palace; on the other, the city government headquarters. At the lower end is an elegant public theater that hosts the symphony and companies devoted to the preservation of Mexican folklore. Radiating out from the civic center are a number of broad avenues, each one in its course passing through public parks replete with fountains and gardens.

One of the most widely chronicled events in the urban renovation of the city was the widening of a major avenue that runs from the downtown area westward through some of the more elegant neighborhoods. The initial plan suggested a route that would have cut through a large building housing the headquarters of the federally owned telephone company. Undaunted in their ambitions to so beautify the city, local officials commissioned an engineering firm to raise the building from its foundation and move it backward some sixty feet to allow the street to pass. While this is undoubtedly a dramatic illustration, it does reflect the costly priorities given to urban development.

The communications system based on major arteries radiating out from the civic center is complemented by several principal thoroughfares that circle the city. On the basis of this layout the city has been able to build a truly remarkable system of public transportation. A large fleet of buses regularly traverses such intricate routes that one's doorstep is literally no more than thirty minutes from any place in town.

Certainly a large part of Guadalajara's attractiveness has to do with the fact that it is not a center of heavy manufacturing. Nevertheless, a growing number of industrial enterprises could pose a threat to the city. Such an eventuality was recognized by local authorities and has resulted in the creation of an industrial park to the south, where new firms are gradually beginning to locate.

Like Guadalajara, Medellín is well planned and exceptionally attractive. The downtown central business district is both fashionable and busy. Several broad avenues are fronted by modern high-rise buildings that house the major financial institutions, and these intermingle with ornate structures of the city and state governments. Immediately adjacent is a bustling area of restaurants, hotels, shops, a large shopping mall, parks, and the main cathedral. Notable here, as in Guadalajara, is the fact that many exclusive residential sites continue to be maintained within a few blocks of the center.

New industry has followed the earlier lead of the large textile firms by locating mainly in satellite municipalities a few miles to the north and south. Thus, a fairly effective zoning is accomplished by historical tradition. Oddly enough for this strongly Roman Catholic and sometimes austere or puritanical population, implicit notions of urban planning extend to open and regulated houses of prostitution cordoned off in a district several miles north of the center.

Along other comparative dimensions, few bona fide slums exist in Medellín. Again, lower-class housing and some wooden or tar paper shacks line the river that bisects the city. But these are minimal and the object of eradication through provision of decent public housing. Most sections of the city are served by a complete range of urban services, including electricity, water, drainage and sanitation, telephones, and transportation. To be sure, some outlying neighborhoods newly settled by rural migrants are well below standard; yet it is significant that public agencies have anticipated these demands and initiated programs for expanded and integrated services.

As one might expect by now, important parallels prevail in the cases of Monterrey and Cali. Perhaps most fundamental is the generally unkempt, even neglected, character of the central city. Monterrey and Cali, unlike their intranational counterparts, reflect what is often, though erroneously, termed the "North American" pattern of urban spatial patterning[7]—namely, the tendency for central city properties to be converted to commercial uses and lower-class housing, while higher status and income groups retreat to the most prestigious city locations (e.g., hillsides, lake, or ocean front) and, particularly, to the less densely settled urban fringe.

Cali's unprepossessing central plaza is surrounded by a two-block radius of stores, cafes, and office buildings cramped along narrow and congested streets. Across the Cali River and up the hillsides to the west are expensive homes and high-rise apartments. An industrial satellite town lies to the north and new suburban developments to the south. Fanning out in an easterly pointed semicircle are the small shops and artisan industries of the lower middle class as well as extensive slums and squatter settlements that some have estimated as including a third of the population.[8]

Sometimes the product of land invasions,[9] these settlements are acutely deficient in urban services. Paved streets are rare to nonexistent, a problem made worse by seasonally heavy rains and flooding. Water is available only at neighborhood faucets and is seldom potable. Sanitation and electricity are conspicuously absent in the poor neighborhoods. Public housing is very limited and typically far beyond the means of the average slum dweller.

Moreover, the poor are merely the most seriously affected by these problems that impinge upon most social classes. Inadequate transportation reduces everyone's mobility. The privileged automobile owner must contend with congested and poorly maintained streets. Electrical service is frequently interrupted. And civic life is restrained by the absence of public meeting and recreational places. A notable rarity for Latin American cities is the absence of any centrally located public market places for petty traders and middle-class shoppers.

Some Quantitative Comparisons of Urban Development

The foregoing descriptions reveal a higher level of urban development, as defined earlier, in Guadalajara and Medellín than in Monterrey and Cali. Nevertheless, much of the evidence so far is observational or impressionistic, and the skeptic could justifiably ask for further corroboration.

In the Mexican case, comparative data on a wide variety of indicators are not available, although the census does provide some interesting figures on housing and sanitation. It is important to keep in mind that these figures are reported by local governments and may be subject to self-serving biases. Still, they indicate that in Monterrey 41.4 percent of the population live in one-room dwelling units; in Guadalajara 33.5 percent live in such units. Similarly, the proportion living in one- or two-room units is 69.7 in Monterrey and 59.6 in Guadalajara. In Guadalajara 16.7 percent of dwelling units are without piped-in water, whereas the figure for Monterrey is 24.7 percent. The situation is more disparate in the case of sewage facilities with 20 percent of the dwelling units in Guadalajara and 34.4 percent in Monterrey without them. One might argue that these differentials are due to greater demand in Monterrey because of its population, size, and rate of growth. In fact, the reverse is true. In 1960, the date of these census figures, Guadalajara's population (740,394) was larger than Monterrey's (601,085) and had increased somewhat faster between 1950 and 1960.

Public expenditures by state agencies conform to the above patterns. In the period of 1965–1967, Guadalajara-Jalisco spent in excess of 100 million pesos on public housing. During the same years Monterrey–Nuevo León had no such item in the state budget and, generally, spent a much smaller fraction on standard services, such as water and electricity. A university study in Monterrey concluded that 42,000 new single-family units were necessary to solve the immediate problem of dual-home occupancy; yet no such action was planned. By contrast, Guadalajara, with fewer problems in this area, was committing public funds to new housing.

Data by cities, as opposed to departments, are not routinely assembled in Colombia so that some approximations are required. While the urban populations of the Departments of Antioquia (Medellín) and Valle del Cauca (Cali) are similar, Antioquia has 50 percent more dwelling units. A census of housing indicates that in Antioquia 73 percent are private homes and only 55 percent in Valle del Cauca. Again the percentages of substandard housing are 1.1 vs. 13.1 in the same relation. Vast disparities exist in the comparative tax effort of these two cities, particularly in taxes earmarked for urban works. In Medellín the assessed tax value per capita is 5,750 pesos vs. 4,230 in Cali. Taxes for urban works (the *valorización* tax), however, are 54 pesos vs. 3 pesos per capita in favor of Medellín.[10] Isolated reports indicate that two-thirds of Cali's streets are unpaved or in ill repair while Medellín leads the nation in telephones per capita; fragments of information to be sure, but they fit a consistent pattern.

In 1964, Medellín's principal public utility company launched a new program for extending water, electricity, and sanitation services to recently settled neighborhoods. By 1968, some 22 million pesos had been spent providing the services to 46 *barrios*, 11,000 dwelling units, and 80,000 residents. Plans for the next two years envisioned a 50 million peso expenditure serving 12,000 units and 84,000 people. Regrettably, the data at hand require us to make gross categorical judgments, but that scarcely detracts from the fact that Cali, plagued by more serious and extensive deficiencies, had mounted no program of comparable scope.

Urban Planning: An Initial Explanation

What seems most compelling about the differences in urban development documented here with observational and statistical data is the wide gap between the paired cities that represent the second- and third-largest population concentrations in their respective countries. Clearly there must be some rather dramatic forces operating to produce these disparities. Yet these forces are not readily evident. The most obvious explanation is that the less developed cities have experienced greater demands in the form of migration and natural population increase. But, while that is moderately true for Medellín and Cali, the reverse is true for the Mexican cities. Another ready explanation is that industrial cities crassly exploit the urban worker and environment with no thought to civic welfare. But, again, patterned differences here crosscut the more or less industrialized dimension. Finally, sheer affluence or economic development is not the answer since all of these cities are "developing," and Monterrey is the most impressive example.

It is our thesis that the explanation must be sought in the realm of politics—and politics at two levels. First, we shall look into politics at the operational level, that is, in the presence of organizational means for coping with urban development. Assuming that differences exist here, we shall probe further into politics at the level of institutionalized structures of power.

The contrast between Guadalajara and Monterrey is by no means a recent discovery. Bemoaning Monterrey's urban development lag, an editorial in one of the local papers once noted that "the city of Guadalajara has beautified several of its principal streets through important and continuing works of asphalt paving" paid for by local property owners. The editorial concluded, "Let us hope we will be able to do something similar"; this plea appeared July 17, 1906.

Apparently Monterrey has not been "able to do something similar," or, at best, it has been unable to keep pace with needed improvements in urban services. Part of the explanation lies in its failure to create and empower specialized public agencies for dealing with urban problems.

Historically, urban development and public works were assigned a high priority as Guadalajara evolved into a colonial administrative and ecclesiastical center. The initial step toward achieving its present level of development came in 1941 with the passage of the first of a series of urbanization laws. The principal provisions of this law established a committee on construction to evaluate proposed works and a municipal urbanization council with the power to tax beneficiaries of new works through a special assessment procedure. As might be expected, the initial legislation met with a number of difficulties in its application, not the least of which included a distrust by property owners of the financial dealings of the new tax authority and a suspicion of inefficiency in the agency itself. Between 1941 and 1948, several modifications of the law were introduced, and, although the initial works were slow in coming, it was then that the system first began operation. The second major step came in 1948 with the ascension to the governorship of Jesús González Gallo, a colorful, aggressive, and, on occasion, reportedly ruthless man, who made the renovation of the city a top priority item for his administration. A 1948 law created a new planning commission, and in 1950 the Council for Municipal Collaboration was established, which endowed the present system with its character as a mixed, public and private, regulatory agency. With these instruments in hand González Gallo took up his work of remodeling the city and, in addition to creating many of the present landmarks, set the process of urban development in Guadalajara on its inexorable course.

A third step came in 1959 under Governor Juan Gil Preciado

with the passage of the State Planning and Urbanization Law. This legislation expanded the number of Councils for Municipal Collaboration by authorizing one for every city in the state. It also established the right of the state to expropriate private property for new urban works and set up a new state agency for urban planning. Much of the success of González Gallo's programs was owed to his personal charisma; Gil Preciado was most responsible for providing the present system with its efficiency and scope.

The operation of the system can be summarized rather briefly. The Council for Municipal Collaboration is a mixed body of fourteen persons, five from the public sector (the mayor, director of public works, representative of the state urban planning agency, and so on) and nine from the private sector (chamber of commerce; service clubs; architectural, engineering, banking, and industrial associations, etc.). The group elects its own officers; traditionally the president is from the private sector and the chamber of commerce. Members of the council receive no financial compensation and decisions are by majority vote.

The principal work of the council is to determine priorities, based on the advice of its own members, public agencies, and citizen groups. For the most part these include street construction, maintenance, and lighting; piped-in drinking water; drainage; and electricity. Having decided on the need for a new work, the council publicly advertises for sealed bids and awards contracts to the lowest bidder whose plans also meet technical standards. This is determined by a technical group of the council. Finally, the cost for each beneficiary, or property owner, is determined according to a sliding scale—a person whose property fronts a new street pays more than one a block or two away. In a public meeting with the council, registered property owners are allowed to vote on whether they want the project, and approval requires a 75 percent majority. Following an approval, the financial end is turned over to a public bank. No money passes through the council; beneficiaries make installment payments directly to the bank.

It should be apparent that this system has been designed to instill public confidence in urban development projects. While it is interesting that this has been done by reducing government autonomy in the decision-making process, it should be emphasized that the system seems to work rather well. An indication of its success is found in the observable availability of services. Another indication is suggested by the fact that of the many rumored scandals that circulate in any city of this size, to my knowledge, none in recent years has concerned the council. Part of the explanation for these successes lies in the structure of local leadership, a matter we shall turn to later.

The historical record of efforts to initiate urban development programs in Monterrey is one of a long series of frustrations and failures. As the quoted editorial comment indicates, local concern over urban problems goes back at least as far as 1906. In 1926 a planning commission was established, and a program for improving city streets was begun. All indications suggest these efforts were of the same scale as those made in Guadalajara twenty years earlier. In 1931 private sector efforts were begun, particularly under the direction of the chamber of commerce, to create a comprehensive plan for development. The initiative failed because of a "lack of resources and collaboration from the government." Similar attempts were made in 1933, 1942, 1943, and 1946 with the same result. The most apparent explanation for this inaction in the face of mounting problems was a persistent conflict between public officials and local industrialists and businessmen.

In 1950 the long awaited "Points for the Regulatory Plan of the City of Monterrey" finally appeared under the auspices of the privately endowed Institute for Social Studies. The plan contained recommendations for needed streets and highways, channeling of the river that bisects the city, land usage, zoning, schools, recreational facilities, and so forth. Among these proposed works, only one, channeling the river, was realized in the ensuing years, and, generally speaking, this first serious effort at attacking urban problems fell on deaf ears.

Perhaps as a result of continuing local concern in some quarters, the state government in 1963 finally established within the old planning division a new department charged with the task of producing an official, updated regulatory plan. Although the resources and support made available were minimal, this new group under the direction of architect Cortés Melo initiated an elaborate study of Monterrey's urban needs, which was some four years in the making. In addition to a good deal of basic information, the first report of this group made certain modest recommendations, which, according to Cortés Melo, were "apparently considered but later ignored by local authorities."

Fortunately for the new planners, a change in governors occurred in October of 1967, bringing in a man much more sympathetic to their ideas. In his inaugural address Eduardo Elizondo stated that the "general condition of the city is deplorable and without any parallel" among the problems to be attacked by the new administration. On his instructions new legislation was quickly passed, and by December of 1967 the legal basis had been laid for municipal and state citizenship councils. Their primary task was to promote urban works through organizational methods similar to those employed in Guadalajara. It is, in fact, widely acknowledged that Monterrey (like many other Mexican cities) patterned its system after that which Guadalajara had initiated some twenty-six years earlier. By 1969, when this study was carried out, work had begun on the widening and rerouting of small stretches of several downtown streets. In a variety of other areas of needed urban services, no new projects have been initiated locally, although the federal government is continuing work on water and electrical problems. Given its belated beginning, one has to wonder whether Monterrey will be able to meet even its most pressing urban needs in the foreseeable future.

Unique among these four cities was the early development in Medellín and Antioquia of a system of local political autonomy and civic-mindedness. Observers variously account for this in terms of geographical isolation requiring self-sufficiency, colonization, and the legal creation of new towns governed by resident commissions, equalitarian patterns of landownership, and the relative absence of latifundia. Certainly all of these elements were important, and we would add the need for efficient urban services and transportation engendered by a growing economy.

Illustrative of this last point, in the late nineteenth and early twentieth centuries local entrepreneurs and public officials promoted a system of "coffee railways" eventually linking Medellín to Bogotá and Caribbean and Pacific seaports. In the early years key services, such as water and electricity, were provided by a series of private utility companies, each one incapable of meeting the demands of new industry and the growing city. As a result, in 1919 the public Municipal Enterprises Corporation was established to supply integrated and regulated services to the metropolitan area. In 1955 this institution was expanded to become the Public Enterprises of the Department of Antioquia. Taking advantage of the national legislation of 1954 that created decentralized, public-private development corporations—intentionally fashioned along lines of the Tennessee Valley Authority—Public Enterprises moved rapidly to expand and jointly regulate services of electricity, water, sanitation, and telephones. In Medellín, amid the presence of several of Latin America's largest private corporations, Public Enterprises is an imposing institution because of its high-rise central offices, professional and technical staff, payroll and budget, and, most notably, its active efforts to maintain quality services in all areas.

For both the city and department, parallel agencies (called *Valorizaciones*) exist for planning and administering local urban works (e.g., street lighting, paving, and maintenance; drainage; feeder lines for indoor plumbing; and so on). In its essential operation this system is similar to that of Guadalajara; local residents participate in the determination of needed works and pay for them according to a sliding scale of assessment. What is important for present purposes is the fact that Medellín, which was the first Colombian city to adopt this system (in the 1940s), adopted it without incidents of noncooperation and, consequently, has accomplished much more through its implementation, as the figures on urban development would suggest (e.g., an assessed taxation of 54 pesos per capita in Medellín to 3 in Cali).

In urban planning, Cali presents something of an enigma. On the one hand, a plethora of agencies, albeit of comparatively recent origin, exist at the municipal, departmental, and federal levels within the public sector, and several private foundations and civic groups are jointly concerned with urban works. On the other hand, each of these groups is underfinanced and coping piecemeal with problems within a context of political and administrative fragmentation, which produces noncooperation.

Public, low-cost housing is essential. Departmental programs languish in various states of noncompletion. A federal housing credit agency is so limited by funds and recipient qualifications that only a small part of the least needy are benefited. Meanwhile, upper-class speculation in urban real estate proceeds unchecked. Municipal and departmental public works agencies are alleged to be launching programs of street paving and repair, but public charges of political kickbacks and contractor graft are the most discernable consequence. Neighborhood civic action *juntas* organize to create minimal sanitation services and claim that any accomplishments are the result of communal efforts in the face of governmental inaction.[11] Local elites imperfectly organized in the Civic Union argue that Cali's urban needs are ignored by the federal government. Practical strategies pioneered in other cities, such as long-term financing of urban works through beneficiary assessments (*valorización*), are limited because they require two scarce commodities: agency-resident collaboration in determining what projects to undertake and the ability of needy residents to pay nominal assessments.

Nevertheless, the picture is not totally unrelieved. The Regional Development Corporation (CVC) is a decentralized development corporation that has made substantial strides in electrical power generation and flood control on the departmental level. Emcali, a municipal public utility working in collaboration with the CVC, has expanded such local services as electricity, drainage, and telephones. Interestingly, the limited success of these agencies may be the result of their decentralization and autonomy, which allow them to work outside the constraints of local political conflict. Apart from these unique and specific programs, Cali's larger urban problem grows in the absence of effective organizational policy.

Structures of Power and Decision Making: A Basic Explanation

In the final aspect of this study, the problem is one of accounting for the differential progress of these cities in creating effective organizational methods for the promotion of urban development. In such an accounting, let us recognize first that any explanation is somewhat intermediate in character by its necessity of focusing on a truncated sequence of causal (independent) and consequent (dependent) variables. However elaborate that sequence, it will always be open at both ends in the sense that we can always pose more fundamental *why* questions and more immediate "So What?" questions. So far in this explanation, we have argued that the most obvious factors accounting for different levels of urban development are the organization and efficiency of certain working agencies. We shall demonstrate this is not accidental but stems from more fundamental features of politics and political culture, namely, the structure of power and decision making. What should be emphasized is that this factor, in turn, has deeper roots in history and economic organization.

In the course of this research the organization of power and decision making was analyzed in each city. Although the methods employed in that analysis will not be elaborated on, they essentially involved a combination of reputation and event analysis techniques.[12] In each city approximately fifty organizational leaders holding key positions in the public and private sectors were interviewed concerning important projects, organizations, and people in the area's development. Because urban development was frequently mentioned as an important issue, case study analyses were carried out to ascertain patterns of actual participation and decision making in this field.

Employing a cutoff point after which nominations abruptly fan out, some twenty top influentials were identified in each city. In Monterrey these people disproportionately represent the industrial sector. The second most frequently mentioned occupational category includes lawyers and financiers closely connected with the industrial firms. The only public official mentioned is the governor, who, until recently, worked as an attorney representing the industrial group. The term *industrial group* is widely used in Monterrey to designate not only the great influence of these people but also their cohesiveness. Many of the major industries (e.g., glass, beer, synthetic fibers, and one of the two steel mills) are owned by a single, extended family. Most of the major industrialists are allied in investment groups. In short, Monterrey's reputed influentials are a small, close-knit group occupying top industrial command posts.

Guadalajara's influential group is substantially different in character. The most apparent contrast is in the relative prominence of the political sector, with the governor ranking highest in importance and four other public leaders included on the list. Industrialists are well represented but these come from a wide variety of enterprises with little overlapping control.

Guadalajara's reputed influentials are best described as a coalition of public leaders and independent industrialists-businessmen.

In Medellín the same broad representation of institutional sectors is apparent in the occupations and backgrounds of influential people. Given the regional economy, it is not surprising that industrialists and financiers occupy a plurality of influential positions, but these people represent more than the textile group. Industrialists come from enterprises devoted to chemicals, glass, tobacco, and construction, while financiers deal in industrial investment as well as export trade. Further, political leaders, such as the governor, mayor, and director of Public Enterprises are well represented. As in Guadalajara, power is organized in Medellín within a coalition of public officials and key economic actors, the important difference being that in Medellín the latter group seems to lead the coalition.

Cali's influential group is unusual. It seems to represent most key institutions, such as government, commerce, industry, services, education, and their interest-group affiliates. While this representation is true in some senses, it is also true that, beneath the surface, influence is often concentrated by multiple position holding and the tendency of high-status people to circulate among top posts sometimes irrespective of any special expertise. In the extreme some leaders have formerly held as many as three of the positions that make up a list based on current occupancy. In short, Cali seems to have a close-knit status elite resembling that of Monterrey but with the important exception that the structure of power does not rest on institutionally integrated bases.

In summary, power and influence are more dispersed in Guadalajara and Medellín, where coalitions with contrasting leadership prevail. Monterrey and Cali reflect more cohesive elite arrangements, although their institutional roots differ. These data assume a good deal more meaning when we turn to the actual process of decision making and the political context within which it operates.

The history of conflict between government and private industry in Monterrey is long and well chronicled. The city began its development under the prerevolutionary dictatorship of Porfirio Díaz, and its economic elites were understandably sympathetic with the policies of that regime. Many of the top industrialists spent the revolutionary years of 1910–1917 in the United States. Despite several violent worker-employer conflicts in the early years of the Republic, a détente was reached between the federal government and Monterrey's industrialists. Both needed each other and tacitly agreed to pursue their separate interests as harmoniously as possible. This was made easier by the fact that in the Monterrey region little agricultural property was worthy of seizure under land-reform acts and no major foreign investment was available for expropriation. Indeed, the federal government was content to see Monterrey's industry continue to profit as long as it abided by minimal standards of employee benefit programs.

Nevertheless, an atmosphere of tension and potential conflict persisted, with the government opposed to Monterrey's company unions and the industrialists fearful of public intervention. The net result of this situation has been a weak governmental sector in the region, public officials handpicked by and serving the interests of the industrialists, and little or no joint collaboration in providing public services. In nearly classical free enterprise fashion, the industrial group took a paternal attitude toward workers through company unions and company-provided benefits (e.g., housing developments and social clubs). They also acted unilaterally in areas of higher education and economic infrastructure by creating their own private technological institute and bringing in natural gas for industrial use through several privately financed projects. While these works have had importance for the development of the region as a whole, they were completed chiefly to serve the self-interests of the industrial elite. Other equally important projects have been ignored because of the powerlessness of the public sector.

Recent events may indicate that the situation is changing. In that regard it is interesting to note that many local leaders feel the new governor is in a better position to accomplish his urban development goals precisely because he is intimate with the industrial group, an observation that accords with this analysis.

The historical roles of the public and private sectors in Guadalajara are the reverse of the Monterrey experience. With the backing of the federal government Guadalajara's public sector acquired considerable influence after the revolution since this agrarian region contained many large property holdings that were broken up under the land-reform program. The revolution had eliminated the old propertied elites, and, in the absence of large industrial or commercial concerns, a new political elite moved into the power vacuum. The importance of the public sector was further enhanced by a series of powerful governors who advanced their own careers by working for the goals of the postrevolutionary government (such as regional urban and economic development) in a relatively congenial setting.

As Guadalajara's economic development got under way it did so on the basis of commercial and medium-sized industrial firms coming into a scene already dominated by a strong public sector. Because of that fact and because economic power was widely dispersed, Guadalajara's private sector, out of necessity, developed a variety of collaborative organizations, which provided some semblance of internal coordination as well as a channel for influence in public decisions. The net result was a coalition of public and private agencies in the area of development decision making. This arrangement is well illustrated in the area of urban development where the organizational means for joint participation were established and have borne fruit. Further evidence of the participation of public and private groups in urban development projects is provided by the fact that Guadalajara's Council for Municipal Collaboration is mixed and many of the top influentials have served on it over the years.

Medellín's relative isolation from a history of national political strife and its unique endowments of economic resources and entrepreneurship combined to produce a collaborative civic elite. This is not to say that conflict was unknown or that contemporary achievements were easily won. In the early years slavery and commercial exploitation were common in the mining areas. Slave rebellions took place. Economic crises followed the depletion of surface ore and misadventures in the export of tobacco. Foreign interests initially exercised a heavy hand in improved mining and transportation technology. Whether because of a marked regional pride or, more likely, an equalitarian and resilient class structure, Antioquia seemed always capable of responding to these historical challenges. More importantly, it responded with legal-political instruments (e.g., mining laws, new towns, public corporations) designed to cope with public problems in the public interest. And it took these steps early, thereby establishing traditions that the contemporary observer, for want of a better explanation, would call a "civic political culture."

Again we would stress that a multitude of circumstances facilitated these developments, but certainly one of the most crucial was the absence of the *latifundia* and powerful landed elites as dominant features of social organization. Some large agricultural interests were present, but they coexisted with large and small mining operators, urban commercial elites and traders, a rural middle class, and, later, an industrial bourgeoisie. Economic interdependence bred social collaboration, and through it all political institutions hammered out the appropriate procedures and agencies. A close, even incestuous, working relationship developed between government and various sectors of the economy bearing mutually advantageous works, such as urban development.

The Cali story now appears in greater relief, for here the *latifundia* system and a rural aristocracy were the historical fulcrums of power. Industrial and commercial expansion was less the result of new urban groups than of the expansion of some traditional elites into new activities. Not only were these elites the predominant holders of power, but they also tended to be self-sufficient in following insular developmental policies in the production of primary products for distant markets. The fact that local opportunities were ignored or defaulted is attested to by the high proportion of foreign-owned firms in industry.

Overlying these characteristic patterns of social and economic organization is a history of political conflict going back to colonial times when local officials fought the landlords to provide beef to the undernourished market rather than selling it at great profit in Quito. More recently, landlords and the federal government have quarreled over land-reform laws with the result of much mutual animosity and little redistribution of land. Perhaps the most damaging consequence of this conflict at the local level has been an inability to recruit and retain qualified public servants. Governors, as well as agency heads, come and go; policies are discontinuous and, therefore, not taken seriously. Prophecy fulfills itself as powerful groups withhold cooperation from public agencies whose subsequent faltering is taken as justification for a lack of trust.

We should hasten to add that this, like most, generalizations has its notable exceptions. The Regional Development Corporation (CVC) prevailed over opposition from landlords and has made gains because of relatively autonomous powers and financing. The same is true in the case of the state university and municipal utility. But each of these institutions provides services the elites need as much as the general public. Indeed, they share more of the advantages. Much different is the case of inadequate housing and services for the urban poor in which little action has been taken.

Some Concluding Theoretical Observations

From this discussion it would be inappropriate to conclude that urban development is the sole prerogative of elites or that elites who fail to place a high priority on the needs of the city necessarily perform poorly in other areas of development and public interest. Among the many external constraints that set limits on what decision makers can do about the urban condition one would have to include topography and climate, rates of population growth and migration, timing of industrialization, disposable wealth and resources, the economy generally and the labor market specifically, national and local legal systems, and historical watersheds, such as revolution and civil war. Similarly, appropriate combinations of such influences in conjunction with elite structures may have different effects for different policy areas. Illustratively, the performance characteristics of Guadalajara and Monterrey in the field of urban development are reversed in matters of education. Elite differences grow out of determinate socio-structural conditions and entail different values and priorities.

Lest we be misunderstood, another caveat should be entered. Out of methodological choice and necessity this is a broad-gauged comparison of urban regions. In that sense we believe it to be accurate, but one should not infer that all is well or poor within any of the four cases. The urban poor of Guadalajara and Medellín are certainly not effective political forces, nor do they enjoy a proportionate share of available public services. Similarly, Monterrey and Cali, as we have endeavored to suggest, are not without efforts to cope with the urban problem. Nevertheless, having noted *patterned variation,* we have chosen to probe the sociological question of "Why?"

What we have attempted to demonstrate is that distinctive, historically conditioned elite structures operate in determinate policy-making ways that are associated with characteristic patterns and levels of urban development. A final question of general interest is what this might mean theoretically.

Taking an oblique tack momentarily, it should be noted that several conventional lines of thinking do not suggest themselves as general explanations. Most important here is the matter of *need.* Cities with the most pressing urban service needs are doing the least to meet them, and this is true even where local leaders are fully conscious of those needs and describe them in the rhetoric of urgency. Further, it cannot be argued that these needs are historical legacies or the result of some untoward event, such as an abrupt upturn in migration, that is now being attended to since those cities with the most pressing needs are at the present doing less about them than their counterparts.

In a similar vein we may question the influence of *articulated needs* via *organization of the poor.* Deprivation, no doubt, gives rise to parapolitical attempts by the urban poor to solve their housing problems. And in some measure these are successful as illustrated by permanent settlements in Monterrey and Cali that originated from land invasions. But neighborhood action groups (*acción comunal, juntas vecinales*), most in evidence in Cali, have a dismal record in redressing any of the larger problems that prompt their organization. Widespread and sustained organization that included disruptive or violent threats to the status quo would probably have much greater success. But such organizations are extremely rare, the tendency being for organizations among the urban poor to be defused by tacit recognition of de facto land tenure, co-opted by leftist political party factions,[13] or otherwise coerced into acquiescence.[14]

Further, a number of factors, such as city size, growth rate (from migration and natural increase), industrial and technological level, general development, and national location, are, in effect, "controlled for" in this study. That is, variation along these larger dimensions is not systematically associated with levels of urban development among the four cases. Obviously it would be foolhardy to dismiss such basic considerations with a small, controlled sample study. Nor would we imply that their significance is slight in conceivable, large sample studies of cities.[15] What we can conclude, however far these global factors carry us in explaining levels of urban development, is that some, perhaps large, proportion of the variance will remain to be explained by more precise comparisons.

On a more positive note, several general factors from this study appear to be intimately related to urban development. The first is *social class structure* and the extent to which it is more or less equalitarian. When small, close-knit elites (whether agricultural, industrial, or some other) and the working class are widely separated in terms of power and privilege without a large buffer group, one can expect the greatest absence and maldistribution of public services. Other things being equal, without viable groups below that engender a rationale for conciliation and negotiation, the privileged classes cannot be expected to share their bounty. While that may sound platitudinous, it is nevertheless true that much research and thinking about urban politics and power in the United States or Latin America typically ignores class structure.

A second general factor is the nature of the *political system*, not the formal but the functional political system. Across the formal political systems of Mexico and Colombia, developmental differences may be noted that are better appreciated by a closer look at our urban regions. A fundamental point is that the political systems of Guadalajara and Medellín are relatively cooperative when compared with their counterparts. Such cooperation is characteristic of the relations between the public and private sectors as well as among levels of government from the local to the national. Inquiring into why this is the case, one can reason that these are *cliental political systems* based on proprietary necessity. In the two cases proprietary necessities are somewhat different. Guadalajara's one-party political directorate rules and enjoys its power at the behest of the federal government. The political mobility of local and state leaders, as well as a continuing fat share of the federal largesse, depends in large part on how well the region distinguishes itself in national circles through the accomplishment of those developmental objectives that are most feasible and appropriate for the region. Lacking spectacular industry but with a long tradition of civic and social achievements, local regimes play to this strength (as they do to certain others, such as tourism, agricultural productivity, and "clean" industries). Importantly, that objective entails a conciliatory approach to the needs of the city and the urban poor, not necessarily out of good will (or connivance), but as a matter of good political sense. In a similar vein, Medellín's sometimes paternal political system is constrained or influenced by a strong Catholic church and the economic need of a committed labor force. A nevertheless legitimate civic pride has grown out of these influences. In both regions civic improvement is closely tied to the peculiar nature of collective goals and is implemented through a cliental political system.

Such is not the case in Monterrey and Cali where, respectively, the constraints of the official party, as opposed to the self-interest of the industrialists, and economic interdependence, as opposed to self-sufficiency, are less compelling. Certainly these two regions and their elites depend on proprietorship. But it is a proprietorship based on the need of factory worker and agricultural laborer clients so that what is returned in the bargain is *private* rather than *public* goods, notably, housing, amenities, and paternal protection donated by the factories and *haciendas* to their own.

While these general explanations seem cogent, they may be disappointing to both the theoretically oriented scholar looking for tightly reasoned propositions and the policy-oriented reformer in search of a clear recipe to remedy urban woes. Much of the argument hinges less on the presence or absence of certain elements than on the ways in which they combine in particular historico- and socio-structural circumstances. Whether for good or ill, such are the limitations placed on any analysis that attempts to combine historical and empirical methods. Yet, if complex realities do not yield easily to the ambitions of theoretical neatness, we may be better advised to keep faith with the former as we hopefully move in small steps toward the latter. No claim is made here to have initiated a theory of urban development. The phrase itself is likely to be misleading apart from related concerns in developmental theory and welfare economics. What we hope to further is comparative research on the politics of urban development that addresses some of the explanations suggested. As the process of urbanization continues to accelerate, and the problems of cities increasingly overlap with the problem of the Third World, these issues would appear to provide a particularly crucial focal point.

5

Structures of Power
in Latin American Cities:
Toward a Summary and
Interpretation

John Walton

If social science could be built on impressionistic evidence, the Latin American city would be well understood. Few observers of these places lack a rich collection of anecdotes about slum dwellers, street beggars, petty traders, a faceless middle class of bureaucratic functionaries, the military mobilized for domestic purposes, and a small privileged oligarchy that seems to orchestrate the activities of diverse groups in ways that serve its own interests. Typically a wealth of lurid detail is woven into a relatively general and inflexible interpretation that envisions a tightly structured power elite superimposed on a society rent by the tensions of poverty and uncontrolled urban growth.

Two interesting observations may be made with respect to this portrait. First, although it is largely based on folk wisdom and casual encounters, it does not materially differ from the modal description derived from more informed or quasi-scientific sources.[1] That is, few rigorous analyses would challenge or supplement the portrait. Second, while a reasonable consensus about the contemporary urban condition in Latin America exists, this view lends itself equally to both optimistic and pessimistic forecasting.

Illustratively, students of political development interpret trends in urbanization and industrialization as conducive to the establishment of an autonomous middle class capable of a moderating influence and a more democratic political process,[2] while critics of this "evolutionary functionalism" claim that the same set of changes has brought more subtle and pernicious forms of elite domination.[3] In a related vein, other observers regard rapid urbanization as either a source of conflict and instability[4] or a stabilizing force promoting political integration.[5]

It would be fruitless to take issue with these very general views. Obviously some of their advocates have different realities in mind, and one has no prima facie reason to expect a generalization true of Chile or Mexico to be true for Peru or Brazil. Further, some of these statements are of an intentionally speculative nature calling for test and evaluation rather than allegiance. Indeed, many of these competing views survive as a result of the relative paucity of systematic, comparative research on politics and power in Latin American cities.

Fortunately this situation is changing. Several years ago Francine Rabinovitz wrote a discursive "review of community power research in Latin America" based on the dozen or so studies available at that time.[6] Since that ground-breaking endeavor a number of new, comparative, and relatively sophisticated research reports that provide an opportunity for systematic codification and evaluation of hypotheses have appeared. Such is the purpose of this essay. In what follows we shall first set down a number of representative hypotheses related to the structure of power in Latin American cities. Next, a method for the secondary analysis of available studies will be presented, followed by a schematic summary of their principal findings. Third, we shall evaluate the set of hypotheses by reference to this codification. And, finally, an attempt will be made to develop a theoretical interpretation of the results, pointing simultaneously to their implications for subsequent research.

Theoretical Generalizations and Testable Propositions

In the theoretical literature and commentary on Latin American cities a wide variety of propositions have been set forth dealing with the structural correlates and consequences of the distribution of power. The theoretical level of these propositions varies; some are general tendency statements (e.g., community power is becoming . . .), while others are genuine contingent propositions (e.g., the greater the x the more competitive the structure of power). Moreover, a number of these propositions are closely related, sometimes expressing essentially the same idea in different words. These conditions militate against any neat ordering of a list of independent and uniquely operational propositions. Rather we shall attempt to indicate a representative and varied set of propositions drawn from major statements in this field. These are listed in order from the more general to the more explicitly testable and with the recognition that frequent, substantive overlap requires evaluation of related propositions with a single set of data. Despite the lack of a good fit between data and propositions, this alternative does allow a more elaborate presentation of the varieties of theoretical thinking and some indication of how well the data match up.

> Proposition 1. Power structures in Latin American cities may be concentrated or elitist but they are seldom dominated by a single elite.

This general or descriptive proposition is based on the assumption of variability in the centralization of control. It suggests that the notion of "oligarchy," while valuable and capable of precise definition, is often carelessly applied to substantially different power arrangements. Most typical is the blurring of differences between monopolistic and competitive elites. A comparable statement of the idea is "the shape of community power may be oligarchic but it is not a single pyramid or monolith."[7]

> Proposition 2. The structure of power in cities is strongly influenced by the national political system and will tend to mirror it in terms of degree of democratization.

Here the reasoning is elementary. Latin American cities exist within a variety of national political cultures ranging from military governments and one-party states to highly competitive, multiparty arrangements. Further, Latin American states tend to be highly centralized, meaning that local structures within a country are less varied than refracted images of the state system. Again Rabinovitz states the matter succinctly: "Community power structure is in large part dependent on the nature and demands of national political systems."[8]

> Proposition 3. Urbanization, or the growth in size and scale of cities, is directly related to increasingly open and competitive structures of power.

This proposition represents the dominant theme in theoretical discussions of political change in Latin America.[9] Urbanization engenders greater political competition through a variety of mechanisms, including forced interdependence, the necessity of cooperation within a more complex social organization, more rapid communication, rising levels of expectation as well as education and political skills, the pressing material needs of the new urban groups that inspire political action, and so forth. All of these influences are summarized in the appearance of new, organized political interests, pressure groups, and counterelites that compete for the available and expanding sources of power. "Increases in the level of urbanization will lead to an increasing openness of the system of social power . . ."[10]

> *Proposition 4. Paralleling trends in urbanization, but with an independent and additive effect, the transformation of the economy from an agricultural to a commercial-industrial base is directly related to increasingly open and competitive structures of power.*

The reasoning here is familiar and similar to the urbanization argument. Unlike more self-sufficient forms of agricultural production (e.g., the *hacienda* system, though by no means all forms), commercial and industrial activities, on the one hand, require greater cooperation and, on the other, generate new resources that may be subject to redistributional claims. A variety of possibilities are illustrative: "Relative to the urban sector, these agrarian upper-class interests are increasingly losing ground as they become (i) merged with commercial activities in the cities; (ii) engaged in combat with radical or revolutionary forces; and (iii) lose their indispensability to the structure of the national economy."[11] Similarly, "the reorganization of the economy imposed by the advance of industrialization brought about noteworthy modifications in the composition of the entrepreneurial elites. New members of the economy's leading groups appeared: state entrepreneurs and professional administrators of foreign concerns. Private sector enterprises become leaders equally concerned with the economy of the enterprise and with national development policy."[12]

> *Proposition 5. In addition to internal changes of the population and economy, local political systems become increasingly open and competitive to the extent that they become interdependent with the larger society.*

Far from constituting an autonomous unit of analysis, the urban political process is continually influenced by extralocal factors. Vertical ties of the city to the carrying society tend to introduce new power resources into the community and to provide local groups with a broader base of political power. These external alliances may easily tend to fortify traditional elites, but, typically, they will also provide a new source of potential influence to competitive groups that arise in the urbanization-industrialization process. ". . . the linkage of cities into urban systems has an effect analogous to increasing city size."[13]

> Proposition 6. The broad social changes taking place in Latin America, such as urbanization and industrialization, have not altered the fact of elite domination but only its form.

This proposition challenges the modal interpretation expressed in the three preceding statements. Essentially it claims that, while change in the number and variety of urban interest groups is undeniable, these groups have forged alliances that parallel earlier structures of privilege and inequality. "It is an error to assume that the generalized process of social transformation in Latin America has given rise to an entrepreneurial elite which opposes the traditional elites, or oligarchies. On the contrary, the reorganization of Latin American societies reaches a new synthesis through a system of alliances among social groups which insures the pivotal importance of the elite in the form of the amalgamation of a traditional oligarchy with an entrepreneurial sector."[14] "Thus, the political alliances of the middle class will depend on whether or not the social system proves capable of satisfying their minimum aspirations. Where that satisfaction is provided, the middle sectors will be likely to seek alliance with the powerful and privileged groups in the community, and will thus contribute to the maintenance of the existing order."[15]

> Proposition 7. Urbanization, industrialization, and vertical integration are necessary but not sufficient conditions of more open and competitive structures of power. In addition to these factors the decisive influences producing a redistribution of political power are found in the interplay of political institutions and the class structure.

Stated somewhat differently, "to sum up these complex considerations, it appears that urbanization does potentially produce a setting in which tensions develop. These may be channeled into behaviors positive for political development and for stimulating change. On the other hand, such positive effects are by no means automatic. They depend on the presence of integrating forces, such as political parties and labor unions as well as effective governmental agencies, which exercise some degree of control over the new pressures while not suppressing them through severe sanctions, as do some military-dominated regimes."[16]

This proposition is admittedly vague and may hint at a tautology with terms like *political institutions* or *integrating forces*. What it does endeavor to say is that, because urbanization and industrialization are not sufficient conditions for competitive structures of power, a satisfactory explanation must probe further into the stratification and political system. What may emerge as a more exacting explanation is largely an open question. Indeed, it is a question that may be informed by our analysis of the available evidence.

For present purposes, this list of seven propositions is ample. Although the propositions do not span any theoretical continuum ranging from the correlates of highly competitive to highly monopolistic arrangements of power, they do represent the effective range within which seasoned obervers believe the Latin American republics operate. If anything these propositions may go beyond the available data suggesting that there are now enough issues on the table to turn to a summary of the evidence.

Codification of Studies and Secondary Analysis

The term *secondary analysis* usually refers to studies based on a reworking of data from earlier research. There is, however, a fairly well established variant of this method in which earlier studies themselves are used as data in a "study of studies." This method was pioneered by anthropologists working with large numbers of ethnographic studies in the Human Areas Research File. Among the methodological nuances they developed were techniques of "data quality control," which allowed for the control of bias (error) and, therefore, a statistical rationale for treating research monographs as reliable sources of primary data.[17] Recently this technique has been applied to studies of community power in North American cities in an effort to pool the evidence and evaluate rival hypotheses from a comparative standpoint.[18]

In attempting to extend this method to studies of Latin American communities, the first task was to identify the relevant "universe" of studies. Here a number of commonplace procedures were followed, including a literature search beginning with the Rabinovitz piece and cross-referencing more recent books and articles, checking with colleagues knowledgeable in the area, and running down several dissertations recently completed or still in progress. The result was the identification of twenty studies dealing with twenty-six communities (or 22 communities eliminating duplications, i.e., cases where the same town was separately studied by different researchers). While this collection may approximate the "universe," it is technically an availability sample. Several criteria defined the sample. The studies had to be focused explicitly on the structure of community power. Reports dealing with social stratification, the electoral process, urban planning, and so forth were thus excluded when such phenomena were not linked to control of the political process. Another criterion was the employment of relatively standardized or systematic research methods. Here the conventional reputational and decisional strategies were prototypical, although case studies were also included in which it was clear that the investigators had employed some other systematic data collection procedure (e.g., participant observation, interviewing, analysis of newspapers and documents, etc.). Finally, ethnographic reports dealing with small villages were excluded on both methodological and conceptual grounds. Often the procedures employed in these studies are, of necessity, rather unsystematic and idiosyncratic. Further, the sample was designed to embrace towns and cities and to exclude such incomparable places as rural villages, farming cooperatives, or *ejidos,* and so forth. This is not to be understood as any reflection on the quality of such work, some of which is quite good.[19]

In table 16 the twenty studies and twenty-six communities are summarized. The first five columns are self-explanatory, indicating authors and dates of the study, country and town names (only one, "Saragosa," is a pseudonym), and population. In the next three columns a presentation of important themes in the study was chosen in preference to risking a loss of information via coding. Although these themes were coded later, their initial presentation in this form conveys something of the substance of the findings and allows for alternate coding schemes.

Four of the columns require some comment on how the information was subsequently coded. First, the data employed as a basis for the coding were drawn exclusively from the research monographs rather than from cross-checks with other observers or documents. The idea here was to be faithful to the author's account. Second, two coders, myself and a Colombian sociologist, reviewed the material, with the result of almost total intercoder reliability, albeit based on a less than desirable number of checks; the point is, a check was made. Third, the categories within coded variables were defined as follows:

1. *Economic Characteristics.* These were divided into two complementary variables.
   a. *Economic Base:* i.e. the origin of a majority of economic activities. Here, for example, a city that was predominantly based on agricultural pursuits would be so classified, even though agriculture per se was less than 50 percent of its gross product, provided industrial and commercial activities were predominantly based on agricultural products (e.g., processing and marketing agricultural products).
      The categories were:
      i. *Agricultural Base*
      ii. *Commercial-Industrial Base*
   b. *Principal Economic Activity:* operational on the basis of the leading sector of the labor force or gross product.
      i. *Agriculture*
      ii. *Commerce*
      iii. *Industry*

2. *Structure of Power*
   a. *Elitist* (EM): an elite monopoly of power, including a single dominant elite, within which there may be

competition, or a dominant faction with one or more consistently lesser factions (lesser factions were included in the category since no cases of a totally dominant and cohesive elite emerged).

b. *Competitive Elites* (CE): power narrowly distributed but among several (at least two) factions of relatively equal strength across a range of issues.

c. *Coalitional* (CO): reasonably diversified bases of power and broad representation of issue-oriented interests typically operating through bargaining mechanisms or collaborative institutions.

d. *Fragmented or Amorphous* (FA): an unstructured situation, highly fragmented interest groups with little institutional integration, typically characterized by divisiveness and conflict.

3. *External Ties*

a. *Strong-Pervasive:* extensive ties between the urban region and the economic and political institutions of the larger society or international economy so that a number of basic policy decisions are made by extra-local interests.

b. *Weak-Minimal:* relative isolation and local autonomy in policy making.

4. *Research Methods*

a. *Reputational:* informants asked to identify the most influential people in the community; typically these lists are narrowed through a "snowball technique" based on increasing consensus above some cutoff point.

b. *Decisional:* focuses on specific local issues, and leaders are taken to be those participants active in their resolution.

c. *Case Study:* less explicit methods based on observation, selective though unsystematic interviewing, and examination of documents.

d. *Combined:* simultaneous use of any two above.

Inclusion of this last variable deserves comment. In the long and heated controversy over interpretations of community power in North American cities, contending schools of thought (the elitists vs. the pluralists) charged one another with employing research methods that favorably biased the conclusions.[20] Comparative evaluation of these claims found them to be valid, and the finding has been sustained in most subsequent replications.[21]

In the case of the Latin American studies it was therefore necessary to determine if such methodological biases were operating and, if so, to employ data quality controls in the analysis of results. The variable was included for these precautionary reasons.

The summary at the bottom of table 16 gives some indication of the representativeness or unrepresentativeness of the sample. By national context Mexico and Colombia are heavily overrepresented, accounting for nearly 70 percent of the sample (i.e., 18 of 26). Although the distribution by political status of the city appears more normal, the real "universe" contains many more *manicipios* than state and national capitals; thus the latter are overrepresented here. Similarly, 60 percent of the cities are over one hundred thousand in population (i.e., 15 of 25 reporting size) adding an urban bias. In short, this availability sample is heavily biased toward large cities and capitals in Mexico and Colombia.[22]

Because it would be awkward to continually refer to these biases, the reader is advised that the subsequent findings should be interpreted cautiously because of the narrowness of their generalities. Of course, this is necessarily so since we are dealing with what is available. While it is interesting to note in passing that researchers (most of whom are U.S. citizens) demonstrate an attraction to large cities and capitals in Mexico and Colombia, one should proceed with the understanding that the results will, at best, be suggestive and far from conclusive for all Latin America because of the restricted range of the sample. However, eighteen large cities and capitals in Mexico and Colombia make a respectable number on which to base some generalizations about cities in these two countries, and in others insofar as cities in those other countries resemble the eighteen in key dimensions.

Table 17 presents a quantitative summary of six independent variables cross-tabulated with the dependent variable "structure of power." Recognizing that the small N of twenty-six does

Table 16. A Descriptive Summary of Studies on Community Power and Politics in Latin America

Study/Date	Country	Town (#)	Political Status	Population Size and Characteristics	Economic Characteristics	Power and Political Characteristics	External Ties	Research Methods
1. Klapp & Padgett, 1960	Mexico	Tijuana (1)	Municipality	160,000 Increasing rapidly	Border town, U.S. satellite, many residents employed in U.S. tourism, among more developed Mexican cities, little industry	Unintegrated, amorphous leadership, no factions, individualized not institutional leadership, cleavage between government & business, opposition party viable (FA)	Pervasive via state & federal governments, official party, dependence on U.S., little autonomy	Reputational
2. D'Antonio & Form, 1965	Mexico	Ciudad Juárez (2)	Municipality	300,000 Increasing rapidly	Border town, U.S. satellite, many residents employed in U.S., tourism and commercial center, little industry, unionized	Factionalism and cleavage, political and party groups strongest but growing opposition party and business influence, competitive elites, conflict (CE)	Pervasive via state & federal governments, official party, dependence on U.S.	Combined reputational & decisional; issues: 1) elections 2) welfare campaign 3) hospital drive
3. Blasier, 1966	Colombia	Cali (3)	Department capital	730,000 Increasing rapidly	Agricultural base, commerce & food processing, growing industry with much foreign ownership	Elitist, dominant clique of land-owners-industrialists, weak government & unions, local & local-national conflict (EM)	Important but characterized by conflict with central government, dependent on foreign firms and trade	Case study
4. Holden, 1966	Costa Rica	Pejivalle (4)	Municipality	Small Stable, rural	Agricultural, coffee cultivation, hacienda system	Monolithic, elitist, small group of cohesive leaders (EM)	Minimal	Reputational

5. Edwards, 1966	Costa Rica	San José (5)	National capital	100,000	Political, commercial, and manufacturing center	Factional (not monolithic), two cliques based in agriculture vs. government and the professions with ties to separate political parties (CE)	Strong, center of national life, trade and foreign industry, city politics closely tied to national	Reputational
6. Padgett, 1967; Dent, n.d.	Colombia	Cali (3)	Department capital	800,000 Increasing rapidly	See 3 above	Bifurcation of power between more dominant economic and less dominant political influentials, "immobilism," conflict and lack of cooperation, no unified political leadership, fragmentation of power among landowners and industrialists (CE)	See 3 above	Reputational
7. Graham, 1968	Mexico	"Saragosa" (6)	Municipality	58,000 Increasing	Agricultural base, commercial and educational center	Factionalism, no cohesive power structure, cliques within businesses and professions, factions within party, by contrast to the "lower" sector, a business-professional elite but one lacking in integration, cooptation of local factions by state government (CE)	Pervasive via state & federal government, official party, little autonomy	Case study, interview; issues: 1) new industry 2) university 3) urban services 4) dam 5) agricultural prices

Table 16—Continued

Study/Date	Country	Town (#)	Political Status	Population Size and Characteristics	Economic Characteristics	Power and Political Characteristics	External Ties	Research Methods
8. Hoskin, 1969	Venezuela	San Cristóbal (7)	State capital	122,000 Increasing, assimilated mestizo population	Agricultural base, commerce and governmental services, incipient industry, by national standards less diversified & developed	Competitive elites, no single cohesive group, six power clusters, multiparty competition, predominance of government leaders in local decisions, professional and society-wealth leaders active in certain issues of direct interest, ideological diversity, high degree of political conflict (CE)	Less integrated into national society than is typical, but external political influences in local issues	Combined reputational & decisional; issues: 1) plant construction 2) new market 3) hydroelectric project 4) nomination of governor
9. Ebel, 1969	El Salvador	San Salvador (8)	National capital	250,000	Diversified agricultural base, commerce, banking, industry, foreign firms	Competitive parties, Christian Democrats with city and popular base, National Conciliation with federal and business-industrial support, coalition, weak city government, no "civic elite" (CO)	Strong, small country with nearly all national politics concentrated in the city, politics influenced by national, also international influence in finance	Case study; issues: 1) municipal tax reform 2) street lighting

	Country	City	Type	Population	Economic base	Power structure	Government relation	Method
10. Alisky, 1969	Mexico	Nogales (9)	Municipality	60,000	Border town and free port, commerce, tourism, agricultural base	Elitist, top leaders active in official party and the economic community of commercial property owners, 75% associated with management vs. labor, a "civic family" of close-knit business and social networks [EM]	Pervasive via state and federal government ties, official party, U.S. contact	Reputational
11. Torres-Trueba, 1969	Mexico	Zacapoaxtla (10)	Municipality	30,000 Heterogeneous 60% Indian	Rural, agricultural, one factory-distillery	Factional, split between old aristocracy and new political-economic leader, also economic, religious and political factionalism along indio-mestizo lines (CE)	Pervasive via state and party	Case study
12a. Forni, 1970	Argentina	Maciel (11)	Municipality	3,000 Increasing	Agricultural base, packing house absentee owned, commerce	Two cliques of traditionalists and new comers based in politics and the economy respectively, relatively equalitarian class structure, local political initiative, also cliques within the economy (agriculture & professions) but these cooperate (CE)	Closely tied to nearby large town but a good deal of local autonomy	Combined reputational & decisional; issues: 1) rural credit

Table 16—Continued

Study/Date	Country	Town (#)	Political Status	Population Size and Characteristics	Economic Characteristics	Power and Political Characteristics	External Ties	Research Methods
12b.		Puerto Gaboto (12)	Municipality	2,000 Stable	Fishing, former port in decline, rudimentary commerce	Elitist, single power-prestige group based in the economy (business, farming) but this group is fragmented internally, little organization or local action (FA)	Strong, little local initiative, dependent	2) train service
13. Ugalde, 1970	Mexico	Ensenada (13)	Municipality	65,000 Increasing	Fishing, tourism, free trade zone, commerce with U.S., among more affluent Mexican towns, many residents employed in U.S., food processing industry	"Pluralistic" or factional, competitive political parties, business and party based unions equally powerful and that arrangement is maintained by larger government in order to keep peace and act as broker, countervailing powers, by Mexican standards a good deal of open conflict or, at least, competition (CO)	Strong via centralized state & federal governments and party, ties to U.S. economy, but also independent in some areas from national system	Case study, interview; issues: 1) street lighting 2) tourist development 3) union conflict 4) toll road
14a. Miller, 1970	Argentina	Córdoba (14)	State capital	600,000 Increasing	Industrialized, foreign owned firms, commercial-administrative-educational center	Under military government at time of study, segmented power structure including representatives of religion, business, local government,	Strong dependence on military government, foreign investment ties	Reputational

	Country	City	Status	Population	Economic Base	Power Structure	Dependency / Ties	Method & Issues
14b.	Peru	Lima (15)	National capital	2,000,000 Rapidly increasing	Industrialized, foreign-owned firms, commercial-administrative-educational center	labor, and the military, "low profile" of the church and military, a "high degree of pluralism" (CO) — Competitive political parties, segmented power structure composed of representatives and institutions from the military, political parties, local and national government, business, labor, & religion, no single elite (CO)	Convergence of national & local politics, foreign investment ties	Combined reputational & decisional; issues: 1) social welfare groups 2) unions 3) popular housing
15. Drake, 1970	Colombia	Manizales (16)	Department capital	200,000	Commercial-administrative-educational center, locus of substantial coffee export, moderate industry	An oligarchy based on wealth, status, and political office holding, elite cohesiveness based on kinship and joint business holdings, top leaders from economic sector, cliques within the elite based on agricultural vs. national & foreign-owned industry but this is "in group" competition, not counterelites, conservative elite (EM)	Only moderate traditional regional autonomy, resistance to national interventions (e.g., in unions), yet some ties to national government and more with international economy	Combined reputational & decisional; issues: 1) social welfare groups 2) unions 3) popular housing
16a. Walton, 1970, 1972	Mexico	Guadalajara (17)	State capital	1,300,000 Increasing	Agricultural base, commercial-administrative-educational center, light to medium industry especially food processing, foreign investment	Coalitional power structure led by state government and including business, industry, and finance, coordinated and collaborative (CO)	Pervasive via federal government, party & foreign firms	Combined reputational & decisional; issues: 1) infrastructure

Table 16—Continued

Study/Date	Country	Town (#)	Political Status	Population Size and Characteristics	Economic Characteristics	Power and Political Characteristics	External Ties	Research Methods
16a. (continued)								2) industrial promotion 3) urban development 4) agricultural development 5) economic planning
16b.		Monterrey (18)	State capital	1,200,000 Increasing	Heavy industry, commercial-administrative-educational center, export of beer, steel, glass, chemicals, financial center	Elitist power structure dominated by close-knit industrial-financial community, subservient public sector, occasional conflict between unified elite and federal government [EM]	Moderate, dependence on federal investment but much political independence and regional autonomy due to economic base and export	1) industrial promotion 2) urban development
16c.	Colombia	Cali (3)	Department capital	900,000 Increasing	Agricultural base, commercial-administrative-educational center, light to medium industry in food processing, chemicals, paper, much foreign investment	Predominance of a high status elite based in large agricultural holdings and industry, intra-elite conflict between progressive industrialists & land-owners, & particularly	Substantial dependence on foreign investment & the federal government, but conflictual relations with	1) Regional Development Corp. 2) agricultural development

	City	Status	Population	Economic base	Power structure	Government ties	Issues/Methods
					between economic & political leaders, conflict (EM)	the latter	3) state university 4) Pan American Games 5) industrial promotion
16d.	Medellin (19)	Department capital	1,000,000 Increasing	Industrialized especially in textiles, commercial-administrative-educational center, export of coffee & textiles, financial center	Coalitional power structure lead by the industrial-financial community but including public sector leaders and institutions, coordinated & collaborative (CO)	Moderate, tradition of regional autonomy & independence from federal government, yet some ties via federal investment & the export economy	1) Public Services Corp. 2) industrial promotion
17. Fagen & Tuohy, 1972	Mexico Jalapa (20)	State capital	85,000 Increasing	Agricultural base particularly in coffee production, commercial-administrative-educational center	Elite coalition led by political leaders with labor union support, but including influential segments of the economic community, university students occasionally exercise influence, some overt conflict, but generally a division of privilege between excluded popular groups & the externally controlled coalition of top economic & political leaders (CE)	Pervasive via state & federal governments, official party	Case study, interview; issues: 1) urban development 2) taxes

Table 16—Continued

Study/Date	Country	Town (#)	Political Status	Population Size and Characteristics	Economic Characteristics	Power and Political Characteristics	External Ties	Research Methods
18. Ocampo, 1972	Colombia	Manizales (16)	Department capital	200,000	See 15 above	Oligarchy, center of nationally influential coffee export monopoly (EM)	Pervasive due to economic dependency	Case study of political economy
19a. Dent, 1973	Colombia	Medellin (19)	Department capital	1,000,000 Increasing	See 16d above	Institutionalized coordination of power between public & private sectors, greater mobilization of power & resources as well as broader participation in their exercise, little factionalism or conflict, much local initiative & cooperation (CO)	See 16d above	Combined; issues: 1) urban services
19b.		Barranquilla (21)	Department capital	650,000 Increasing	Seaport, commerce, manufacturing, economic decline in recent years	Factionalism & conflict between public & private sectors, political instability, cliques & individualism in private sector, no organizational networks of power (i.e., institutionally amorphous); what leadership is exercised tends to be nonlocal in origin (FA)	Strong dependence on central government	Combined; issues: 1) urban services

| 20. Dávila & Ogliastri, 1972; Ogliastri, 1973 | Colombia | Bucaramanga (22) | Department capital | 350,000 | Agricultural base especially coffee, commercial-administrative-educational center, artisan & small industry | An upper-class elite with diversified & multiple economic bases, intra-elite conflict, elite-sponsored political sector that emulates privileged groups & aspires to higher status through political office [EM] | Strong, dependence on national government & economy, regional independence opposed by Bogotá | Combined reputational & decisional; issues: 1) industrial investment 2) public works to prevent erosion 3) electrification 4) road construction 5) airport construction |

Summary:
20 Studies

Mexico—	9	
Colombia—	9	
Costa Rica—	2	
Venezuela—	1	
El Salvador—	1	
Argentina—	3	
Peru—	1	
	26	

26 towns including duplications.

National capital—	3
State or department capital—	14
Municipality—	9
	26

22 towns excluding duplications.

<10,000—	2
10–50,000—	1
50–100,000—	4
100–500,000—	8
500,000—	5
1,000,000—	5
1,000,100+—	
	25
	+1 n.a.

not permit meaningful statistical analyses, we describe the patterns in this table and in table 18 (which simply collapses categories for a more compact presentation) in terms of the strength of association. It should be noted that, while appropriate for the level of measurement here, the use of gross categories and qualitative judgments of what appear to be strong or weak associations will obscure associations that exist in the data. Important, however, is the converse; where moderate to strong associations appear, we can be all the more confident of them since, in effect, they persist despite the necessarily unrefined analysis.

Tables 17 and 18 demonstrate that the kind of methodological biases found in analyses of North American cities are not carried over to Latin America; that is, there is no association between the type of research method used and the pattern of power structure identified. The absence of association may be a result of more sophisticated methods developed in the recent years that coincide with most of the studies of present concern. It could also reflect the possibility that U.S. researchers (the majority of the investigators here) are less biased and more objective outside their own culture. The fact that research methods are not systematically associated with one kind of conclusion or another on the dependent variable means that we need not be concerned about bias and data quality control and may proceed to a straightforward analysis of the remaining associations.

Proposition 1. Supported. Proposition 1 stated that Latin American community power structures may tend to be concentrated but are seldom dominated by a single elite. Supporting evidence for this proposition is presented in the column marginals or row of totals at the bottom of tables 17 and 18. In table 17 only eight of twenty-six studies report the existence of an elite monopoly, and even then the category definition allowed for some internal competition within the elite (i.e., if anything, this test was liberal and allowed the elitist interpretation a wide latitude from which to emerge). The first three power-structure categories are equally common, sustaining the assumption of wide variability in patterns across cities. Finally, if the "elite monopoly" and "competitive elite" categories are combined into a "centralized" one and compared with a combination of the other two "decentralized" alternatives (table 18 column totals), then a majority (16 of 26) represents more concentrated power or the elitist case. But again, the modal finding is not overwhelming, with about 40 percent (i.e., 10 of 26) representing decentralized power arrangements. In short, the evidence indicates substantial variability in the distribution of cases from centralized to decentralized power structures.

A final note of caution should be added. Those doing elite studies inevitably encounter problems of access to information on the more totalitarian features of a political system and, therefore, necessarily suggest a pluralist bias. Elites are eager to show their democratic faces but guard closely the secrets of their coercive methods. However, since it is reasonable to assume that this is a directionally systematic bias, the same amount of variation reported (and the basic point) will likely be valid, even though one may want to shift the range of that variation toward the elitist end of the continuum. Also, while it is true that elites try to guard their secrets, field experience shows that they generally fail because counterelites and opposition groups usually expose them.[23]

Proposition 2. Not supported. Proposition 2 argued that local political structures, particularly in the highly centralized governments of Latin America, tend to reflect national patterns of democratization or competitiveness in the political system. Under the variable heading "national democratization" the seven countries are ranked from high to low on an index of competitiveness within the political system. The order, adjusted for recent changes, such as the fall of a military regime in Venezuela and the rise of another in Argentina, is based on several others that have appeared in the literature.[24] Most of the studies under examination were conducted in the late 1960s. Needless to say, this kind of a ranking is highly judgmental, and other observers might argue certain scale locations. Venezuela, for example, is ranked high for its present government, but it endured years of the Jiménez dictatorship, which probably influenced local governments more substantially than has the current government. Peru provides the converse, a reasonably long period of democratic rule (except when elections went in favor of Haya de la Torre) prior to the present military regime. Argentina's military government during the period of reference may have been more decentralized and tolerant than the Mexican one-party system. Nevertheless, visual inspection of the

Table 17. Structure of Power by Selected Independent
Variables

	Structure of Power				
	Elite Monopoly	Competitive Elites	Coalitional	Fragmented, Amorphous	Total
1. Research method					
Reputational	2	2	2	1	7
Combined, case study	6	6	5	2	19
2. National democratization					
High: Costa Rica	1	1	0	0	2
Venezuela	0	1	0	0	1
Colombia	5	1	2	1	9
Mexico	2	4	2	1	9
El Salvador	0	0	1	0	1
Peru	0	0	1	0	1
Low: Argentina	0	1	1	1	3
3. City size					
<10,000	1	1	0	1	3
10–50,000	0	1	0	0	1
50–100,000	1	2	1	0	4
100–500,000	3	3	1	1	8
500–1,000,000	2	1	1	1	5
1,000,000+	1	0	4	0	5
4. Economic base					
Agriculture	7	6	3	1	17
Commerce-industry	1	2	4	2	9
5. Principal economic activity					
Agriculture	1	2	0	1	4
Commerce	6	4	2	2	14
Industry	1	2	5	0	8
6. External ties					
Strong-pervasive	5	7	5	3	20
Weak-minimal	3	1	2	0	6
Total	8	8	7	3	26

Table 18. Structure of Power by Selected Independent Variables
(Collapsed Version of Table 17)

	Structure of Power		
	Centralized (Elite Monopoly & Competitive Elites)	Decentralized (Coalitional & Fragmented, Amorphous)	Total
1. Research method			
Reputational	4	3	7
Combined, case study	12	7	19
2. National demo-cratization			
High: Costa Rica	2	0	2
Venezuela	1	0	1
Colombia	6	3	9
Mexico	6	3	9
El Salvador	0	1	1
Peru	0	1	1
Low: Argentina	1	2	3
3. City size			
<100,000	6	2	8
100–500,000	6	2	8
500,000+	4	6	10
4. Economic base			
Agriculture	13	4	17
Commerce-industry	3	6	9
5. Principal economic activity			
Agriculture	3	1	4
Commerce	10	4	14
Industry	3	5	8
6. External ties			
Strong-pervasive	12	8	20
Weak-minimal	4	2	6
Total	16	10	26

table suggests any reasonable reordering would still reflect more intranational variation than systematic associations by nation.

Reading across the rows in table 17, one sees that if a pattern is discernable it would suggest the reverse of the hypothesis. Cities in the more democratic countries tend to have less competitive structures of power. Conversely, as is more evident in table 18, cities in the less democratic countries have more competitive power structures.

One is tempted to speculate on this result. Perhaps a competitive national system encourages the centralization of power in cities that act as quasi-interest groups in competition for the spoils of the federal system. While such reasoning may have its own merits, it obviously goes beyond the available evidence. Mexico and Colombia, which share adjacent positions toward the upper end of the index, are overrepresented because the other countries offered insufficient examples to establish a pattern. Nevertheless, the evidence is adequate for rejecting the proposition since it demonstrates again substantial intranational variation as opposed to the convergence of local-national patterns, even under a reordering of national scale locations.

Proposition 3. Moderately Supported. The third proposition posits a direct relation between urbanization and open or competitive power structures. Since all of the larger cities have experienced rapid population increases in recent years, city size provides a valid indicator of the urbanization process. Although the evidence is equivocal, the pattern is clearly in the predicted direction: larger, urbanizing cities tend to have more competitive structures of power.

Proposition 4. Supported. The fourth proposition argues that cities based on an agricultural economy tend to be elitist, while industrial and commercial economies foster greater interdependence, cooperation, and political competition. The relationship is strongly supported by our data. *Rural towns, as well as cities whose principal wealth is derived from agricultural pursuits (both farming and processing), are characterized by centralized power structures in contrast to cities with commercial and industrial economic bases.*

The fifth variable in tables 17 and 18 refers also to this proposition and merely operationalizes it on the basis of principal economic activity (i.e., the leading sector of the labor force or gross product) rather than economic base. Largely because of the separation of the categories of commerce and industry, the proposition receives only mild support here. Most interesting is the fact that two-thirds (10 of 14) of the cities whose wealth and employment are generated in commerce and services tend to have centralized structures of power. While the evidence is thin, it would suggest that only with industrialization do elitist arrangements begin to lose their predominance and to accommodate competing interests.

Proposition 5. Weakly supported. The fifth proposition alleges that vertical integration, or the extent of linkage between the city and the larger society, produces a more competitive arrangement of power at the local level. Interestingly, considering the number of its exponents[25] and its apparent substantiation in the North American example,[26] the proposition receives only slight support here. At least two explanations come to mind. The most obvious is the poor quality of the data. Beyond that, vertical integration may mean several things for Latin American cities. The meaning implicit in the hypothesis is the introduction of new community resources—jobs, interest groups, national parties, or unions—that provide alternative power bases. Equally important, however, is the integration of local economies into dependent trade relations and monopolistic national and multinational corporate structures, either of which would reinforce local patterns of privilege and inequality. With the available evidence these are difficult to separate, although it seems that external ties of the first sort would have the predicted effects, while those of the latter sort would have the reverse effects.

Qualitative Analysis: Propositions 6 and 7. Propositions 6 and 7 are not amenable to straightforward quantitative tests, since they entail, not so much the documentation of variegated urban interest groups, but a judgmental determination of the ways in which these groups form alliances. Illustratively, moderate support for propositions 3 and 4 could be interpreted as a negation of proposition 6. That, however, would oversimplify the latter statement, which does not deny the plurality of urban political interests but asserts that these interests are allied in ways that represent a "new synthesis" of patterns of inequality. The internal composition of the elite may be broad; yet that elite may continue to enjoy the same (or even greater) disproportionate power and privilege vis-à-vis the similarly increasing nonelite.

The heart of the problem, of course, is that few of the available studies deal (methodologically or theoretically) with such *multiple dimensions* of power distribution as concentration, integration or cohesiveness, and total amount.[27] As a result analysis of these propositions must rely on selective examination of those studies that provide relevant qualitative evidence.

Support for the sixth proposition can be found in several studies that probe beneath surface appearances for a more comprehensive description. Illustrative is the experience of a middle-sized Mexican town. "What exists in Saragosa is a factional style of politics, *monopolized by the upper sector*, operating within the framework of a democratic regime. Since 1942 there *has been no challenge to business-professional leadership from the lower sector*, either in the city or in the countryside. A system of relationships has developed in which the electorate in principle selects public officials. In *form*, power is distributed in such a way that equal weight is given to the three sectors represented in the local PRI. In *reality* the worker and peasant sectors have accepted elite leadership as proper and just."[28]

With reference to a similar community that reflects clear-cut differences between upper and lower groups on a variety of measures of influence, Fagen and Tuohy observe: "Unless real democratization of party membership and participation takes place, the only change will be to substitute competitive elitism for controlled elitism."[29]

Among the twenty-six city studies summarized in table 16, Cali, Colombia, was studied in three separate investigations.[30] These reports are in substantial agreement concerning the existence of a close-knit economic elite whose wealth, derived originally from large-scale agricultural holdings, in recent years has been invested in local industry, thereby simply expanding the political power base of traditional classes. "What does stand out in this study is somewhat of an oligarchy of local industrialists and landowners who operate with the approval or consensus of national decision makers in Bogotá and, at times, with the blessings of the Catholic Church. Although middle elites were found to have relatively little contact with the public sector, the primary elites possessed a substantial amount of contact in *both* the public and private sectors."[31]

Similarly, the studies of Edwards[32] and Torres-Trueba[33] conclude that seemingly competitive interests are tied together in alliances that exclude effective influence by the middle or lower classes. Conversely, several reports attest to the emulative character of the middle classes.[34] Rather than acting as autonomous moderating influences, the new middle classes reinforce and broaden traditional structures of inequality by their deference to elitist values. In short, qualitative examination of the evidence suggests a good deal of support of the sixth proposition.

Nevertheless, several "deviant cases" require equal attention. Ebel's study of San Salvador describes a multiparty situation that became increasingly competitive during the 1960s. Ebel characterized this city–national capital as a "national municipal system" with the following characteristics:

(1) a system of political competition not limited to the political forces and groups within the city itself but also embracing national governmental institutions and the political elites controlling them. In this situation, the political contests are likely to be between coalitions of political groups and governmental agencies, often embracing both the national and local levels;

(2) a multiple access system whereby interest groups may utilize decisional points at either the national or local levels to either thwart or implement demands for municipal services and/or other actions; and

(3) a tie-in with the international political system—particularly the international banking community—due to the fact that municipal improvements are sometimes financed by international loans.[35]

Miller's study of Lima appears to share many of these same features.[36]

The Mexican border cities of Tijuana,[37] Ciudad Juárez,[38] and Ensenada[39] provide interesting parallels to the foregoing examples. In each town investigators observed more political-party and interest-group competition than is found in other cities of the Republic. In part this stems from the diminishing influence of Mexico's dominant party (PRI) in more urbanized areas.[40] But more important may be the effects of international contacts, border trade, and U.S. ("green card") employment opportunities, all of which promote greater affluence in the border towns and, consequently, less dependence on PRI and its component unions.

A third variety of competitive or coalitional power arrangements is found in Guadalajara and Medellín, where representative groups of public and private sectors share relatively equal influence and cooperate in decision making. These cities have two things in common: strong local-state governments, evolved from economic necessity in Medellín and postrevolutionary imposition in Guadalajara, and relatively equalitarian class structures, which are reflected in a broader distribution of power.

The fourth type of power arrangement is fragmented, amorphous, or unstructured. Despite its relative infrequency, it suggests the theoretically interesting limiting case in which factionalism reaches the point of stalemate and competing groups become immobilized. Typically, this situation stems from the absence of effective control at the local level and, similarly, from a lack of legitimate political institutions.

In summarizing these deviant examples, three points require emphasis. First, the comments here apply only to deviant examples and do not contradict the modal results presented earlier. Second and more specifically, the examples do not appear to refute proposition 6: in no case was there reported a viable and representative pattern of political pluralism similar to that found in certain North American cities.[41] Seldom do middle-class interests constitute an independent source of political power, and there are no cases of regularized lower-class access to policy-making circles. Therefore, what is demonstrated in the deviant cases should be understood as moderate, though not insignificant, departures from new styles of elite domination. Third, more competitive power structures in this sense seem to emerge where there are (1) strong, competitive political parties at the national level that provide leverage to a variety of local groups (e.g., nonelites that may be able to influence city and state governments through indirect appeals), or (2) substantial convergence of the local and the national-international systems that may indirectly confer new resources on the local community (e.g., employment, less unilateral local control, etc.), or (3) relatively equalitarian class structures resulting in a broader distribution of occupations and income that may be converted into political resources. It would be a mistake to regard these factors as mere tautologies or as elements entailed in the definition of competitive power structures. Logically, they cannot be considered tautologies because they apply only to a subsample of the cases, not to the larger sample. Substantively, they represent potential resources of power rather than power itself. These three generalizations would seem to support and add substance to the seventh proposition. That is, any one or a combination of these three factors may, along with the necessary conditions of urbanization, industrialization, and vertical integration, provide sufficient conditions for more open and competitive structures of power. This, of course, is a hypothesis-generating speculation that necessarily ventures beyond the data.

Some Observations on Theory and Research

Despite the relatively small and unrepresentative sample of research monographs dealing with the structure of power in Latin American cities, and recognizing the necessarily crude level of secondary analysis, this discussion has, nevertheless, succeeded in identifying a number of tentative empirical generalizations. Power arrangements reflect substantively significant variability, albeit within a truncated range of theoretical possibilities. The structural correlates of more competitive structures include urbanization, transition from an agricultural to an industrial economy, and integration of a national hierarchy of cities. Yet these must be regarded as necessary rather than sufficient conditions of any "democratization"; they compel alternatives to agrarian-based and more rigid systems of stratification and power without determining the forms of those alternatives.[42] Perhaps the major finding is that these forces produce "dynamics without change"[43] in fundamental patterns of privilege and inequality to the extent that they encourage new alliances among agricultural-industrial-export-political-foreign elites arrayed over sycophantic middle and indemnified working classes. Equally important, however, is the fact that a number of studies deviate from this modal pattern and suggest the tentative generalization that competitive political parties, convergence of local and national-international systems, and equalitarian class structures may provide the sufficient condition for a broader distribution of power.

One theoretical implication of these results is to cast further doubt on the utility of evolutionary or trend-continuum notions of political change. The pattern described is not one of covariant trends leading inexorably to "political development" but, rather, a conjunction of necessary and sufficient conditions. The critical factors adduced here may conjoin, but no evolutionary logic suggests that they must. This statement does not deny the possibility of theoretical generalization but implies that such a generalization must be grounded in the historical, political, and external systemic patterns that characterize cities.

A second and less oblique theoretical implication is that effective explanations of the redistribution of political power seem to rest ultimately on those "integrating forces"[44] represented by political parties, extra local institutions (e.g., national unions and reform movements), organizational manifestations of a more distributive class structure (e.g., cooperatives, associations of small entrepreneurs, a professional civil service, etc.), and, doubtless, others not addressed here. But such institutions do not promote "democratization" in the normative sense of the word. As Horowitz observes: "The redistribution of power is not necessarily more democratic because it is based in cities, but it must be more facile and opportunistic (i.e., responsive to the will of the people) to survive."[45]

And this raises a third theoretical implication-problem concerning how we are to conceptualize the dimensions of political change. Since an elitist-to-pluralist gradient does not capture the effective range of possibilities, we need better-informed typologies. Alternatively, it may be useful to think of the distribution of power and benefits in terms of curvilinear functions similar to income distribution and expressible in numerical coefficients. Undoubtedly, this poses some tough problems at the operational level, but some precedents exist[46] and others may be derived from the field of welfare economics.

Finally, an implication of equal importance from a methodological and theoretical standpoint concerns the unit of analysis employed in research into Latin American urban politics. As dependency theorists have argued vigorously and as the findings here confirm, the Latin American city-region or nation-state does not provide an appropriate or comprehensive unit of analysis when we are concerned with economic and political changes that often stem from an international system of stratification.[47] Efforts to trace the origins and consequences of forces affecting politics and development in Latin America that focus exclusively on *either* the city-region (or nation-state) or government and corporate institutions of the advanced countries necessarily exclude key aspects of the transactional flow of influences. It is not suggested that the future researcher must "do everything" or follow the vacuous directive of "looking at the total system" to correct this myopia. More practically, what can and should be done is to delineate a *transnational unit of analysis* and follow it with respect to delimited issues. Illustratively, observation of a Latin American city may suggest that certain foreign-owned industries or commercial enterprises have important effects on the local economy—say on labor-force distribution and wages, concentration of ownership, monopolization, decision-making priorities, and so on. To deal effectively with this situation, the researcher needs to trace not only local repercussions but also national ones to determine the conditions and trade-offs of foreign entrance into the particular region, and he needs to trace the international level or institutional headquarters to determine policies and purposes of the transnational enterprise. The same unit or model would appear to be equally applicable to governmental influences in the areas of trade, development loans, and so forth. It may be that current renditions of dependency theory, in an effort to balance the surfeit of intranational analyses, have overemphasized the determinacy of influences from the top that work their way down through a nested set of metropolis-satellite relations. Certainly national and regional political forces are also at work and contribute uniquely to specific developmental policies. But, ultimately, this question is an empirical one that can be addressed through the adoption of a transnational unit of analysis.

Conclusion

Looking back over this discussion, I feel I may have left the reader with an unduly tentative or equivocal set of observations. However, certain conclusions may be drawn with assurance.

The uncoded summary of studies in table 16 organizes much of the available evidence and provides a tentative overview subject to elaboration, analysis, and alternative coding. The present "tests" of a series of hypotheses are indecisive but provide a baseline for subsequent analyses. While the evidence, such as it is, appears to support both the propositions that predict more competitive power arrangements coming in train with urbanization and the interpretation of these arrangements as a new synthesis of competitive elite alliances and perpetuated inequalities, this very ambiguity testifies that current conceptualization and research do not go to the heart of the issue; that is, they are not yet equipped to answer questions about the structure of representation versus manipulation or accumulative versus distributive inequalities. If one may draw inferences from the evidence, however, it would appear that the pivotal proposition 6 is best supported. The emergence of new urban elites based on alliances among the class interests of landowners, industrialists, exporters, development-minded politicians, and foreign investors has at least perpetuated, if not exacerbated, earlier structures of inequality. Nowhere do we encounter evidence of a net gain in the power or privilege of the peasantry and the urban worker.

Understanding, then, that the increased political competition we are observing is a competition largely among elites (whose internal differences may indirectly benefit nonelite groups), we can identify certain factors associated with this change. Attention was called to the role of "integrating institutions" such as political parties, vertical ties to the national-international system, and patterns of class structure. Let me suggest that a parsimonious interpretation of these and related factors centers on the *vertical integration of cities in a national-international stratified, though transactive, system.* It is perhaps a basis for broader generalization that similar interpretations have been advanced for changing structures of power in North American cities.[48] Assuming that this line of thinking may have potential, we conclude the discussion with a suggestion on methodological implementation.

6 Conclusion

The process of urbanization in developing countries has been evaluated from two different perspectives. For one, urbanization is a correlate of industrialization and, more generally, modernization. As such, it constitutes both an impulse and a reflection of dynamic nationhood. For another, urbanization, as it occurs today, is a sign of the growing imbalances of underdeveloped economies. Urban growth is not a sign of national progress; on the contrary, it lies at the core of the circle of excessive centralization, inequality, and economic stagnation.

The first (classic) viewpoint has had to yield in the face of overwhelming evidence that underdeveloped urbanization is less a consequence of nascent industrialism than of stagnant agriculture. Yet, its proponents still maintain that urban resource concentration will pay off in the long run. It facilitates economies of scale and, thus, makes possible rapid industrial growth. While such developmental strategy is clearly unbalanced, it is argued that countries with scarce resources can ill afford a massive push on all fronts. They must take advantage of those dynamic factors available to them, of which rapid urban growth is a crucial one.[1]

The second (modern) position views rapid urbanization as a factor feeding on the stagnating processes that gave rise to it in the first place. Thus, the solution lies in checking the uncontrolled growth of a few metropolitan centers and concentrating on efficient agricultural production and the development of alternative industrial poles of growth. This is the rationale for current strategies of regional planning and development.[2]

The controversy about the value of urbanization for national development belongs more properly to the realm of planning and economics. The contribution of the preceding chapters lies, however, in describing the structural framework within which past urbanization has occurred and future plans must take place. The second, critical, perspective on urbanization seldom penetrates in detail into the historical arrangements conditioning massive rural-urban migration. The first, favorable, perspective seldom questions the extent to which power arrangements in the city can affect the results of resource concentration.

By looking at historical and ecological settings and at the varying urban structures of power, the preceding chapters warn against sweeping economic prescriptions. Depending on the varying integration of elites and the distribution of power, similar plans of resource concentration or decentralization may yield quite different results. The varying dynamism of cities of similar size and in the same country, such as Monterrey and Guadalajara, documents the importance of political structure for development.

Students of urbanization often note that the political and economic structure of cities cannot be studied apart from the national and even the international system to which they belong. While such an observation is true in Latin America, the converse also holds, namely, that the urban situation is a reflection of and an accurate commentary on the national situation. The array of empirical findings reviewed in the preceding chapters leads to one fundamental conclusion: *the elitist character of urban social structure has remained, despite major processes of differentiation and growth.*

The Iberic conquest and colonization set the framework for the emergence of monopolistic control, distinct class differences, and the absorption of migrant masses without granting them access to effective political power. This early colonial order carried into the republican period with minor modifications until, by the second quarter of this century, its own internal dynamics promoted massive processes of rural-urban migration. Waves of migrants quickly overwhelmed the simple cephalic pattern of earlier years and promoted both social and ecological differentiation. Major cities became polarized into "established" and "marginal" sectors, increasingly isolated from each other. Many observers of the migration process predicted that the movement was destined to subvert in a few years the tight elitist control over political and economic structures.

Evidence from the last decade points, however, to the failure of this result to materialize. Elite control proved more resilient than expected, while new marginal masses proved more adaptable than initially predicted. In bringing together these two sets of results we have tried to cast light over the totality and the mutually reinforcing character of these processes. The stability produced by the fit of orientations between the two great urban sectors is often lost in studies from above or below: research on power structures often leave unanswered the question of potential rebelliousness of the masses; research on marginal populations often leave unanswered the question of potential inability of elites to cope with major changes in the social structure.

Changes have been registered in Latin American cities. Elites have lost their homogeneous character, new powerful groups have claimed their share of control, and new patterns of coalition and elite competition have been added to the old monopolistic arrangement. Yet, underlying all changes in response to social differentiation, the evidence suggests that neither middle nor marginal groups have gained access to power or a voice in fundamental decisions.

The surprising political stability of Latin American cities in the face of rapid growth and perennial economic scarcity is not only the product of elite political skills or mass adaptability but also the integration of the two. Yet, if in the short run this complementarity will guarantee continuing stability, in the long run the growing economic and ecological imbalances will make the requirement of change increasingly evident. Repeated analyses of Latin American economic development suggest that the conditions of neocolonialism and dependency have grown more acute in the post–World War II era. The now classic Prebisch thesis on deteriorating terms of trade, albeit a subject of considerable controversy, has been vastly amplified by studies of structural dependency, trade and aid policies, income distribution, and monopolization.[3]

Without resorting to the sense of inevitability implied in Marx's "iron law of capitalism," it is nevertheless demonstrable that these conditions of neocolonialism and internal colonialism have produced a new and reasonably radical, nationalistic consciousness among certain intellectual and political groups. Contemporary Peru, Panama, and Argentina provide the clearest illustrations of this nationalism, but the mood is even more prevalent, as evidenced by extensive trade agreements with Soviet bloc countries.

Certain elites, most notably in export trade and manufacturing under foreign ownership or licensing, may come to be defined as part of the problem inhibiting indigenous national development. This definition, in turn, may lead to a bifurcation of elites in which the more progressive splinter groups seek alliances with or become accessible to those masses that suffer most under the conditions of internal colonialism. If accurately assessed, the new mood of nationalism may be projected to entail a good deal of realignment among existing coalitions of power. Until the present, and depending on the country and specific circumstances, it has been military officers, professionals and intellectuals, and university students who have taken the lead in revolutionary or reformist enterprises. However, the efforts at rapid change by such groups cannot succeed apart from basic transformations in the nation as a whole. Also crucial to their success are those sources that increase the vulnerability of a previously monolithic order to radical challenges.

Having stressed the firm entrenchment of urban elites, at this point we must shift perspectives and examine the converse problem of potential elite vulnerability. What follows then is a "counter-system" analysis[4] based on available elite studies. To caution against political naïveté, it should be stressed that we are talking about elite *vulnerability,* as opposed to any outright weakness or patent formula for the seizure of power. Sources of vulnerability will have little practical importance unless there are organized groups capable of exploiting these openings. Latin American urban elite studies suggest three more or less distinct sources of vulnerability:

Elite Factionalism. As shown in chapter 5, urban power structures in Latin America have become increasingly differentiated and less cohesive. In many cities elite factions and even broader coalitions are able to rule because certain negotiated arrangements ensure all parties some acceptable share of influence and largesse. For present purposes the essential point is that these arrangements may become unstable. This instability, in turn, suggests that certain powerful groups either may be willing to make concessions to nonelites in order to enhance their support or may be separating from old allies in an attempt to form a new and possibly more representative coalition.

Illustrations are abundant and would include the post-revolutionary PRI in Mexico and the contemporary Peruvian military government. More germane, perhaps, would be cases similar to the Cauca Valley in Colombia, where serious cleavages divide large agricultural landowning interests and more progressive urban industrialists. Some years ago the latter group, in opposition to the former, successfully established a regional development corporation, elitist in control but dedicated to broad infrastructure works. Advocates of land reform have attempted to trade their support for the precariously financed corporation in exchange for greater services (e.g., flood control, electricity) and land reform.

It should be stressed, however, that few well-documented successes exist in this area. Part of the reason may well be that short-run concessions are soon forgotten once elite groups secure a renegotiated position of power. Nevertheless, this strategy is always available and may be more effective when counterelite groups are able to identify the likely numerous and serious sources of elite cleavage.

Elite Dependence. Urban and regional elites (and to some extent national ones) are dependent upon external sources of support. Mexico provides a choice illustration. In the highly centralized party-government system local elites depend heavily on federal budgetary support, which tends to be correlated with both regional developmental potential and demonstrated commitment or achievement. Similarly, the career mobility of public officials depends on their track record in the promotion of developmental projects and the maintenance of political peace. In both respects local officials are notably vulnerable to opposition. Serious local strikes or demonstrations regularly result in the federal ouster of governors and mayors. Regions noted for a lack of tranquillity are systematically disadvantaged in the federal largesse. This situation makes it essential for ambitious politicians and private interests desirous of services to accede to serious counterelite demands. In their attempts to attract external loans and investments national elites may be similarly compromised by the threat of "instability."

There is a second aspect of elite dependency, namely, that for their realization of goals and system-legitimizing purposes elite policies require some form of mass cooperation. Obviously, coercion goes a long way in helping to assure the success of elite-sponsored strategies. But, to a greater or lesser extent, noncompliance (e.g., strikes, sit-downs, slowdowns, sabotage, etc.) is always available. Once again, while this kind of dependency may not be a great disadvantage, it does provide another wedge available to groups that would seek to promote structural changes.

The Fragility of Mystification. All social classes propagate certain self-serving myths about their own motives and respectability. Marxist theory uses the term *mystification* to refer to those self-interested constructions of social reality fostered by the ruling classes in their own defense and justification. The difficulty with mystification, however, is that it requires a high degree of mass consensus in order to function effectively. Resting on such a base, it is conversely subject to dissolution once formerly agreed upon normative definitions become political issues. The importance of the politicization of such basic questions is that elites, no longer able to rely on consensual normative support of their interests, must necessarily turn to more overt and coercive measures, which carry greater risks.

The point takes us back to the relation between elite use of force and cognitive inhibition of popular radicalism. Under certain historical circumstances, swift repression may reinforce the "impregnable" image of the existing order and, in fact, strengthen its legitimacy vis-à-vis its own middle- and upper-class constituency. Under others, however, a circle of progressive loss of credibility, followed by increasingly blatant repression, can effectively weaken elite hold of power and facilitate counterelite mobilization of the masses. It is in these circumstances that Merriam's dictum applies: "power is not strongest when it uses violence, but weakest."[5] The last instance of undebated revolutionary takeover in the hemisphere—Cuba—vividly documents this possibility. The rebel army and the underground mobilized to their own advantage the increasingly desperate and cruel use of force by the Batista regime.[6]

For a variety of reasons the demystification process is spreading rapidly in Latin America. We could not begin to list and evaluate the sources of this change here, but, certainly, among major factors we would have to include the following: a stronger and increasingly sophisticated nationalism in the hemisphere, the successful seizure of power by socialist and left-of-center elites and the subsequent experimenting with original social change strategies, and recent military and economic setbacks suffered by the United States in maintaining its interests abroad. Added to these trends is a rapid resurgence of intellectual interest in the demystifying theories of dependency. Few writers can match the precision debunking of Illich:

> Underdevelopment as a state of mind occurs when mass needs are converted to the demand for new brands of packaged solutions which are forever beyond the reach of the majority. Underdevelopment in this sense is rising rapidly even in countries where the supply of classrooms, calories, cars, and clinics is also rising. The ruling groups in these countries build up services which have been designed for an affluent culture; once they have monopolized demand in this way, they can never satisfy majority needs ... The only way to reverse the disastrous trend to increasing underdevelopment, hard as it is, is to learn to laugh at accepted solutions in order to change the demands which make them necessary.[7]

Assuming that challenges to the modus operandi or public image of the elite are mounted effectively, one may see typical responses either of opening-wedge concessions or of greater defensiveness. Both, however, tend to strengthen the position of counterelites. Concessions may, under certain circumstances, produce an accumulating sense of political efficacy, not to mention substantive gains. Defensiveness, on the other hand, may lead to greater exposure, confrontations, and possibly even greater concessions following protracted conflict. In all events, an elite forced into defending its interests will thereby begin spending its political capital, which is never inexhaustible.

Finally, having reviewed results of past empirical studies in Latin American cities, it remains for us to examine which research topics deserve primary emphasis in the future. The following two are not exhaustive of all important concerns, but they merit special attention. Both focus on structural issues of power exchange and dependence, the first by examining a key manifestation internal to the city, the second by concentrating explicitly on external determinants.

Urban Land Markets. The issue of urban land use and land prices is still a vital and neglected topic. Research problems here are the evolution of land prices in time and across regions and its relations with broader social and economic phenomena; the official land policy and regulating mechanisms; the fate of squatter invasions and their relations with alternative uses and interests on the land; the major influences and controls on the urban land market and current speculative methods; and the gradient of land prices and its specific determinants in each city.

Urban land markets are not the primary, but a key intervening, variable in processes leading to the physical manifestations of poverty in Latin America. They are determined by economic phenomena of a national and international order but, in turn, directly affect the housing options open to the poor and, hence, the likelihood of illegal settlement. Despite being a logical entry point for studies of the housing economy of marginal masses, research has usually concentrated on the specific behavior of the poor without full comprehension of its broader structural determinants.

The External Setting. Statements on the need to place urban studies within a broad national and international framework have seldom been accompanied by relevant research pursuits. The topic is probably the most general and most important one for future investigation. If the present volume has attempted to integrate current knowledge of structural features of Latin American cities, an urgent need to understand the network of relationships linking the city to external institutions still remains. Four such sets of relations deserve mention:

1. Relations between the city and its hinterland. The latter includes satellite towns, major sources of urban-bound migration, and the rural periphery. Relevant problems include the social and political interactions between the city and its rural/town hinterland, participation of elites and masses in these interactions, and the extent to which economic and political changes in the city affect the surrounding area and vice versa.

2. Relations among different cities within the national system. This requires examination of national urban hierarchies; the integration of primary, secondary, and tertiary centers; and the network of political and economic relationships linking

them. Equally important is the specific manner in which this interurban integration is effected: whether relations of larger to smaller centers are monopolistic and exploitative; whether, on the contrary, smaller cities can maintain diversified relations with larger centers; and whether the hierarchy of cities is integrated via a plurality of echelons or whether smaller cities are directly linked with one or a few national centers.

3. Relations between the city and the national political and economic order. Obviously, there are wide differences in the relative structural location of cities vis-à-vis national centers. A city like Monterrey, despite its size and industrial dynamism, offers a clear separation of local and national structures and decision-making bodies. Thus, it is possible to speak of patterns of conflict and/or cooperation between national and local institutions. At the other extreme, a city like San Salvador, with half the population of Monterrey, cannot be clearly differentiated from the national system. Being the capital of a small country, San Salvador has urban and national institutions that overlap to such an extent that it is difficult to speak of an autonomous urban structure.[8]

4. Relations between the city and international concerns. These include direct relations of city government with international cultural and welfare organizations, foreign foundations, and financial institutions. More importantly, however, they include relations between the city and international industrial and financial concerns. Crucial questions here are the ability of the local system to attract, reject, and regulate foreign concerns and the impact that their presence and investments have on such phenomena as rural migration, the land market, urban ecology, and class structure.

This treatise on the Latin American city ends with the somewhat paradoxical conclusion that the city per se is not the appropriate unit of analysis for future urban research. Rather, our findings suggest the need for a unit of analysis based on distinctive *vertically integrated processes* passing through a network of dimensions from the international level to the urban hinterland. The four nodes of the network *within* such a unit of analysis are the international, national, urban/regional, and urban hinterland. In substantive applications, specific actors and influences would be identified and followed through each level. Such an integrative perspective is conceptually defined by a focus on *patterns of influence and power,* rather than on concrete geographic locations.

Illustrative is the above question of dependent capitalism. To understand fully the influence of this factor on the city, it is necessary to look beyond the urban confines. A vertically integrated unit of analysis compels us to raise questions about the aims of multinational corporations whose subsidiaries appear on the local scene: why the particular site was selected, what conditions or concessions attended its entrance into the nation, how did the decision articulate with national development strategies, what has been its impact on the urban economy (e.g., in terms of monopolization, employment, income distribution, and indigenous capital formation), how has it affected the balance of political power locally, and how has it affected migration, markets, and so forth.

So "urban" an issue as the above-cited problem of land allocation and use is also imperfectly understood unless one brings to bear the demand pressure built by migration from the urban hinterland and other cities, the actions of governmental regulating bodies and legal definitions of private property at the national level, and the impact of foreign aid and corporate investment on the local use and demand for land.

While multinational corporate entities and patterns of land use are key but isolated illustrations, the same case and the same vertically integrated analytic framework is applicable to most of the major problems confronting the Latin American city today.

Notes

1. Introduction

1. See, for example, Terry N. Clark, ed., *Comparative Community Politics;* Ira Lapidus, ed., *Middle Eastern Cities;* William Hanna and Judith Hanna, *Urban Dynamics in Black Africa; Latin American Urban Research,* vols. 1–4. Recent journals on the subject include *Comparative Urban Research* and *New Atlantis.*
2. Scott Greer, *The Emerging City.*
3. For example, Robert T. Daland, ed., *Comparative Urban Research;* Guillermo Geisse and Jorge Hardoy, eds., *Latin American Urban Research,* vol. 2, *Regional and Urban Development Policies.*

2. The Economy and Ecology of Urban Poverty

1. Jorge Hardoy, "Dos mil años de urbanización en América Latina," in *La urbanización en América Latina,* ed. Jorge Hardoy and Carlos Tobar; Jorge Hardoy and Carmen Aranovich, "Cuadro comparativo de los centros de colonización española existentes en 1580 y 1630," *Desarrollo Económico* 7, no. 27 (1967): 349–360; Charles Gibson, *The Aztecs under Spanish Rule;* Ralph Gakenheimer, "The Peruvian City of the Sixteenth Century," in *The Urban Explosion in Latin America,* ed. Glenn H. Beyer; Richard Morse, "Some Characteristics of Latin American Urban History," *American Historical Review* 67, no. 2 (1962): 317–338; Richard Morse, "Trends and Issues in Latin American Urban Research, 1965–1970," *Latin American Research Review* 6, no. 1 (Spring 1971): 3–52, continued in no. 2 (Summer 1971): 19–75.
2. Morse, "Trends and Issues"; Jorge Hardoy, "El rol de la ciudad en la modernización de América Latina," in *Las ciudades en América Latina,* ed. Jorge Hardoy; Gakenheimer, "The Peruvian City."
3. Gibson, *The Aztecs;* Gakenheimer, "The Peruvian City"; Hardoy, "El rol."
4. Hardoy, "Dos mil años"; George Foster, *Culture and Conquest.*
5. Gakenheimer, "The Peruvian City"; Morse, "Trends and Issues."

6. Hardoy, "Dos mil años."

7. Morse, "Some Characteristics"; Gakenheimer, "The Peruvian City."

8. Hardoy, "Dos mil años"; Gakenheimer, "The Peruvian City."

9. Jorge Hardoy, "La influencia del urbanismo indígena en la localización y trazado de las ciudades coloniales," quoted in Morse, "Trends and Issues."

10. Hardoy, "Dos mil años"; Morse, "Trends and Issues"; Herminio Portell Vila, *Historia de Cuba en sus relaciones con EE. UU. y España.*

11. Hardoy, "Dos mil años"; Hardoy and Aranovich, "Cuadro comparativo."

12. Morse, "Some Characteristics."

13. Bernardo de Vargas Machuca, *Milicia y descripción de las Indias;* Rafael Altamira, *A History of Spain;* Clarence H. Haring, *The Spanish Empire in America.*

14. Haring, *The Spanish Empire.* An interesting account of the origins of elite families in Buenos Aires stemming from this custom is found in Juan Sebreli, *Apogeo y ocaso de los Anchorena.*

15. Gakenheimer, "The Peruvian City."

16. Portell Vila, *Historia de Cuba;* Gibson, *The Aztecs.*

17. Gakenheimer, "The Peruvian City."

18. Hardoy, "Dos mil años."

19. Ibid.

20. Charles Gibson, "Spanish-Indian Institutions and Colonial Urbanism in New Spain," in *El proceso de urbanización en América desde sus orígenes hasta nuestros días,* ed. Jorge Hardoy and R. Schaedel; Juan Sebreli, *Buenos Aires.*

21. Hardoy, "Dos mil años."

22. Jorge Hardoy, "El paisaje urbano de América del Sur," in *Las ciudades,* ed. Jorge Hardoy; Peter Amato, "Papel de la elite y patrones de asentamiento en la ciudad latinoamericana," *Revista de la Sociedad Interamericana de Planificación* 4 (March–June 1970): 22–34; Leo F. Schnore, "On the Spatial Structure of Cities in the Two Americas," in *The Study of Urbanization,* ed. Philip M. Hauser and Leo F. Schnore.

23. Hardoy, "Dos mil años."

24. Ibid., p. 52.

25. Hardoy, "El paisaje urbano"; Amato, "Papel de la elite"; Gino Germani, "Hacía una democracia de masas," in *Argentina,* ed. Torcuato Di-Tella, Gino Germani, and Jorge Graciarena.

26. Hardoy, "El rol."

27. Amato, "Papel de la elite"; Hardoy, "El paisaje urbano."

28. Homer Hoyt, *The Structure and Growth of Residential Neighborhood in American Cities;* Homer Hoyt, "Recent Distortions of Classical Models of Urban Structure," *Land Economics* 40 (May 1964): 199–212.

29. Amato, "Papel de la elite"; Joaquin Errasuriz and Josefina Rossetti, *Tipología habitacional del Gran Santiago;* Guillermo Geisse, "La desigualdad de los ingresos: Punto de partida del círculo de la pobreza urbana."

30. Luis Uniquel, *La dinámica del crecimiento de la Ciudad de México;* Sebreli, *Buenos Aires;* José Bacigalupo, "Proceso de urbanización en la

Argentina," in *La urbanización*, ed. Jorge Hardoy and Carlos Tobar.

31. Peter Amato, *An Analysis of the Changing Patterns of Elite Residential Areas in Bogotá, Colombia.*

32. Alejandro Portes, "Urbanization and Politics in Latin America," *Social Science Quarterly* 52 (December 1971): 697–720.

33. Portes, "Urbanization and Politics"; Andrew Gunder Frank, "Urban Poverty in Latin America," in *Masses in Latin America*, ed. Irving L. Horowitz; Irving L. Horowitz, *Three Worlds of Development*; Frederick Pike, "Aspects of Class Relations in Chile, 1850–1860," in *Latin America*, ed. James Petras and Maurice Zeitlin.

34. Julio Cotler, "The Mechanics of Internal Domination and Social Change in Peru," *Studies in Comparative International Development* 12 (1967–1968): 229–246; Anibal Quijano, "Dependencia, cambio social y urbanización en América Latina"; José Nun, "Superpoblación relativa, ejercito industrial de reserva y masa marginal," *Revista Latinoamericana de Sociología* 5 (July 1969): 178–236.

35. Anthony Leeds, "The Significant Variables Determining the Character of Squatter Settlements," *América Latina* 12 (July–September 1969): 44–86.

36. Leeds, "The Significant Variables"; Jorge Hardoy, "Política urbanística y política del suelo urbano y suburbano en América Latina," in *Las ciudades*, ed. Jorge Hardoy.

37. C. A. Frankenhoff, "Elements of an Economic Model for Slums in a Developing Economy," *Economic Development and Cultural Change* 16, no. 1 (1967): 27–35.

38. John F. C. Turner, "Uncontrolled Urban Settlement: Problems and Policies," *International Social Development Review* 1 (1968): 107–130.

39. Barbara Ward, "The Uses of Prosperity," *Saturday Review*, August 29, 1964, pp. 191–192.

40. Gunnar Myrdal, *Rich Lands and Poor.* On the dependence of demographic movements on the broader economic infrastructure, see Anibal Quijano, "La urbanización de la sociedad en Latinoamérica," *Revista Mexicana de Sociología* 39 (October–December 1967): 669–703.

41. Oscar Lewis, "The Culture of Poverty," *Scientific American* 215 (October 1966): 19–25; Oscar Lewis, *Antropología de la pobreza*; Marshall Clinard, "Urbanization, Urbanism, and Deviant Behavior in Puerto Rico," in *Social Change and Public Policy*, ed. Social Science Research Center; Roger Vekemans and Ismael Fuenzalida, "El concepto de la marginalidad," in *Marginalidad en América Latina*, ed. DESAL.

42. Leeds, "The Significant Variables."

43. William Mangin, "Latin American Squatter Settlements: A Problem and a Solution," *Latin American Research Review* 2 (Summer 1967): 65–98; Bryan Roberts, "The Social Organization of Low-Income Urban Families," in *Crucifixion by Power*, by Richard Newbold Adams; Larissa Lomnitz, "The Social and Economic Organization of a Mexican Shantytown," in *Latin American Urban Research*, vol. 4, ed. Wayne A. Cornelius and Felicity M. Trueblood.

44. Celso Furtado, *Development and Underdevelopment*; Celso Furtado, *Dialéctica del desarrollo*; Myrdal, *Rich Lands and Poor*; Hla Myint, The

Economics of the Developing Countries; Albert Hirschman, *The Strategy of Economic Development;* Raúl Prebisch, "Commercial Policy in the Underdeveloped Countries," *American Economic Review* 49 (1959): 251–273.

45. See especially the above-cited works by Jorge Hardoy, as well as others published by the Center for Urban and Regional Studies (CEUR) of the Instituto Torcuato DiTella in Buenos Aires and those of the Interdisciplinary Center for Urban Development (CIDU) in Santiago. The works of Amato, Turner, and Gakenheimer also deserve mention in this regard.

46. Jorge Hardoy, Raúl Basaldua, and Oscar Moreno, *Política de la tierra urbana y mecanismos para su regulación en América del Sur.*

47. Ibid.; Leeds, "The Significant Variables"; Uniquel, *La dinámica.*

48. Amato, "Papel de la elite."

49. Ibid.; Hardoy, "Política urbanística."

50. Hardoy, "Política urbanística"; Elizabeth Leeds, "Forms of 'Squatment' Political Organization: The Politics of Control in Brazil."

51. Hardoy et al., *Política de la tierra.*

52. Ibid.; Unikel, *La dinámica.*

53. Alejandro Portes, "Rationality in the Slum: An Essay on Interpretive Sociology," *Comparative Studies in Society and History* 14, no. 3 (1972): 268–286.

54. Jorge Hardoy, "La ciudad y el campo en América Latina: Un análisis de las relaciones socioeconómicas," in *Las ciudades,* ed. Hardoy; Daniel Goldrich, "Political Organization and the Politicization of the Poblador," *Comparative Political Studies* 3 (July 1970): 176–202.

55. Luis M. Morea, "Vivienda y equipamiento urbano," in *La urbanización,* ed. Hardoy and Tobar.

56. Hardoy et al., *Política de la tierra.*

57. Ibid.; MINVU, "Programa de descentralización del MINVU para 1970–71."

58. CORHABIT, *Operación Sitio 1965–1966;* CORHABIT, *Plan de vivienda popular;* "Plan de la vivienda: Un esfuerzo nacional y popular," *La Nación,* August 20, 1967.

59. Francisco J. Moreno, "Caudillismo: An Interpretation of Its Origins in Chile," in *Conflict and Violence in Latin American Politics,* ed. Francisco J. Moreno and Barbara Mitrani; Portes, "Urbanization and Politics"; Rodolfo Stavenhagen, "Class, Colonialism, and Acculturation," in *Masses in Latin America,* ed. Horowitz.

60. Luis Alberto Sánchez, "Urban Growth and the Latin American Heritage," in *The Urban Explosion,* ed. Beyer; Portes, "Urbanization and Politics"; Ivan Vallier, "Las elites religiosas en América Latina: Catolicismo, liderazgo y cambio social," in *Elites y desarrollo en América Latina,* ed. Seymour M. Lipset and Aldo Solari.

61. Goldrich, "Political Organization"; Goldrich, "Toward the Comparative Study of Politicization in Latin America," in *Contemporary Cultures and Societies of Latin America,* ed. Dwight B. Heath and Richard Newbold Adams; Quijano, "Dependencia."

62. Ward, "The Uses of Prosperity"; Tad Szulc, *Winds of Revolution.*

63. Frankenhoff, "Elements of an Economic Model."

64. R. Hoffmann, N. García, O. Mercado, and F. Uribe, "La marginalidad

urbana," in *Marginalidad en América Latina*, ed. DESAL; Guillermo Rosenbluth, "Problemas socio-económicos de la marginalidad y la integración urbana"; Clinard, "Urbanization."

65. CELADE, *Encuesta sobre inmigración en el Gran Santiago—Informe general*; Harley Browning and Waltraut Feindt, "The Social and Economic Context of Migration to Monterrey, Mexico," in *Latin American Urban Research*, vol. 1, ed. Francine F. Rabinovitz and Felicity M. Trueblood.

66. Portes, "Rationality in the Slum." A study by ECLA characterizes lower-class settlements as representing "the rejection by the city of native or other people who lived in it, who differ from the rest of the urban population more in the degree of their poverty than in their origins," quoted in Frank, "Urban Poverty in Latin America," p. 216.

67. William L. Flinn and James W. Converse, "Eight Assumptions concerning Rural-Urban Migration in Colombia: A Three Shantytowns Test," *Land Economics* 46 (November 1970): 456–464.

68. Roberts, "The Social Organization."

69. Anthony Leeds and Elizabeth Leeds, "Brazil and the Myth of Urban Rurality: Urban Experience, Work, and Values in 'Squatments' of Rio de Janeiro and Lima," in *City and Country in the Third World*, ed. A. J. Field.

70. Alejandro Portes, "The Urban Slum in Chile: Types and Correlates," *Land Economics* 47 (August 1971): 235–248.

71. Turner, "Uncontrolled Urban Settlement"; Charles Abrams, *Squatter Settlements*; ECLA, "La participación de las poblaciones marginales en el crecimiento urbano"; Adolfo Gurrieri, "Situación y perspectivas de la juventud en una población urbana popular."

72. Turner, "Uncontrolled Urban Settlement"; Portes, "The Urban Slum."

73. Flinn and Converse, "Eight Assumptions"; Abrams, *Squatter Settlements*.

74. Leeds, "Forms of 'Squatment' Political Organization."

75. Rosenbluth, "Problemas socio-económicos."

76. Mangin, "Latin American Squatter Settlements"; Henry Dietz, "Urban Squatter Settlements in Peru: A Case History and Analysis," *Journal of Inter-American Studies* 11 (July 1969): 353–370; Goldrich, "Political Organization"; Daniel Goldrich, Raymond B. Pratt, and Charles R. Schuller, "The Political Integration of Lower-Class Urban Settlements in Chile and Peru," *Studies in Comparative International Development* 3 (1967–1968): 3–22.

77. Flinn and Converse, "Eight Assumptions"; Ramiro Cardona, "Investigación nacional sobre marginalidad urbana en Colombia," *América Latina* 11 (October–December 1968): 128–134; Mangin, "Latin American Squatter Settlements"; Elsa Usandizaga and A. Eugene Havens, *Tres barrios de invasión*; Roberts, "The Social Organization."

78. Lucy Behrman, "Political Development and Secularization in Two Chilean Urban Communities," *Comparative Politics* 4 (January 1972): 269–280.

79. Flinn and Converse, "Eight Assumptions"; Roberts, "The Social Organization"; Turner, "Uncontrolled Urban Settlement"; Edward Wilkus, "Urban Stratification: A Case Study of Mexico City"; Fundación Salvadoreña de Desarrollo y Vivienda, "Bases para un proyecto de investigación evaluativa sobre cambio social y económico derivado de los proyec-

tos de la fundación"; Roland H. Ebel, "The Decision-Making Process in San Salvador," in *Latin American Urban Research*, vol. 1, ed. Francine F. Rabinovitz and Felicity M. Trueblood.

80. Portes, "The Urban Slum."

81. Ibid.; Leeds, "The Significant Variables."

82. Leeds, "Forms of 'Squatment' Political Organization"; Frank, "Urban Poverty."

83. Mangin, "Latin American Squatter Settlements"; Turner, "Uncontrolled Urban Settlement."

84. Turner, "Uncontrolled Urban Settlement."

85. Goldrich et al., "The Political Integration"; Goldrich, "Political Organization."

86. Hoyt, *The Structure*.

87. Flinn and Converse, "Eight Assumptions"; Roberts, "The Social Organization"; Talton F. Ray, *The Politics of the Barrios of Venezuela*; Mangin, "Latin American Squatter Settlements"; Alejandro Portes, *Cuatro poblaciones*.

88. Turner, "Uncontrolled Urban Settlement."

89. Alejandro Portes, "Los grupos urbanos marginados: Nuevo intento de explicación," *APORTES* 18 (October 1970): 131–147.

90. Portes, *Cuatro poblaciones*.

91. Turner, "Uncontrolled Urban Settlement."

92. Mangin, "Latin American Squatter Settlements."

93. Browning and Feindt, "The Social and Economic Context"; Jorge Balán, "Are Farmers' Sons Handicapped in the City?" *Rural Sociology* 33, no. 2 (1968): 160–174.

94. Browning and Feindt, "The Social and Economic Context."

95. Amato, "Papel de la elite"; Sebreli, *Buenos Aires*.

96. Hardoy et al., *Política de la tierra*; Unikel, *La dinámica*.

97. Schnore, "On the Spatial Structure."

98. Rosenbluth, "Problemas socio-económicos"; ECLA, "The Social Development of Latin America in the Post-War Period"; Richard Patch, *Life in a "Callejón"*; Oscar Lewis, "The Culture of the 'Vecindad' in Mexico City: Two Case Studies," *Actas del III Congreso Internacional de Americanistas*.

99. The point was first made by Charles Stokes and supported ever since by field researchers ("A Theory of Slums," *Land Economics* 38 [August 1962]: 187–197).

100. Joaquin Errasuriz and Josefina Rossetti, *Tipología habitacional del Gran Santiago*; Flinn and Converse, "Eight Assumptions."

101. Portes, "Urbanization and Politics."

102. ECLA, "Los servicios públicos en una población de erradicación"; Mangin, "Latin American Squatter Settlements."

3. The Politics of Urban Poverty

1. Review and critical comment of this literature are found in Joan Nel-

son, *Migrants, Urban Poverty and Instability in Developing Nations,* and Wayne A. Cornelius, "The Political Sociology of Cityward Migration in Latin America: Toward Empirical Theory," in *Latin American Urban Research,* vol. 1, ed. Francine F. Rabinovitz and Felicity M. Trueblood.

2. The notion originated with the work of Oscar Lewis *(Antropología de la pobreza).* Lewis was less guilty of overgeneralization and characterization of the urban poor in terms given above than his followers and commentators. See, for example, Marshall Clinard, "Urbanization, Urbanism, and Deviant Behavior in Puerto Rico," in *Social Change and Public Policy,* ed. Social Science Research Center, and Peter Marris, "A Report on Urban Renewal in the United States," in *The Urban Condition,* ed. Peter Marris. In Latin America, the notion has been subsumed under the more encompassing term "marginality." See R. Hoffmann, N. García, O. Mercado, and F. Uribe, "La marginalidad urbana," in *Marginalidad en América Latina,* ed. DESAL. For a recent comprehensive critique, see Lisa Peattie, "The Concept of Marginality as Applied to Squatter Settlements," in *Latin American Urban Research,* vol. 4, ed. Wayne A. Cornelius and Felicity M. Trueblood.

3. Elizabeth Leeds, "Forms of 'Squatment' Political Organization: The Politics of Control in Brazil"; William Mangin, "Latin American Squatter Settlements: A Problem and a Solution," *Latin American Research Review* 2 (Summer 1967): 65–98; John F. C. Turner, "Uncontrolled Urban Settlement: Problems and Policies," *International Social Development Review* 1 (1968): 107–130; Daniel Goldrich, "Political Organization and the Politicization of the Poblador," *Comparative Political Studies* 3 (July 1970): 176–202; Talton F. Ray, *The Politics of the Barrios of Venezuela;* Wayne A. Cornelius, "Political Involvement among Low-Income Migrants to Mexico City," in *Poverty and Politics in Urban Mexico,* ed. Wayne A. Cornelius.

4. The estimate is provided by Anthony Leeds, "The Significant Variables Determining the Character of Squatter Settlements," *América Latina* 12 (July–September 1969): 44–86.

5. Ibid.; Anthony Leeds and Elizabeth Leeds, "Brazil and the Myth of Urban Rurality: Urban Experience, Work, and Values in 'Squatments' of Rio de Janeiro and Lima," in *City and Country in the Third World,* ed. A. J. Field.

6. Max Weber, *The Theory of Social and Economic Organization.*

7. José Nun, Juan Carlos Marin, and Miguel Murmis, "La marginalidad en América Latina."

8. Frank Andrews and George Phillips, "The Squatters of Lima: Who They Are and What They Want," *Journal of Developing Areas* 4 (January 1970): 211.

9. Joaquin Errasuriz and Josefina Rossetti, *Tipología habitacional del Gran Santiago;* Torcuato DiTella, Gino Germani, and Jorge Graciarena, eds., *Argentina.* For an impressionistic account of the spatial distribution of working-class groups in Buenos Aires, see Juan Sebreli, *Buenos Aires.*

10. Sandra Powell, "Political Participation in the Barriadas: A Case Study," *Comparative Political Studies* 2 (July 1969): 212. See also Ray, *Politics of the Barrios;* Nelson, *Migrants;* and Wayne A. Cornelius and

Henry Dietz, "Urbanization, Demand-Making, and Political System Overload: Political Participation among the Migrant Poor in Latin American Cities."

11. Daniel Goldrich, Raymond B. Pratt, and Charles R. Schuller, "The Political Integration of Lower-Class Urban Settlements in Chile and Peru," *Studies in Comparative International Development* 3 (1967–1968): 3–22; Alejandro Portes, *Cuatro poblaciones.*

12. Reynaldo A. Tefel, *El infierno de los pobres;* Antonio Ugalde, *The Urbanization Process of a Poor Mexican Neighborhood;* Wayne A. Cornelius, *Political Learning among the Migrant Poor.*

13. MINVU, "Programa de descentralización del MINVU para 1970–71."

14. Goldrich, "Political Organization."

15. James Petras, "Chile: Nationalization, Socioeconomic Change, and Popular Participation"; Jorge Fiori, "Campamento nueva La Habana: Estudio de una experiencia de auto-administración de justicia," *Revista Latinoamericana de Estudios Urbanos Regionales* 3 (April 1973): 84–101.

16. Fiori, "Campamento nueva"; CIDU, "Reivindicación urbana y lucha política: Los campamentos de pobladores en Santiago de Chile," *Revista Latinoamericana de Estudios Urbano Regionales* 2 (November 1972): 55–81.

17. The following section leans heavily on the paper by Elizabeth Leeds ("Forms of 'Squatment' Political Organization"), which is, to my knowledge, the most insightful account of developments in Rio's lower-class settlements.

18. Ibid.; Janice Perlman, "The Fate of Migrants in Rio's Favelas."

19. Leeds, "Forms of 'Squatment' Political Organization."

20. Irving L. Horowitz, "Electoral Politics, Urbanization, and Social Development in Latin America," *Urban Affairs Quarterly* 2 (March 1967): 3–35; Gino Germani, "The City as an Integrating Mechanism," in *The Urban Explosion in Latin America,* ed. Glenn H. Beyer.

21. Carolina María de Jesús, *Child of the Dark;* Ray, *Politics of the Barrios;* Elsa Usandizaga and A. Eugene Havens, *Tres barrios de invasión.*

22. Ramiro Cardona, *Dos barrios de invasión;* Goldrich, "Political Organization."

23. Fritz Heider, *The Psychology of Interpersonal Relations;* Leon Festinger, *A Theory of Cognitive Dissonance;* Elliott Aronson, "Dissonance Theory: Progress and Problems," in *Current Perspectives in Social Psychology,* ed. Edwin P. Hollander and Raymond G. Hunt.

24. Nelson, *Migrants;* François Bourricaud, *Poder y sociedad en el Peru contemporáneo;* Fernando Cardoso, "Le Prolétariat brésilien," *Sociologie du Travail* 4 (1961): 50–65; Gino Germani, "Social and Political Consequences of Mobility," in *Social Structure and Mobility in Economic Development,* ed. Neil J. Smelser and Seymour M. Lipset; Barry Ames, "Bases of Support for Mexico's Dominant Party," *American Political Science Review* 64 (March 1970): 153–167.

25. Seymour M. Lipset, *Political Man;* Maurice Zeitlin, "Economic Insecurity and the Political Attitudes of Cuban Workers," *American Sociological Review* 31 (February 1966): 31–51; Denton Morrison and Allan Steeves, "Deprivation, Discontent, and Social Movement Participation,"

Rural Sociology 32 (December 1967): 414–434; Nelson, *Migrants.*

26. Writers in the Marxist tradition have stressed the importance of this factor for political action under the label "class consciousness." The classic statement on the problem was provided, however, by Max Weber: "The degree in which 'communal action' and possibly 'societal action' emerge from the 'mass actions' of the members of a class is especially linked to the 'transparency' of the connections between the causes and the consequences of the class situation. For however different life changes may be, this fact in itself by no means gives birth to 'class action' . . . The fact of being conditioned and the results of the class situation must be distinctly recognizable" ("Class, Status, and Party," in *From Max Weber,* ed. Hans H. Gerth and C. Wright Mills, p. 184).

27. Mangin, "Latin American Squatter Settlements," p. 84.

28. Ray, *Politics of the Barrios.*

29. Goldrich et al., "Political Integration."

30. Alex Inkeles, *Becoming Modern;* Daniel Lerner, *The Passing of Traditional Society.* In Latin America, Roger Vekemans and Ismael Fuenzalida, "El concepto de marginalidad," in *Marginalidad en América Latina,* ed. DESAL.

31. Goldrich et al., "Political Integration." Findings running contrary to this prediction are presented by Cornelius, "Political Involvement."

32. Hoffmann et al., "La marginalidad urbana," p. 302.

33. A. Cabala Darghan, *Estudio sobre participación dentro de un tipo de asociación voluntaria.*

34. H. E. Freeman, E. Novak, and L. G. Reeder, "Correlates of Membership in Voluntary Associations," *American Sociological Review* 22 (October 1957): 528–533; Charles Wright and Herbert Hyman, "Voluntary Association Memberships of American Adults: Evidence from National Sample Surveys," *American Sociological Review* 23 (June 1958): 284–294.

35. Goldrich et al., "Political Integration."

36. Cornelius, *Political Learning.*

37. Mangin, "Latin American Squatter Settlements"; Tefel, *El infierno,* pp. 128, 157.

38. Cornelius, *Political Learning,* p. 44.

39. Adolfo Gurrieri, "Situación y perspectivas de la juventud en una población urbana popular."

40. Goldrich, "Political Organization," p. 191.

41. William Mangin, *Peasants in Cities;* Henry Dietz, "The Politics of Squatter Assimilation in Lima, Peru"; Goldrich, "Political Organization."

42. Ames, "Bases of Support"; Ugalde, *The Urbanization Process.*

43. Goldrich, "Political Organization."

44. Alejandro Portes, "Political Primitivism, Differential Socialization, and Lower-Class Leftist Radicalism," *American Sociological Review* 36 (October 1971): 820–835.

45. See, for example, the collection of essays in *Latin American Radicalism,* ed. Irving L. Horowitz, Josue de Castro, and John Gerassi, and the older, but more detailed, one in *Latin America,* ed. James Petras and Maurice Zeitlin.

46. In Cuba, for example, support for the revolution among the marginal

population of Havana did not materialize until the Batista forces had been decisively defeated in the field. On the class composition of the revolutionary groups, see Nelson Amaro, *Class and Mass in the Origins of the Cuban Revolution.*

47. The origins of this tendency may perhaps be traced to the militant rhetoric of the *Communist Manifesto* and certain rhetorical passages in Marx's *Capital*. The historical interpretation of the Parisian Commune as rehearsal for the final confrontation to come also lent support to this orientation (Karl Marx, *The Eighteenth Brumaire of Louis Bonaparte*). Journalistic derivations are innumerable. See, for example, Tad Szulc, *Winds of Revolution.*

4. Elites and the Politics of Urban Development

1. Irving L. Horowitz, "Electoral Politics, Urbanization, and Social Development in Latin America," *Urban Affairs Quarterly* 2 (March 1967): 3–35.

2. Gerald Breese, *Urbanization in Newly Developing Countries.*

3. Leo F. Schnore, "On the Spatial Structure of Cities in the Two Americas," in *The Study of Urbanization*, ed. Philip M. Hauser and Leo F. Schnore, pp. 347–398.

4. Don J. Bogue, *The Structure of the Metropolitan Community*; Roland L. Warren, *The Community in America.*

5. Herbert J. Gans, *The Urban Villagers*; Scott Greer, *The Emerging City*; Stanley Milgram, "The Experience of Living in Cities," *Science* 13 (March 1970): 1461–1468.

6. Isidro Vizcaya Canales, *Los origenes de la industrialización de Monterrey, 1867–1920.*

7. Schnore, "On Spatial Structure."

8. Charles Abrams, *Squatter Settlements*; see chapter 2, table 4, for an indication of the extent of this phenomenon in Cali in relation to other Latin American cities.

9. J. P. Powelson, "The Land-Grabbers of Cali," *Reporter*, January 16, 1964, pp. 30–31.

10. Richard M. Bird, *Taxation and Development.*

11. Chapter 3 provides an extended discussion of the way residents of lower class settlements view the problem of urban services and government action in this area.

12. See John Walton, "Development Decision Making: A Comparative Study in Latin America," *American Journal of Sociology* 75 (March 1970): 828–851.

13. William Mangin, "Squatter Settlements," *Scientific American* 217 (October 1967): 21–29; D. L. Bayer, "Urban Peru—Political Action as Sellout," *Transaction* 7 (November 1969): 36, 47–51.

14. Chapter 3 deals in some detail with alternative political perspectives adapted by the urban poor under these circumstances.

15. See Anthony Leeds, "The Significant Variables Determining the

Character of Squatter Settlements," *América Latina* 12 (July–September 1969): 44–86.

5. Structures of Power in Latin American Cities

1. See, e.g., Tad Szulc, *Winds of Revolution*.
2. Seymour M. Lipset, *Political Man*; James S. Coleman, "The Conclusion," in *The Politics of the Developing Areas*, ed. Gabriel A. Almond and James S. Coleman; George Blanksten, "The Politics of Latin America," in *Politics of the Developing Areas*, ed. Almond and Coleman.
3. François Bourricaud, "Structure and Function of the Peruvian Oligarchy," *Studies in Comparative International Development* 2 (1966): 17–31; Julio Cotler, "The Mechanics of Internal Domination and Social Change in Peru," *Studies in Comparative International Development* 12 (1967–1968): 229–246; Luis Ratinoff, "The New Urban Groups: The Middle Classes," in *Elites in Latin America*, ed. Seymour M. Lipset and Aldo Solari.
4. Marvin Olsen, "Rapid Growth as a Destabilizing Force," *Journal of Economic History* 23 (December 1963): 529–552; Lucian W. Pye, "The Political Implications of Urbanization and the Developmental Process," in *The City in the Newly Developing Countries*, ed. Gerald Breese; Russell H. Fitzgibbon, "Measuring Democratic Change in Latin America," *Journal of Politics* 29 (November 1967): 129–166.
5. John Friedmann and Thomas Lackington, "Hyperurbanization and National Development in Chile," *Urban Affairs Quarterly* 2 (June 1967): 13–21; Gino Germani, "The City as an Integrating Mechanism," in *The Urban Explosion in Latin America*, ed. Glenn H. Beyer; Wayne A. Cornelius, "Urbanization as an Agent of Political Instability: The Case of Mexico," *American Political Science Review* 63 (September 1969): 833–857; Seymour M. Lipset and Stein Rokkan, *Party Systems and Voter Alignments*.
6. Francine F. Rabinovitz, "Sound and Fury Signifying Nothing: A Review of Community Power Research in Latin America," *Urban Affairs Quarterly* 3 (March 1968): 111–122.
7. Ibid., p. 112.
8. Ibid., p. 113.
9. John Friedmann, "The Role of Cities in National Development," *American Behavioral Scientist* 12 (May–June 1969): 13–21; Irving L. Horowitz, "Electoral Politics, Urbanization, and Social Development in Latin America," in *Latin American Radicalism*, ed. Irving L. Horowitz, Josue de Castro, and John Gerassi; Robert T. Daland, "Urbanization Policy and Political Development in Latin America," *American Behavioral Scientist* 12 (May–June 1969): 22–33.
10. Friedmann, "Role of Cities," p. 15.
11. Horowitz, "Electoral Politics."
12. Fernando Cardoso, "Entrepreneurial Elites in Latin America," *Studies in Comparative International Development* 2 (1966): 147–158.
13. Friedmann, "Role of Cities."

14. Cardoso, "Entrepreneurial Elites in Latin America."

15. Ratinoff, "The New Urban Groups."

16. Daland, "Urbanization Policy and Political Development," p. 26.

17. Raoul Naroll, Data Quality Control.

18. Michael Aiken, "The Distribution of Community Power: Structural Bases and Social Consequences," in The Structure of Community Power, ed. Michael Aiken and Paul E. Mott; Claire W. Gilbert, "Community Power and Decision-Making: A Quantitative Examination of Previous Research," in Community Structure and Decision-Making, ed. Terry N. Clark; Claire W. Gilbert, Community Power Structure; John Walton, "Substance and Artifact: The Current Status of Research on Community Power Structure," American Journal of Sociology 71 (January 1966): 430–438; John Walton, "A Systematic Survey of Community Power Research," in The Structure of Community Power, ed. Aiken and Mott.

19. Norman E. Whitten, "Power Structure and Sociocultural Change in Latin American Communities," Social Forces 43 (March 1965): 320–329; T. L. Norris, "Decision-Making Activity Sequences in a Hacienda Community," Human Organization 12 (1953): 26–30; Antonio Ugalde, "Contemporary Mexico: From Hacienda to PRI, Political Leadership in a Zapotec Village," in The Caciques, ed. Robert Kern and Ronald Dokart.

20. Aiken and Mott, eds., The Structure of Community Power; Clark, ed., Community Structure; Willis D. Hawley and Frederick M. Wirt, The Search for Community Power.

21. Walton, "Substance and Artifact"; Gilbert, "Community Power and Decision-Making"; Gilbert, Community Power Structure; Aiken, "The Distribution of Community Power"; John W. Curtis and James Petras, "Community Power, Power Studies, and the Sociology of Knowledge," Human Organization 29 (Fall 1970): 204–218; S. H. Hildahl, "A Note on '. . . A Note on the Sociology of Knowledge,'" Sociological Quarterly 11 (September 1970): 405–415.

22. The twenty studies appearing in table 16 in chronological order of appearance are: Orin Klapp and L. Vincent Padgett, "Power and Decision-Making in a Mexican Border City," American Journal of Sociology 65 (January 1960): 400–406; William V. D'Antonio and William H. Form, Influentials in Two Border Cities; Cole Blasier, "Power and Social Change in Colombia: The Cauca Valley," Journal of Inter-American Studies 8 (July 1966): 399–425; D. E. W. Holden, "La estructura del liderazgo y sus características en una comunidad de Costa Rica," Journal of Inter-American Studies 8 (January 1966): 129–141; H. T. Edwards, "Power Structure and Its Communication Behavior in San José, Costa Rica," Journal of Inter-American Studies 8 (July 1966): 236–247; L. Vincent Padgett, "The Power Structure of Cali"; David Dent, "Oligarchy and Power Structure in Urban Colombia: The Case of Cali"; Lawrence S. Graham, Politics in a Mexican Community; Gary Hoskin, "Power Structure in a Venezuelan Town: The Case of San Cristóbal," in Case Studies in Social Power, ed. Hans-Dieter Evers; Roland H. Ebel, "The Decision-Making Process in San Salvador"; Marvin Alisky, "Power Structure and Decision-Making in Nogales, Sonora"; H. E. Torres-Trueba, "Factionalism in a Mexican Municipio: A Preliminary Study of the Political, Economic, and Religious Expressions of

Factionalism in Zacapoaxtla, Puebla," *Sociologus* 19 (1969): 134–152; F. H. Forni, "The Decision-Making System in Two Small Communities in Argentina"; Antonio Ugalde, *Power and Conflict in a Mexican Community;* Delbert G. Miller, *International Community Power Structures;* George F. Drake, *Elites and Voluntary Associations;* John Walton, "Development Decision-Making: A Comparative Study in Latin America," *American Journal of Sociology* 75 (March 1970): 828–851; John Walton, "Political Development and Economic Development: A Regional Assessment of Contemporary Theories," *Studies in Comparative International Development* 7 (Spring 1972): 39–63; Richard R. Fagen and William S. Tuohy, *Politics and Privilege in a Mexican City;* José F. Ocampo, *Dominio de clase en la ciudad colombiana;* David Dent, "Community Cooperation in Colombia: A Comparative Study of Public-Private Sector Relationships in Two Urban Centers"; Carlos Dávila and Enrique Ogliastri, "Elite y desarrollo: Un estudio en Bucaramanga, Colombia"; Enrique Ogliastri, "Elite, Class, and Power in the Economic Development of a Colombian City: Bucaramanga."

23. Blasier, "Power and Social Change"; Bourricaud, "Structure and Function"; Drake, *Elites and Voluntary Associations;* Graham, *Politics in a Mexican Community;* Ocampo, *Dominio de clase en la ciudad colombiana.*

24. Gabriel A. Almond and James S. Coleman, eds., *The Politics of the Developing Areas;* Seymour M. Lipset, *Political Man;* Russell H. Fitzgibbon, "A Statistical Evaluation of Latin American Democracy," *Western Political Quarterly* 9 (1956): 607–619.

25. Friedmann, "The Role of Cities"; Rabinovitz, "Sound and Fury"; Whitten, "Power Structure and Sociocultural Change."

26. Herman Turk, "Interorganizational Networks in Urban Society: Initial Perspectives and Comparative Research," *American Sociological Review* 35 (February 1970): 1–19; John Walton, "Differential Patterns of Community Power Structure: An Explanation Based on Interdependence," in *Community Structure,* ed. Clark.

27. Walton, "Development Decision-Making."

28. Graham, *Politics in a Mexican Community,* pp. 55–56.

29. Fagen and Tuohy, *Politics and Privilege,* p. 167.

30. Blasier, "Power and Social Change"; Padgett, "The Power Structure of Cali"; Walton, "Development Decision-Making."

31. Dent, "Oligarchy and Power Structure," p. 22.

32. Edwards, "Power Structure and Its Communication Behavior."

33. Torres-Trueba, "Factionalism in a Mexican Municipio."

34. Miller, *International Community Power Structures;* Fagen and Tuohy, *Politics and Privilege;* Dávila and Ogliastri, "Elite y desarrollo."

35. Ebel, "The Decision-Making Process in San Salvador," pp. 33–34.

36. Miller, *International Community Power Structures.*

37. Klapp and Padgett, "Power and Decision-Making in a Mexican Border City."

38. D'Antonio and Form, *Influentials in Two Border Cities.*

39. Ugalde, *Power and Conflict in a Mexican Community.*

40. John Walton and Joyce A. Sween, "Urbanization, Industrialization, and Voting in Mexico: A Longitudinal Analysis of Official and Opposi-

tion Party Support," *Social Science Quarterly* 52 (December 1971): 721–745.

41. Robert A. Dahl, *Who Governs?*; Roscoe C. Martin et al., *Decisions in Syracuse*; Aaron Wildavsky, *Leadership in a Small Town*.

42. Arthur L. Stinchcombe, "Agricultural Enterprise and Rural Class Relations," *American Journal of Sociology* 67 (September 1961): 165–176.

43. Robert R. Alford, "The Political Economy of Health Care: Dynamics without Change," *Politics and Society* 3 (Winter 1972): 127–164.

44. Daland, "Urbanization Policy and Political Development."

45. Horowitz, "Electoral Politics."

46. Edward C. Hayes, *Power Structure and Urban Policy*.

47. Paul Baran, *The Political Economy of Growth*; Andrew Gunder Frank, *Capitalism and Underdevelopment in Latin America*; Theontonio dos Santos, "The Structure of Dependence," *American Economic Review* 50 (May 1970): 231–236; James Petras and Maurice Zeitlin, eds., *Latin America*.

48. Aiken, "The Distribution of Community Power"; Turk, "Interorganizational Networks in Urban Society," pp. 1–19; Walton, "Differential Patterns of Community Power Structure."

6. Conclusion

1. An extensive discussion of this and the opposing point of view is found in Oscar Yujnovsky, "La investigación para el planeamiento del desarrollo urbano en América Latina."

2. Jorge Hardoy, "Urbanization Politics and Urban Reform in Latin America," in *Latin American Urban Research*, vol. 1, ed. Francine F. Rabinovitz and Felicity M. Trueblood.

3. See, for example, David Chaplin, "Industrialization and the Distribution of Wealth in Peru," *Studies in Comparative International Development* 3 (1967–1968): 55–66; Osvaldo Sunkel, "The Structural Background of Development Problems in Latin America," in *Latin America*, ed. Charles Nisbet, pp. 3–37; Celso Furtado, *Economic Development in Latin America*; Teresa Hayter, *Aid as Imperialism*; Dale Johnson, "The National and Progressive Bourgeoisie in Chile," *Studies in Comparative International Development* 4 (1968–1969): 63–86.

4. Gideon Sjoberg and Leonard Cain, "Negative Values, Counter-system Models, and the Analysis of Social Systems," in *Institutions and Social Exchange*, ed. Herman Turk and Richard Simpson.

5. Charles E. Merriam, *Political Power*.

6. Nelson Amaro, *Class and Mass in the Origins of the Cuban Revolution*.

7. Ivan Illich, "Outwitting the Developed Countries," *New York Review of Books*, November 6, 1969.

8. Roland H. Ebel, "The Decision-Making Process in San Salvador," in *Latin American Urban Research*, vol. 1, ed. Francine F. Rabinovitz and Felicity M. Trueblood, pp. 189–213.

Bibliography

Abrams, Charles. *Squatter Settlements: The Problem and the Opportunity.* Report to the U.S. Agency for International Development. Washington, D.C.: Department of Housing and Urban Development, 1965.

Aiken, Michael. "The Distribution of Community Power: Structural Bases and Social Consequences." In *The Structure of Community Power,* edited by Michael Aiken and Paul E. Mott. New York: Random House, 1970.

Aiken, Michael, and Paul E. Mott, eds. *The Structure of Community Power.* New York: Random House, 1970.

Alford, Robert R. "The Political Economy of Health Care: Dynamics without Change." *Politics and Society* 3 (Winter 1972): 127–164.

Alisky, Marvin. "Power Structure and Decision-Making in Nogales, Sonora." Paper presented at the Southwestern Political Science Association Meeting, Houston, Texas, April 1969.

Almond, Gabriel A., and James S. Coleman, eds. *The Politics of the Developing Areas.* Princeton: Princeton University Press, 1960.

Altamira, Rafael. *A History of Spain.* New York: Van Nostrand, 1949.

Amaro, Nelson. *Class and Mass in the Origins of the Cuban Revolution.* Washington University Series in Comparative International Development, no. 10. St. Louis, 1969.

Amato, Peter. *An Analysis of the Changing Patterns of Elite Residential Areas in Bogotá, Colombia.* Ithaca: Cornell University Latin American Dissertation Series, 1968.

———. "Papel de la elite y patrones de asentamiento en la ciudad latino-americana." *Revista de la Sociedad Inter-Americana de Planificación* 4 (March–June 1970): 22–34.

América en cifras 1972: Situación demográfica, estado y movimiento de la población.

Ames, Barry. "Bases of Support for Mexico's Dominant Party." *American Political Science Review* 64 (March 1970): 153–167.

Andrews, Frank, and George Phillips. "The Squatters of Lima: Who They Are and What They Want." *Journal of Developing Areas* 4 (January 1970): 211.

Aronson, Elliott. "Dissonance Theory: Progress and Problems." In *Current Perspectives in Social Psychology*, edited by Edwin P. Hollander and Raymond G. Hunt. 3d ed. New York: Oxford University Press, 1971.

Bacigalupo, José. "Proceso de urbanización en la Argentina." In *La urbanización en América Latina*, edited by Jorge Hardoy and Carlos Tobar. Buenos Aires: Editorial del Instituto, 1969.

Balán, Jorge. "Are Farmers' Sons Handicapped in the City?" *Rural Sociology* 33, no. 2 (1968): 160–174.

Baran, Paul. *The Political Economy of Growth*. New York: Monthly Review Press, 1957.

Bayer, D. L. "Urban Peru—Political Action as Sellout." *Transaction* 7 (November 1969): 36, 47–51.

Behrman, Lucy. "Political Development and Secularization in Two Chilean Urban Communities." *Comparative Politics* 4 (January 1972): 269–280.

Bird, Richard M. *Taxation and Development: Lessons from the Colombian Experience*. Cambridge: Harvard University Press, 1970.

Blanksten, George. "The Politics of Latin America." In *The Politics of the Developing Areas*, edited by Gabriel A. Almond and James S. Coleman. Princeton: Princeton University Press, 1960.

Blasier, Cole. "Power and Social Change in Colombia: The Cauca Valley." *Journal of Inter-American Studies* 8 (July 1966): 399–425.

Bogue, Don J. *The Structure of the Metropolitan Community*. Ann Arbor: Horace H. Rackman School of Graduate Studies, University of Michigan, 1949.

Bourricaud, François. *Poder y sociedad en el Peru contemporáneo*. Buenos Aires: Sur, 1967.

———. "Structure and Function of the Peruvian Oligarchy." *Studies in Comparative International Development* 2 (1966): 17–31.

Breese, Gerald. *Urbanization in Newly Developing Countries*. New York: Prentice-Hall, 1966.

Browning, Harley, and Waltraut Feindt. "The Social and Economic Context of Migration to Monterrey, Mexico." In *Latin American Urban Research*, vol. 1, edited by Francine F. Rabinovitz and Felicity M. Trueblood. Beverly Hills: Sage Publications, 1971.

Cardona, Ramiro. *Dos barrios de invasión*. División de Estudios de Población, Boletín, no. 21. Bogotá: Asociación Colombiana de Facultades de Medicina, 1968.

———. "Investigación nacional sobre marginalidad urbana en Colombia." *América Latina* 11 (October–December 1968): 128–134.

Cardoso, Fernando. "Entrepreneurial Elites in Latin America." *Studies in Comparative International Development* 2 (1966): 147–158.

———. "Le Prolétariat brésilien." *Sociologie du Travail* 4 (1961): 50–65.

CELADE. *Encuesta sobre inmigración en el Gran Santiago—Informe general*. Santiago: CELADE and Universidad de Chile, 1964.

Chaplin, David. "Industrialization and the Distribution of Wealth in Peru." *Studies in Comparative International Development* 3 (1967–1968): 55–66.

CIDU. "Reivindicación urbana y lucha política: Los campamentos de pobladores en Santiago de Chile." *Revista Latinoamericana de Estudios Urbanos Regionales* 2 (November 1972): 55–81.

Clark, Terry N. *Community Structure and Decision-Making: Comparative Analyses.* San Francisco: Chandler, 1968.

——, ed. *Comparative Community Politics.* New York: Halsted Press, Division of John Wiley & Sons, 1974.

Clinard, Marshall. "Urbanization, Urbanism, and Deviant Behavior in Puerto Rico." In *Social Change and Public Policy,* edited by Social Science Research Center. San Juan: University of Puerto Rico, 1968.

Coleman, James S. "The Conclusion." In *The Politics of the Developing Areas,* edited by Gabriel A. Almond and James S. Coleman. Princeton: Princeton University Press, 1960.

Comisión Nacional de la Vivienda (Argentina), ed. *Informe sobre su actuación y plan integral,* vol. 2. Buenos Aires: Ministerio de Trabajo y Previsión, 1957.

CORHABIT. *Operación Sitio 1965–1966.* Santiago: Vera y Gianini, 1966.

——. *Plan de vivienda popular.* Santiago: Corhabit, 1969.

Cornelius, Wayne A. "Political Involvement among Low-Income Migrants to Mexico City." In *Poverty and Politics in Urban Mexico,* edited by Wayne A. Cornelius. Stanford: Stanford University Press, forthcoming.

——. *Political Learning among the Migrant Poor: The Impact of Residential Context.* Sage Professional Papers, Comparative Political Series. Beverly Hills: Sage Publications, 1973.

——. "The Political Sociology of Cityward Migration in Latin America: Toward Empirical Theory." In *Latin American Urban Research,* vol. 1, edited by Francine F. Rabinovitz and Felicity M. Trueblood. Beverly Hills: Sage Publications, 1971.

——. "Urbanization as an Agent of Political Instability: The Case of Mexico." *American Political Science Review* 63 (September 1969): 833–857.

——, and Henry Dietz. "Urbanization, Demand-Making, and Political System Overload: Political Participation among the Migrant Poor in Latin American Cities." Paper presented at the meeting of the American Political Science Association, New Orleans, September 1973.

Corten, Andre. "Como vive la otra mitad de Santo Domingo: Estudio de dualismo estructural." *Caribbean Studies* 4 (1965): 3–19.

Cotler, Julio. "The Mechanics of Internal Domination and Social Change in Peru." *Studies in Comparative International Development* 12 (1967–1968): 229–246.

Cuevas, Marco Antonio. *Análisis de tres áreas marginales de la Ciudad de Guatemala.* Guatemala City: Ministerio de Educación, 1965.

Curtis, John W., and James Petras. "Community Power, Power Studies, and the Sociology of Knowledge." *Human Organization* 29 (Fall 1970): 204–218.

Dahl, Robert A. *Who Governs? Democracy and Power in an American City.* New Haven: Yale University Press, 1961.

Daland, Robert T., ed. *Comparative Urban Research: The Administration and Politics of Cities.* Beverly Hills: Sage Publications, 1969.

———. "Urbanization Policy and Political Development in Latin America." *American Behavioral Scientist* 12 (May–June 1969): 22–33.

D'Antonio, William V., and William H. Form. *Influentials in Two Border Cities: A Study in Community Decision-Making.* Notre Dame: University of Notre Dame Press, 1965.

Darghan, A. Cabala. *Estudio sobre participación dentro de un tipo de asociación voluntaria: Junta de Vecinos.* Santiago: Consejería Nacional de Promoción Popular, División de Estudios, 1968.

Dávila, Carlos, and Enrique Ogliastri. "Elite y desarrollo: Un estudio en Bucaramanga, Colombia." Report to the Colombian Council of Scientific Research (Colciencias), Bogotá, December 1972.

Davis, Kingsley. *World Urbanization 1950–1970, vol. 1: Basic Data for Cities, Countries, and Regions.* Population Monograph Series, no. 4. Berkeley: University of California Press, 1969.

de Jesús, Carolina María. *Child of the Dark.* New York: Dutton, 1962.

Demographic Yearbook, 1971. New York: Statistical Office of the United Nations, 1972.

Dent, David. "Community Cooperation in Colombia: A Comparative Study of Public-Private Sector Relationships in Two Urban Centers." Ph.D. Dissertation, Department of Political Science, University of Minnesota, 1973.

———. "Oligarchy and Power Structure in Urban Colombia: The Case of Cali." Unpublished paper.

DESAL (Center for Social and Economic Development of Latin America) I. *Marginalidad en América Latina.* Barcelona: Herder, 1969.

DESAL II. "Encuesta sobre la familia y la fecundidad en poblaciones marginales del Gran Santiago 1966/67." Mimeographed. Santiago, 1968.

de Vargas Machuca, Bernardo. *Milicia y descripción de las Indias.* Madrid, 1892.

Dietz, Henry. "The Politics of Squatter Assimilation in Lima, Peru." Ph.D. Dissertation, Department of Political Science, Stanford University, 1974.

———. "Urban Squatter Settlements in Peru: A Case History and Analysis." *Journal of Inter-American Studies* 11 (July 1969): 353–370.

DiTella, Torcuato; Gino Germani; and Jorge Graciarena, eds. *Argentina: Sociedad de masas.* Buenos Aires: Eudeba, 1965.

dos Santos, Theontonio. "The Structure of Dependence." *American Economic Review* 50 (May 1970): 231–236.

Drake, George F. *Elites and Voluntary Associations: A Study of Community Power in Manizales, Colombia.* Madison: Land Tenure Center, 1970.

Ebel, Roland H. "The Decision-Making Process in San Salvador." Paper presented at the Southwestern Political Science Association Meeting, Houston, April 1969. Also in *Latin American Urban Research,* vol. 1, edited by Francine F. Rabinovitz and Felicity M. Trueblood. Beverly Hills: Sage Publications, 1971.

ECLA. "La participación de las poblaciones marginales en el crecimiento urbano." Mimeographed. Santiago: Conferencia Latinoamericana sobre la Infancia y la Juventud, 1965.

———. "Los servicios públicos en una población de erradicación." Mimeographed. Santiago, 1965.

———. "The Social Development of Latin America in the Post-War Period." Mimeographed. Santiago, 1963.

Edwards, H. T. "Power Structure and Its Communication Behavior in San José, Costa Rica." *Journal of Inter-American Studies* 8 (July 1966): 236–247.

Errasuriz, Joaquin, and Josefina Rossetti. *Tipología habitacional del Gran Santiago.* Santiago: Ministerio de Vivienda y Urbanismo, 1969.

Fagen, Richard R., and William S. Tuohy. *Politics and Privilege in a Mexican City.* Stanford University Press, 1972.

Festinger, Leon. *A Theory of Cognitive Dissonance.* Stanford: Stanford University Press, 1957.

Fiori, Jorge. "Campamento nueva La Habana: Estudio de una experiencia de auto-administración de justicia." *Revista Latinoamericana de Estudios Urbanos Regionales* 3 (April 1973): 84–101.

Fitzgibbon, Russell H. "Measuring Democratic Change in Latin America." *Journal of Politics* 29 (November 1967): 129–166.

———. "A Statistical Evaluation of Latin American Democracy." *Western Political Quarterly* 9 (1956): 607–619.

Flinn, William L. "Rural and Intra-Urban Migration in Colombia: Two Case Studies in Bogotá." In *Latin American Urban Research,* vol. 1, edited by Francine F. Rabinovitz and Felicity M. Trueblood. Beverly Hills: Sage Publications, 1971.

———, and James W. Converse. "Eight Assumptions concerning Rural-Urban Migration in Colombia: A Three Shantytowns Test." *Land Economics* 46 (November 1970): 456–464.

Forni, F. H. "The Decision-Making System in Two Small Communities in Argentina." Paper presented at the International Sociological Association Meeting, Varna, Bulgaria, 1970.

Foster, George. *Culture and Conquest: America's Spanish Heritage.* Chicago: University of Chicago Press, 1960.

Frank, Andrew Gunder. *Capitalism and Underdevelopment in Latin America: Historical Studies of Brazil and Chile.* New York: Monthly Review, 1967.

———. "Urban Poverty in Latin America." In *Masses in Latin America,* edited by Irving L. Horowitz. New York: Oxford University Press, 1970.

Frankenhoff, C. A. "Elements of an Economic Model for Slums in a Developing Economy." *Economic Development and Cultural Change* 16, no. 1 (1967): 27–35.

Freeman, H. E.; E. Novak; and L. G. Reeder. "Correlates of Membership in Voluntary Associations." *American Sociological Review* 22 (October 1957): 528–533.

Friedmann, John. "The Role of Cities in National Development." *American Behavioral Scientist* 12 (May–June 1969): 13–21.

————, and Thomas Lackington. "Hyperurbanization and National Development in Chile." *Urban Affairs Quarterly* 2 (June 1967): 3–29.

Fundación Salvadoreña de Desarrollo y Vivienda. "Bases para un proyecto de investigación evaluativa sobre cambio social y económico derivado de los proyectos de la fundación." Manuscript, San Salvador, 1973.

Furtado, Celso. *Development and Underdevelopment.* Berkeley: University of California Press, 1964.

————. *Dialéctica del desarrollo.* Mexico City: Fondo de Cultura Económica, 1965.

————. *Economic Development in Latin America: A Survey from Colonial Times to the Cuban Revolution.* New York: Cambridge University Press, 1970.

Gakenheimer, Ralph. "The Peruvian City of the Sixteenth Century." In *The Urban Explosion in Latin America,* edited by Glenn H. Beyer. Ithaca: Cornell University Press, 1967.

Gans, Herbert J. *The Urban Villagers: Group and Class in the Life of Italian Americans.* New York: Free Press, 1962.

Geisse, Guillermo. "La desigualdad de los ingresos: Punto de partida del círculo de la pobreza urbana." Paper presented at the Seminar on New Directions of Urban Research, University of Texas at Austin, May 1974.

————, and Jorge Hardoy, eds. *Latin American Urban Research,* vol. 2. *Regional and Urban Development Policies: A Latin American Perspective.* Beverly Hills: Sage Publications, 1972.

Germani, Gino. "The City as an Integrating Mechanism." In *The Urban Explosion in Latin America,* edited by Glenn H. Beyer. Ithaca: Cornell University Press, 1967.

————. "Hacía una democracia de masas." In *Argentina: Sociedad de masas,* edited by Torcuato DiTella, Gino Germani, and Jorge Graciarena. Buenos Aires: Eudeba, 1965.

————. "Social and Political Consequences of Mobility." In *Social Structure and Mobility in Economic Development,* edited by Neil J. Smelser and Seymour M. Lipset. Chicago: Aldine, 1966.

Gibson, Charles. *The Aztecs under Spanish Rule.* Stanford: Stanford University Press, 1964.

————. "Spanish-Indian Institutions and Colonial Urbanism in New Spain." In *El proceso de urbanización en América desde sus orígenes hasta nuestros días,* edited by Jorge Hardoy and R. Schaedel. Buenos Aires: Editorial del Instituto, 1969.

Gilbert, Claire W. "Community Power and Decision-Making: A Quantitative Examination of Previous Research." In *Community Structure and Decision-Making: Comparative Analyses,* edited by Terry N. Clark. San Francisco: Chandler, 1968.

————. *Community Power Structure: Propositional Inventory, Tests, and Theory.* Gainesville: University of Florida Press, 1972.

Goldrich, Daniel. "Political Organization and the Politicization of the Poblador." *Comparative Political Studies* 3 (July 1970): 176–202.

———. "Toward the Comparative Study of Politicization in Latin America." In *Contemporary Cultures and Societies of Latin America*, edited by Dwight B. Heath and Richard Newbold Adams. New York: Random House, 1965.

———; Raymond B. Pratt; and Charles R. Schuller. "The Political Integration of Lower-Class Urban Settlements in Chile and Peru." *Studies in Comparative International Development* 3 (1967–1968): 3–22.

Graham, Lawrence S. *Politics in a Mexican Community*. Gainesville: University of Florida Press, 1968.

Greer, Scott. *The Emerging City: Myth and Reality*. New York: Free Press, 1962.

Gurrieri, Adolfo. "Situación y perspectivas de la juventud en una población urbana popular." Santiago: ECLA, 1965.

Hanna, William, and Judith Hanna. *Urban Dynamics in Black Africa*. Chicago: Aldine, 1971.

Hardoy, Jorge. "Dos mil años de urbanización en América Latina." In *La urbanización en América Latina*, edited by Jorge Hardoy and Carlos Tobar. Buenos Aires: Editorial del Instituto, 1969.

———. "El paisaje urbano de América del Sur." In *Las ciudades en América Latina*, edited by Jorge Hardoy. Buenos Aires: Paidos, 1972.

———. "El rol de la ciudad en la modernización de América Latina." In *Las ciudades en América Latina*, edited by Jorge Hardoy. Buenos Aires: Paidos, 1972.

———. "La ciudad y el campo en América Latina: Un análisis de las relaciones socioeconómicas." In *Las ciudades en América Latina*, edited by Jorge Hardoy. Buenos Aires: Paidos, 1972.

———. "Política urbanística y política del suelo urbano y suburbano en América Latina." In *Las ciudades en América Latina*, edited by Jorge Hardoy. Buenos Aires: Paidos, 1972.

———. "Urbanization Politics and Urban Reform in Latin America." In *Latin American Urban Research*, vol. 1, edited by Francine F. Rabinovitz and Felicity M. Trueblood. Beverly Hills: Sage Publications, 1971.

———, and Carmen Aranovich. "Cuadro comparativo de los centros de colonización española existentes en 1580 y 1630." *Desarrollo Económico* 7, no. 27 (1967): 349–360.

———; Raul Basaldua; and Oscar Moreno. *Política de la tierra urbana y mecanismos para su regulación en América del Sur*. Buenos Aires: Editorial del Instituto, 1968.

Haring, Clarence H. *The Spanish Empire in America*. New York: Oxford University Press, 1947.

Harth Deneke, Jorge. "The Colonias Proletarias of Mexico City: Low Income Settlements on the Urban Fringe."

Hawley, Willis D., and Frederick M. Wirt. *The Search for Community Power*. Englewood Cliffs, N.J.: Prentice-Hall, 1968.

Hayes, Edward C. *Power Structure and Urban Policy: Who Rules Oakland?* New York: McGraw-Hill, 1972.

Hayter, Teresa. *Aid as Imperialism*. Middlesex: Penguin, 1971.

Heider, Fritz. *The Psychology of Interpersonal Relations*. New York: Wiley, 1967.

Hildahl, S. H. "A Note on '. . . A Note on the Sociology of Knowledge.'" *Sociological Quarterly* 11 (September 1970): 405–415.

Hirschman, Albert. *The Strategy of Economic Development*. New Haven: Yale University Press, 1958.

Hoffmann, R.; N. García; O. Mercado; and F. Uribe. "La marginalidad urbana." In *Marginalidad en América Latina*, edited by DESAL. Barcelona: Herder, 1969.

Holden, D. E. W. "La estructura del liderazgo y sus características en una comunidad de Costa Rica." *Journal of Inter-American Studies* 8 (January 1966): 129–141.

Horowitz, Irving L. "Electoral Politics, Urbanization, and Social Development in Latin America." *Urban Affairs Quarterly* 2 (March 1967): 3–35.

———. *Three Worlds of Development*. New York: Oxford University Press, 1972.

———; Josue de Castro; and John Gerassi, eds. *Latin American Radicalism*. New York: Random House, 1970.

Hoskin, Gary. "Power Structure in a Venezuelan Town: The Case of San Cristóbal." In *Case Studies in Social Power*, edited by Hans-Dieter Evers. Leiden: Brill, 1969.

Hoyt, Homer. "Recent Distortions of Classical Models of Urban Structure." *Land Economics* 40 (May 1964): 199–212.

———. *The Structure and Growth of Residential Neighborhood in American Cities*. Washington, D.C.: Federal Housing Administration, 1939.

Illich, Ivan. "Outwitting the Developed Countries." *New York Review of Books*, November 6, 1969.

Inkeles, Alex. *Becoming Modern*. Boston: Little, Brown, 1973.

Johnson, Dale. "The National and Progressive Bourgeoisie in Chile." *Studies in Comparative International Development* 4 (1968–1969): 63–86.

Klapp, Orin, and L. Vincent Padgett. "Power and Decision-Making in a Mexican Border City." *American Journal of Sociology* 65 (January 1960): 400–406.

La Nación. "Plan de la vivienda: Un esfuerzo nacional y popular." Special supplement to the Santiago newspaper, August 20, 1967.

Lapidus, Ira, ed. *Middle Eastern Cities: Ancient, Islamic, and Contemporary Middle Eastern Urbanism: A Symposium*. Berkeley: University of California Press, 1969.

Leeds, Anthony. "The Significant Variables Determining the Character of Squatter Settlements." *América Latina* 12 (July–September 1969): 44–86.

———, and Elizabeth Leeds. "Brazil and the Myth of Urban Rurality: Urban Experience, Work, and Values in 'Squatments' of Rio de Janeiro and Lima." In *City and Country in the Third World*, edited by A. J. Field. Cambridge: Schenckman, 1969.

Leeds, Elizabeth. "Forms of 'Squatment' Political Organization: The Politics of Control in Brazil." Master's Thesis, Department of Government, University of Texas at Austin, 1972.

Lerner, Daniel. *The Passing of Traditional Society*. Glencoe, Ill.: Free Press, 1964.

Lewis, Oscar. *Antropología de la pobreza*. Mexico City: Fondo de Cultura Económica, 1962.

———. "The Culture of Poverty." *Scientific American* 215 (October 1966): 19–25.

———. "The Culture of the 'Vecindad' in Mexico City: Two Case Studies." *Actas del III Congreso Internacional de Americanistas*. San José, C.R.: 1959.

Lipset, Seymour M. *Political Man: The Social Bases of Politics*. Garden City, N.Y.: Doubleday, 1960.

———, and Stein Rokkan. *Party Systems and Voter Alignments: Cross-National Perspectives*. New York: Free Press, 1967.

Lomnitz, Larissa. "The Social and Economic Organization of a Mexican Shantytown." In *Latin American Urban Research*, vol. 4, edited by Wayne A. Cornelius and Felicity M. Trueblood. Beverly Hills: Sage Publications, 1974.

Mangin, William. "Latin American Squatter Settlements: A Problem and a Solution." *Latin American Research Review* 2 (Summer 1967): 65–98.

———. *Peasants in Cities*. Boston: Houghton Mifflin, 1970.

———. "Squatter Settlements." *Scientific American* 217 (October 1967): 21–29.

Marris, Peter. "A Report on Urban Renewal in the United States." In *The Urban Condition*, edited by Peter Marris. New York: Basic Books, 1963.

Martin, Roscoe C., et al. *Decisions in Syracuse*. Bloomington: Indiana University Press, 1961.

Marx, Karl. *The Eighteenth Brumaire of Louis Bonaparte*. New York: International Publishers, 1963.

Merriam, Charles E. *Political Power*. New York: Collier, 1964.

Milgram, Stanley. "The Experience of Living in Cities." *Science* 13 (March 1970): 1461–1468.

Miller, Delbert C. *International Community Power Structures: Comparative Studies in Four World Cities*. Bloomington: Indiana University Press, 1970.

MINVU. "Programa de descentralización del MINVU para 1970–71." Circular of the Ministry of Housing and Urbanism to Local-Level Planning Agencies. Santiago, 1969.

Morea, Luis M. "Vivienda y equipamiento urbano." In *La urbanización en América Latina*, edited by Jorge Hardoy and Carlos Tobar. Buenos Aires: Editorial del Instituto, 1969.

Moreno, Francisco J. "Caudillismo: An Interpretation of Its Origins in Chile." In *Conflict and Violence in Latin American Politics*, edited by Francisco J. Moreno and Barbara Mitrani. New York: Thomas Crowell, 1971.

Morrison, Denton, and Allan Steeves. "Deprivation, Discontent, and Social

Movement Participation." *Rural Sociology* 32 (December 1967): 414–434.

Morse, Richard. "Some Characteristics of Latin American Urban History." *American Historical Review* 67, no. 2 (1962): 317–338.

———. "Trends and Issues in Latin American Urban Research, 1965–1970." *Latin American Research Review* 6, no. 1 (Spring 1971): 3–52; 6, no. 2 (Summer 1971): 19–75.

Myint, Hla. *The Economics of the Developing Countries.* New York: Praeger, 1964.

Myrdal, Gunnar. *Rich Lands and Poor.* New York: Harper and Row, 1957.

Naroll, Raoul. *Data Quality Control: A New Research Technique.* New York: Free Press, 1961.

Nelson, Joan. *Migrants, Urban Poverty and Instability in Developing Nations.* Cambridge: Harvard University Center for International Affairs, 1969.

New Encyclopedia Britannica, 15th ed.

Norris, T. L. "Decision-Making Activity Sequences in a Hacienda Community." *Human Organization* 12 (1953): 26–30.

Nun, José. "Superpoblación relativa, ejercito industrial de reserva y masa marginal." *Revista Latinoamericana de Sociología* 5 (July 1969): 178–236.

———; Juan Carlos Marin; and Miguel Murmis. "La marginalidad en América Latina." Joint Program ILPES/DESAL, Working Paper, no. 2. Santiago, 1967.

Ocampo, José F. *Dominio de clase en la ciudad colombiana.* Medellín: Oveja Negra, 1972.

Ogliastri, Enrique. "Elite, Class, and Power in the Economic Development of a Colombian City: Bucaramanga." Ph.D. dissertation, Northwestern University, 1973.

Olsen, Marvin. "Rapid Growth as a Destabilizing Force." *Journal of Economic History* 23 (December 1963): 529–552.

Padgett, L. Vincent. "The Power Structure of Cali." Manuscript, Universidad del Valle, Cali, Colombia, 1967.

Patch, Richard. *Life in a "Callejón": A Study of Urban Disorganization.* American Universities Field Staff Reports, West Coast South American Series, 8, no. 6. Hanover, N.H.: 1961.

Peattie, Lisa. "The Concept of Marginality as Applied to Squatter Settlements." In *Latin American Urban Research*, vol. 4, edited by Wayne A. Cornelius and Felicity M. Trueblood. Beverly Hills: Sage Publications, 1974.

Perlman, Janice. "The Fate of Migrants in Rio's Favelas." Ph.D. dissertation, Massachusetts Institute of Technology, 1971.

Petras, James. "Chile: Nationalization, Socioeconomic Change, and Popular Participation." Paper presented at the meeting of the American Political Science Association, Washington, D.C., September 1972.

———, and Maurice Zeitlin, eds. *Latin America: Reform or Revolution.* Greenwich: Fawcett, 1968.

Pike, Frederick. "Aspects of Class Relations in Chile, 1850–1860." In *Latin*

America: Reform or Revolution, edited by James Petras and Maurice Zeitlin. Greenwich: Fawcett, 1968.

"Plan de la vivienda: Un esfuerzo nacional y popular." La Nación, August 20, 1967.

Portell Vila, Herminio. Historia de Cuba en sus relaciones con EE. UU. y España. Havana: J. Montero, 1938.

Portes, Alejandro. Cuatro poblaciones: Informe preliminar sobre situación y aspiraciones de grupos marginados en el Gran Santiago. Monograph Report, University of Wisconsin Sociology of Development Program, Santiago, 1969.

———. "Los grupos urbanos marginados: Nuevo intento de explicación." APORTES 18 (October 1970): 131–147.

———. "Political Primitivism, Differential Socialization, and Lower-Class Leftist Radicalism." American Sociological Review 36 (October 1971): 820–835.

———. "Rationality in the Slum: An Essay on Interpretive Sociology." Comparative Studies in Society and History 14, no. 3 (1972): 268–286.

———. "Urbanization and Politics in Latin America." Social Science Quarterly 52 (December 1971): 697–720.

———. "The Urban Slum in Chile: Types and Correlates." Land Economics 47 (August 1971): 235–248.

Powell, Sandra. "Political Participation in the Barriadas: A Case Study." Comparative Political Studies 2 (July 1969): 195–215.

Powelson, J. P. "The Land-Grabbers of Cali." Reporter, January 16, 1964, pp. 30–31.

Prebisch, Raul. "Commercial Policy in the Underdeveloped Countries." American Economic Review 49 (1959): 251–273.

Promoción Popular. "Estudio sobre participación en un tipo de asociación voluntaria: Junta de Vecinos." 1968.

Pye, Lucian W. "The Political Implications of Urbanization and the Developmental Process." In The City in the Newly Developing Countries, edited by Gerald Breese. Englewood Cliffs, N.J.: Prentice-Hall, 1969.

Quijano, Anibal. "Dependencia, cambio social y urbanización en América Latina." Unpublished paper, Santiago: ECLA, Department of Social Affairs, 1967.

———. "La urbanización de la sociedad en Latinoamérica." Revista Mexicana de Sociología 39 (October–December 1967): 669–703.

Rabinovitz, Francine F. "Sound and Fury Signifying Nothing: A Review of Community Power Research in Latin America." Urban Affairs Quarterly 3 (March 1968): 111–122.

Ratinoff, Luis. "The New Urban Groups: The Middle Classes." In Elites in Latin America, edited by Seymour M. Lipset and Aldo Solari. New York: Oxford University Press, 1967.

Ray, Talton F. The Politics of the Barrios of Venezuela. Berkeley: University of California Press, 1969.

Roberts, Bryan. "The Social Organization of Low-Income Urban Families."

In *Crucifixion by Power: Essays on Guatemalan National Social Structure, 1944–1966*, by Richard Newbold Adams. Austin: University of Texas Press, 1970.

Rosenbluth, Guillermo. "Problemas socio-económicos de la marginalidad y la integración urbana." Mimeographed. Santiago: Universidad de Chile, 1962.

Sánchez, Luis Alberto. "Urban Growth and the Latin American Heritage." In *The Urban Explosion in Latin America*, edited by Glenn H. Beyer. Ithaca: Cornell University Press, 1967.

Schnore, Leo F. "On the Spatial Structure of Cities in the Two Americas." In *The Study of Urbanization*, edited by Philip M. Hauser and Leo F. Schnore. New York: Wiley, 1965.

Sebreli, Juan. *Apogeo y ocaso de los Anchorena*. Buenos Aires: Siglo Veinte, 1972.

———. *Buenos Aires: Vida cotidiana y alienación*. Buenos Aires: Siglo Veinte, 1965.

Seltzer, Leon E., ed. *The Columbia Lippincott Gazetteer of the World*, 4th ed. New York: Columbia University Press, 1966.

Sjoberg, Gideon, and Leonard Cain. "Negative Values, Counter-system Models, and the Analysis of Social Systems." In *Institutions and Social Exchange: The Theories of Talcott Parsons and George H. Homans*, edited by Herman Turk and Richard Simpson. Indianapolis: Bobbs-Merrill, 1971.

Stavenhagen, Rodolfo. "Class, Colonialism, and Acculturation." In *Masses in Latin America*, edited by Irving L. Horowitz. New York: Oxford University Press, 1972.

Stinchcombe, Arthur L. "Agricultural Enterprise and Rural Class Relations." *American Journal of Sociology* 67 (September 1961): 165–176.

Stokes, Charles. "A Theory of Slums." *Land Economics* 38 (August 1962): 187–197.

Sunkel, Osvaldo. "The Structural Background of Development Problems in Latin America." In *Latin America: Problems in Economic Development*, edited by Charles Nisbet. New York: Free Press, 1960.

Szulc, Tad. *Winds of Revolution: Latin America Today and Tomorrow*. New York: Praeger, 1965.

Tefel, Reynaldo A. *El infierno de los pobres*. Managua: Ediciones Pez y Serpiente, 1972.

Torres-Trueba, H. E. "Factionalism in a Mexican Municipio: A Preliminary Study of the Political, Economic, and Religious Expressions of Factionalism in Zacapoaxtla, Puebla." *Sociologus* 19 (1969): 134–152.

Turk, Herman. "Interorganizational Networks in Urban Society: Initial Perspectives and Comparative Research." *American Sociological Review* 35 (February 1970): 1–19.

Turner, John F. C. "Uncontrolled Urban Settlement: Problems and Policies." *International Social Development Review*, no. 1 (1968), pp. 107–130.

Ugalde, Antonio. "Contemporary Mexico: From Hacienda to PRI, Political Leadership in a Zapotec Village." In *The Caciques: Oligarchical Politics and the System of Caciquismo in the Luso-Hispanic World*, edited by Robert Kern and Ronald Dokart. Albuquerque: University of New Mexico Press, 1973.

———. *Power and Conflict in a Mexican Community: A Study of Political Integration*. Albuquerque: University of New Mexico Press, 1970.

———. *The Urbanization Process of a Poor Mexican Neighborhood*. Special Publication of the Institute of Latin American Studies. Austin, 1974.

Unikel, Luis. *La dinámica del crecimiento de la Ciudad de México*. Mexico City: Fundación para Estudios de la Población, 1972.

Usandizaga, Elsa, and A. Eugene Havens. *Tres barrios de invasión*. Bogotá: Tercer Mundo, 1966.

Vallier, Ivan. "Las elites religiosas en América Latina: Catolicismo, liderazgo y cambio social." In *Elites y desarrollo en América Latina*, edited by Seymour M. Lipset and Aldo Solari. Buenos Aires: Paidos, 1967.

Vekemans, Roger, and Ismael Fuenzalida. "El concepto de la marginalidad." In *Marginalidad en América Latina*, edited by DESAL. Barcelona: Herder, 1969.

Vizcaya Canales, Isidro. *Los origenes de la industrialización de Monterrey, 1867–1920*. Monterrey: Publicaciones del Instituto Tecnológico y de Estudios Superiores de Monterrey, 1969.

Walton, John. "A Systematic Survey of Community Power Research." In *The Structure of Community Power*, edited by Michael Aiken and Paul E. Mott. New York: Random House, 1970.

———. "Development Decision-Making: A Comparative Study in Latin America." *American Journal of Sociology* 75 (March 1970): 828–851.

———. "Differential Patterns of Community Power Structure: An Explanation Based on Interdependence." In *Community Structure and Decision-Making: Comparative Analyses*, edited by Terry N. Clark. San Francisco: Chandler, 1968.

———. "Political Development and Economic Development: A Regional Assessment of Contemporary Theories." *Studies in Comparative International Development* 7 (Spring 1972): 39–63.

———. "Substance and Artifact: The Current Status of Research on Community Power Structure." *American Journal of Sociology* 71 (January 1966): 430–441.

———, and Joyce A. Sween. "Urbanization, Industrialization, and Voting in Mexico: A Longitudinal Analysis of Official and Opposition Party Support." *Social Science Quarterly* 52 (December 1971): 721–745.

Ward, Barbara. "The Uses of Prosperity." *Saturday Review*, August 29, 1964, pp. 191–192.

Warren, Roland L. *The Community in America*. Chicago: Rand McNally, 1963.

Weber, Max. "Class, Status, and Party." In *From Max Weber: Essays in Sociology*, edited by Hans H. Gerth and C. Wright Mills. New York: Oxford University Press, 1958.

———. *The Theory of Social and Economic Organization*. New York: Free Press, 1965.

Whitten, Norman E. "Power Structure and Sociocultural Change in Latin American Communities." *Social Forces* 43 (March 1965): 320–329.

Wildavsky, Aaron. *Leadership in a Small Town.* Totowa, N.J.: Bedminister Press, 1964.

Wilkus, Edward. "Urban Stratification: A Case Study of Mexico City." Manuscript, Department of Sociology, University of Illinois, 1971.

Wright, Charles, and Herbert Hyman. "Voluntary Association Memberships of American Adults: Evidence from National Sample Surveys." *American Sociological Review* 23 (June 1958): 284–294.

Yujnovsky, Oscar. "La investigación para el planeamiento del desarrollo urbano en América Latina." Paper presented at the Seminar on Urbanization and Social Research (CIDU), Santiago, Chile, April 1967.

Zeitlin, Maurice. "Economic Insecurity and the Political Attitudes of Cuban Workers." *American Sociological Review* 31 (February 1966): 31–51.

Index

Lightning Source UK Ltd.
Milton Keynes UK
UKHW011019240519
343257UK00001B/52/P